PRAISE FOR

Get Out of Your Own Way

"Powerful, practical insights that can help many to live more rewarding lives—turning weaknesses into strengths. *Get Out of Your Own Way* to achieve more satisfaction in yourself and all your intimate relationships. Goulston and Goldberg show us specifically how to convert problems into opportunities. A rewarding, clear, and pleasurable book."

—Harold Bloomfield,
author, *How to Survive the Loss of a Love*

"*Get Out of Your Own Way* treats this sensitive subject with rare kindness and common sense. The sincere reader will benefit by learning that they are not alone in the ways they self-interfere and will treat themselves with greater kindness and understanding." —Tim Gallwey,
author, *The Inner Game of Golf*

"This is a valuable book. It provides clear insight, compassionate understanding, and practical solutions to forty self-defeating behaviors that can destroy your life if left unaddressed. Use it as a manual to free yourself from a self-imposed prison and create the life you truly want."

—Jack Canfield,
coauthor, *Chicken Soup for the Soul*

The 6 Secrets of a Lasting Relationship

How to Fall in Love Again— and Stay There

Mark Goulston, M.D.

with
Philip Goldberg

A PERIGEE BOOK

A Perigee Book
Published by The Berkley Publishing Group
A division of Penguin Putnam Inc.
375 Hudson Street
New York, New York 10014

Copyright © 2001 by Mark Goulston, M.D.
Text design by Tanya Maiboroda
Cover design copyright © 2001 by Royce M. Becker
Cover photograph copyright © Simon Battensby/Masterfile
Photograph of Mark Goulston by John Collier

G. P. Putnam's Sons edition: February 2001
First Perigee edition: April 2002

Perigee ISBN: 0-399-52739-7

Published simultaneously in Canada.

Visit our website at www.penguinputnam.com

The Library of Congress has catalogued the
G. P. Putnam's Sons edition as follows:

Goulston, Mark.
The six secrets of a lasting relationship : how to fall in love again—and stay there /
by Mark Goulston, with Philip Goldberg.
p.   cm.
Includes index.
ISBN 0-399-14703-9
1. Marriage.   2. Man-woman relationships.   I. Goldberg, Philip, date.   II. Title.
HQ734.G144   2001   00-044561
306.81—dc21

Printed in the United States of America

10 9 8 7 6 5 4 3 2 1

To Lisa and Lori,
our guides to lasting love.

Acknowledgments

Compassionately connect with, steadfastly believe in, practically advise and never give up. That is how I try to work with couples who come to me for counseling. I never would have known how to do this—and therefore could not have written this book—had it not been for my first mentor, the late Dr. William MacNary, Dean of Students at the Boston University School of Medicine. After Dean MacNary's death, his shoes were filled by Al Dorskind, whose generous, wise and trusted guidance continues even now.

Other guiding lights whose influence made this book possible include Drs. Edwin Shneidman, Judd Marmor, Robert Stoller and Herbert Linden. Thanks to the lessons I learned from these wise and caring professionals, I have been fortunate enough to earn the trust of patients who come to me with their pain, fear, confusion and discouragement.

Thanks are also due to my business partner, Laura Dawn Lewis, CEO and founder of CouplesCompany.com, where we are committed to helping relationships grow and flourish, rather than wither and die. I am also grateful to Dr. Ronald Dozoretz, Elliot Gerson, John Bringenberg, Michael Bollini, Diane Powell and Lisa DeMille at Lifescape.com; Time-Warner's ParentTime.com, and ivillage.com, for the encouragement and freedom that helped me to further hone my experience on relationships.

As Bette Midler sang: "You gotta have friends." This book (and this author) greatly benefited from the support of friends (and family friends), whom I also want to thank, that include A. Raymond Tye, Tom Brennan, Kevin Thranow, Walter Anderson, Kate White, Billy Pittard, Felice Willat, Paul and Sarah Edwards, Jane Applegate, Mark and Mia Silverman, and Preston and Vicki Johnson.

This book would never have been possible without the efforts of my trusted coauthor and friend, Philip Goldberg. The balance of anecdotes, insights and exercises, as well as the entire structure of this book, were all due to his skill and persistence. I cannot thank him enough for making me appear wiser than I really am. Our work together was marked by what could be called the Six Secrets of a Lasting Collaboration: (intellectual) chemistry, respect, enjoyment, acceptance, trust and empathy.

Phil, in turn, would like to personally thank Fanny Levy for her editorial assistance; his parents, Ann and Archie, for modeling a marriage that only death could end; and Lori Deutsch for her indispensable practical help, her unflagging faith, and her devotion.

We would both like to thank our agent, Lynn Franklin, and our publisher and editor, John Duff. Their confidence, patience and deft input helped to guide this book from inception to completion. They served as wise and protective shepherds, guiding us through a minefield of challenges.

My eternal gratitude goes out to my family: my mother, Ruth, and my late father, Irving; my brothers, Noel and Robert, and their wives, Mary and Angela for their love, interest and enthusiasm for this undertaking; my brother-in-law Michael Stotsky; and above all my wife, Lisa, and our children, Lauren, Emily and Billy. They kept me honest every step of the way, ensuring that I practiced what I preached and preached what I practiced. I can't thank them enough for their patience and understanding during the course of this project, which time after time stole from them my undivided attention and some of my participation in their lives.

Finally I want to acknowledge you, the reader, for acquiring this book; trusting me to help you in an area as personal as your intimate relationships; and inspiring me to continue my journey to discover additional ways to help and serve.

Contents

The
6 Secrets
of a
Lasting
Relationship

Introduction

—

> *If only you could love enough you would be the happiest and most powerful being in the world.*
>
> —EMMETT FOX

The ecstasy of falling in love is exceeded only by the anguish of falling out of love. To one degree or another, you have felt that anguish. That is why you were drawn to this book. Fall in love again? "If only," says the skeptical voice in your head. "Way too much water under the bridge for that." You may think that the only way you could ever fall in love again is with someone new—a prospect you've fantasized about and maybe even considered. Or, you may be reconciled to never having that delicious feeling again. You've settled, figuring it might not be what you dreamed of having, but what the hell, it's okay compared to other relationships.

But, despite your skepticism, you're reading this. Your heart and soul ache to recapture what you and your partner once had—and keep it this time. Maybe, just maybe, it's possible.

It *is* possible. In more than twenty-five years as a psychotherapist I have helped hundreds of couples repair, rebuild and restore their love. I have also helped countless single people fall in love again after relationships had left them heartbroken, cautious and skeptical. It is doable, and surprisingly simple.

Based on more than ten thousand hours of couples therapy, I have concluded that these are the six secrets of a lasting relationship:

1. Keep the *chemistry* burning.
2. Treat your partner with *respect*—and earn his or hers.
3. Don't stop thinking about *enjoyment*.
4. Give one another *acceptance* despite your flaws.
5. Deserve each other's *trust*.
6. Always keep in touch with *empathy*.

The structure of an intimate relationship rests on six pillars, which are the core of each of the six secrets. Their initials form the acronym **CREATE**: **C**hemistry, **R**espect, **E**njoyment, **A**cceptance, **T**rust, and **E**mpathy.

We all want to feel a powerful chemistry for our mates—and to know they feel it for us. We all want to be respected by our partners—and to have respect for them. We all want to enjoy being with our beloved—and to be enjoyed. We all want to fully accept our mates—and to be fully accepted in return. We all want to trust our partners—and be trusted by them. We all want to empathize with our lovers—to understand what they are thinking and feeling—and to have them know what it is like to be us.

The cause of all relationship problems is usually a breakdown of one or more of these essential ingredients. If you do not fortify and reinforce them on a regular basis, they invariably begin to give way under the stress of marriage and family life—or the pressures of a long-term bond between two single people. If you do not recognize the damage and take steps to repair it, the deterioration will accelerate and you will soon find that the foundation of your relationship has decayed, and with it the emotional floor you stand on and the ceiling that holds your dreams.

But you *can* strengthen the supporting structure. You just have to know how. Once you do, you'll find that all the specific things that have begun to go wrong between you and your partner will improve—either spontaneously or because you are now better equipped and better motivated to work on your problems together. And while you're at it, you just may fall in love again.

"Yeah, right," you think. "How can we possibly return to the sweet romance and wild passion we once had, now that our flesh sags and our spirits are weighed down by all this heavy baggage?" Well, you won't get those days of innocence back, but you can restore more of the passion and romance than you might imagine. You won't recapture your early love just as it was, but you'll get something better. Something more durable. What you think of as emotional baggage can be transformed into a new, mature love that surpasses in depth and intimacy all your romantic memories.

The steps to accomplish this are simple and clear. But don't confuse simple with easy. It won't be easy. Falling back in love and staying there takes work—and a commitment to continue doing the work even when you don't feel like it. You may be thinking, "I've already worked at this relationship. How much more can I do?" Well, for one thing, you haven't done the work that's laid out systematically in this book. For another, the work you've been doing may have been one-sided. You may have been carrying too much of the burden, maybe even trying to do it all by yourself. In fact, you could be thinking, "Let *him* work at it for a change," or, "I'm tired of taking the initiative, it's *her* turn now."

But what if your partner is willing to match you effort for effort? What if his or her patience, perseverance and commitment matched your patience, perseverance and commitment? Don't you think that would make a difference? One of the great advantages of the CREATE model is that it invariably leads to what marketing people call "buy-in."

When I meet with couples in therapy, I often ask these two questions:

1. Would you agree that when chemistry, respect, enjoyment, acceptance, trust and empathy are strong, the relationship as a whole will be strong?
2. Would you agree that if any or all of those six essentials are weak, the relationship will be in trouble?

Virtually without fail, I get 100 percent agreement from both the man and the woman. Before buying into a new concept, some people need for it to make sense. Others need for it to feel right. While there are many exceptions, most men buy into CREATE because it makes sense, and most women buy in because it feels right. This is extremely important, because once both partners agree on the basic premise of a successful relationship, resistance dissolves and they can work together as a team— and that can make all the difference in the world.

I urge you to stop feeling like a victim. Stop thinking that you're owed something by your partner. The IOU approach hasn't worked yet, and it never will. Instead, get ready to work together to CREATE the love you deserve. How much more time do you have to waste by doing the wrong thing—or doing nothing?

If you take full advantage of the six secrets of lasting love, you will discover:

- renewed involvement with each other
- revived enthusiasm for your relationship
- a stronger sense of partnership and commitment
- an atmosphere of healing
- greater capacity to solve problems effectively
- deepened intimacy and tenderness
- enhanced mutual understanding
- freedom from guilt and blame
- a more durable bond
- a reawakening of love

If you and your partner make your best effort to use the no-blame, no-fault, no-nonsense approach in this book, you *can* fall in love again. If you have no partner at the moment, learn from the book what went wrong in the past and how to do it right in the future. And this time (or next time) you should be able to *stay* in love. You owe it to yourself to at least try.

There is no remedy for love but to love more.

—HENRY DAVID THOREAU

1

The 6 Pillars of Lasting Love

How to Create a Solid Foundation

To love for the sake of being loved is human, but to love for the sake of loving is angelic.

—ALPHONSE DE LAMARTINE

"Our sex life is dead," said Jason.

He had been sitting quietly, barely concealing his impatience, as his wife explained why they had come to my office for marital counseling. Wendy, a marketing executive at a film studio, had given me the facts: married six years, two kids, insanely busy lives. She insisted on therapy because she and Jason had been fighting, and the fights were getting frequent and ugly. "He's hostile toward me," she said. "He won't communicate. He doesn't even *try* to understand me." As Wendy continued, Jason rolled his eyes at what he later called "women's magazine psychobabble." Then he blurted out his bottom-line concern: no sex.

Wendy was obviously annoyed by her husband's remark. "We have a ten-month-old son and a three-year-old daughter, and busy careers on top of it," she said. "You'd think he could delay gratification just a little."

Jason's frustration was palpable. "Delay? You think our chemistry is on hold or something? It's gone!" He turned to me and said, through gritted teeth, "I know that having kids changes things. But this really sucks. We used to be a very hot couple."

Looking at them, there was no reason they shouldn't still be hot. They were in their mid-thirties, attractive and clearly passionate, just not toward each other at the moment.

The discussion quickly deteriorated into tit-for-tat sniping and finger-pointing, with neither spouse listening to the other. Jason, who did not want to be there in the first place, looked like he might bolt for the door if he heard the words "communication" or "feelings" one more time. To get his attention, I had to bring the discussion back to his reality, and I had to do it in his language, avoiding the "touchy-feely" terms that turned him off. He was a no-nonsense guy who had clawed his way up from the streets by single-handedly building a large employment agency. "It sounds like you have a strong sex drive," I said. "If you're not getting enough sex with Wendy, you're either cheating or jerking off."

As I'd hoped, Jason was shocked into paying attention again. He gaped at me, trying to figure out what to say. Wendy was also shocked. She looked at her husband with fear in her eyes, wondering why he hadn't contradicted my statement. It was inconceivable to her that a grown man would be masturbating like a teenager. Could he be having an affair?

Jason extended his right hand. Pointing to it with his left hand, he said, "Meet my mistress."

He had been masturbating to porn sites on the Internet. The shame that he felt at admitting this secret was surpassed only by the relief of finally getting it out in the open.

> **USABLE INSIGHT**
> *Time doesn't heal,*
> *truth heals*

The monkey that Jason had thrown off his back now turned into a huge gorilla that filled the room. I sensed that they were both thinking, "Okay, Doc, you got us into this mess, now get us out."

"Put yourself in your husband's shoes right now," I urged Wendy. "He's a respectable father, husband and businessman. If I were to ask him which feels worse, having to resort to masturbation or you finding out about it, what would he say?"

Wendy tried to discern the answer to my question, then gave up and abruptly started to cry. "He must feel awful," she said.

"You have no idea!" said Jason. The anger had left his voice. He realized from Wendy's response that she understood his frustration and truly cared. He was greatly relieved.

We had achieved something vitally important: *empathy*, the ability to put yourself in another person's shoes and know what it's like to be him or her. Soon we established that Jason had empathy for Wendy as well. He understood the pressures on his wife to be a good mother and maintain her career at the same time. And he understood how stress had caused her to be less than receptive to his sexual advances.

Having achieved this measure of mutual empathy, we were able to move on. To the couple's surprise, I did not zero in on the sexual component of their relationship. In fact, I avoided it. I knew from experience that it would be fruitless to delve into the details without first examining the emotional context that had ripped the rug out from under a once healthy sex life.

"When was the last time you felt respected by your wife?" I asked Jason.

He thought for a moment, then answered, despondently, "It's been so long I can't remember." Like most men, he needed to feel respected, if not admired, by the woman he loved. At the very least, he needed to know that he was not *disrespected*.

Wendy was shocked that Jason did not feel respected by her. "He's a great guy," she said. "I guess I can be critical at times, but I have tremendous admiration for him."

"Not anymore," muttered Jason. He was afraid that the revelation about his masturbating would destroy Wendy's respect. On the contrary, she admired his courage in admitting it.

"I didn't know how hurt you were," she told him. "You should have told me. Don't you trust me?"

She'd hit the nail on the head. Jason didn't trust Wendy to hear his pain without losing respect for him. In his mind, feeling hurt was unmanly. Instead of communicating his feelings directly, he became sullen and secretive and dealt with his frustration in private.

Wendy then admitted to a trust issue of her own: while Jason was hiding his secret, she felt that something was going on and wondered if he was having an affair—only to now feel guilty for not trusting him.

In our next few sessions together, we examined more deeply the issues of trust and respect. We also opened up additional areas of exploration. One was acceptance: both Jason and Wendy had come to feel let down as they discovered traits in each other that they had difficulty accepting. When I asked Wendy how long it had been since she'd felt cherished by Jason, she wistfully said, "I've gone from feeling like a prize to a pain in the ass." We also talked about enjoyment. Once upon a time, they had found joy and delight in one another's company. But they had let their life together grow tedious and businesslike.

Only after these other areas had been explored thoroughly did I let Jason and Wendy return to the issue of sexual chemistry. Now they could focus on that aspect of their relationship without losing sight of everything that was affecting it and, in turn, was being affected by it.

The Web of CREATE

It's curious how, when you're in love, you yearn to
go about doing acts of kindness to everybody.

—P. G. WODEHOUSE

Couples usually come to counseling with specific frustrations, conflicts and areas of pain. They complain about issues surrounding sex, intimacy, communication, money, parenting and the other usual suspects. My challenge and responsibility as a therapist is to get them to look at the relationship as a whole and to view their specific problems in a larger context.

That's where the six secrets of lasting love come in. When I first realized that the key ingredients of a healthy relationship—chemistry, respect, enjoyment, acceptance, trust and empathy—form the acronym CREATE, I could not imagine a happier coincidence. Every couple who comes for counseling wants to do more than fix, correct or repair their marriage. They don't want to settle for coping when it's possible to heal. And they don't want to settle for healing when they can thrive. They want to inject new life, forge a different way of relating to one another and build something deep and durable—in short, to CREATE a strong and lasting love.

> **USABLE INSIGHT**
>
> *Why cope when you can heal? Why just heal when you can thrive?*

The six secrets fit that creative need in a comprehensible and comprehensive way—comprehensible because everyone can understand their importance; comprehensive because they contain all the ingredients for healing and strengthening every aspect of an intimate relationship.

They are presented here in the order of CREATE because acronyms are useful tools for remembering important principles. Like the columns that hold up an arch or the roof of a temple, no single one is more important than any other to the health of the structure as a whole, and each one is profoundly affected by the rest. When one of the six weakens, it places extra strain on the others. If one crumbles to the ground, the others begin to topple in turn, like dominos.

The interdependent relationship among these six building blocks works in a positive direction as well. When any of them is strengthened, a ripple effect is produced in which the others are automatically reinforced and the pressure on each one to support the entire structure is reduced. To switch metaphors, think of the six secrets as the vital organs of the body. If you improve the condition of the heart, for instance, you spontaneously help the lungs, kidneys, liver and other organs as well.

A memorable example of the interaction of the six pillars took place in one of the *Rocky* movies, when Rocky Balboa was training for his rematch with Clubber Lang by running wind sprints on a beach. Struggling to regain his shattered confidence after losing the first bout, Rocky stops and stares out at the sea, apparently ready to give up. Adrian, his wife, doggedly confronts him. She refuses to let up until the fighter finally admits to the most humiliating thing he can imagine: "I'm afraid!"

After Adrian gets him to talk about his fears, she lets him now know she believes in him no matter what. With his confidence restored, Rocky is ready to forge ahead to victory.

As corny as it may sound, the scene is gratifying for the audience because it resonates with something deep in the human psyche: the need for the six pillars. It was Adrian's unflagging respect for her husband that made her want to help him—and his respect for her that forced him to pay attention. It was Adrian's profound empathy that let her know Rocky was holding something back, and she should keep on pushing for the truth. It was Rocky's trust in his wife that enabled him to speak that truth even though it made him vulnerable to rejection and ridicule. Adrian's unwavering acceptance of her husband despite his admitted weakness enabled Rocky to accept himself, respect himself and trust himself. In the playful banter that follows their emotional breakthrough, the pillar of enjoyment is obvious. As for their chemistry, which had declined in proportion to Rocky's loss of confidence, it is abundantly evident in the kiss and embrace that end the scene.

When We Fall in Love

Ecstasy cannot last, but it can carve a channel for
something lasting.

—E. M. FORSTER

It is impossible to remember what it felt like to be in our mother's womb. Our every need was automatically met. It came straight through her placenta into our developing body. Then we were born, and we screamed. Fortunately, we can't truly recall the trauma of birth, nor the awful feeling of being cast into a world where our wishes were not necessarily fulfilled or even understood. As time went by, we adjusted, figuring out how to get our needs met and learning to do without immediate gratification. But we never completely got over the fall from our Eden in the womb.

As we make our way through childhood and adolescence, we find ourselves compelled to break away from our parents. The process is as scary as it is exhilarating, for the price of autonomy is losing the comfort and safety of our dependency. To help us take these additional steps from the womb, we get a boost from emotional, psychological and biological forces within us. Emotionally, we summon the bravado (which we mistake for courage) to rebel, reject and defy much of what our parents say and believe. Psychologically, we assume a grandiosity that parents can barely tolerate and pray will eventually pass. Biologically, we not only become stronger and more self-sufficient, but we go from being disgusted by the opposite sex to finding them fascinating, alluring and irresistible. By the time we hit our middle or late teens, we may be certifiably girl or boy crazy.

Aside from the biological drive to reproduce the species, there are three reasons why our attraction to the opposite sex is so intense. First, nature uses our sexual urges to lure us away from our parents. Deep down, we always longed for the kind of connection that we felt in the womb but had no chance to experience since birth. Every touch, every kiss, every love letter reminds us of that connection, and with our first experiences of sexual passion and orgasm, we experience a kind of euphoric oneness that is the equivalent of going back to the womb. The problem is, once we feel the overwhelming power of that connection, it's very difficult to go back to being alone in the world. There is an almost addictive pull to reconnect. As with other addictions, we go into withdrawal when it's suddenly gone.

The second reason we're compelled to connect is that we're often attracted to those who have qualities we don't possess. The logical guy and the emotional gal. The shy man and the charismatic woman. The intellectual and the artist. The dreamer and the pragmatist. They complete each other. Rather than developing the desired qualities in ourselves (the healthier but rarely exercised option), we use each other to gather from the world that which we want but cannot get on our own.

The third reason sexual and romantic attractions are so intense is that they serve an important developmental function. Falling in love destroys any lingering thought of spending our lives in our parents' home. In essence, we embed and implant our entire being into the other person. Love offers the illusory comfort that we will not fall through the cracks when we separate from our parents. We have the feeling that everything will turn out okay—in fact, more than okay: glorious and spectacular.

It is no coincidence that we fall in love for the first time when we are falling in hate with our parents. As strong as the sexual *chemistry* is that we feel to our boy- or girlfriend, that's how turned off we are to our overanxious, overcontrolling parents. As much as we *respect*—and feel respected by—our sweetheart, that's how much we disrespect our parents and think they disrespect us. As much as we *enjoy* being with our lover, that's how much we want to get away from our parents and the yucky house they live in. As much *acceptance* as we share with our intimate partners, that's how judgmental we are toward our parents and they seem to be toward us. As much as we *trust* and feel trusted by our beloved, that's how suspicious we are of our parents. And as much *empathy* as we and our boy- or girlfriend seem to have for each other, that's how much our clueless parents can't seem to get where we're coming from.

Those three reasons may explain why some individuals, especially teens and young adults, can become despondent and even suicidal when an intense love relationship falls apart. One way to understand the despair of a breakup is to think of it as des-pair—being unpaired in the world after you've had the euphoria of being paired.

What applies to first love applies in its own way to second, third, tenth and thirtieth love. When you first meet that new, wonderful, irresistible dream lover, it doesn't matter whether you're sixteen or sixty, you are driven by those three unconscious forces to connect. Of course you're older and wiser now. Of course you're decades removed from your parents' home. But the primal longing for the bliss of the womb, the urge to complete ourselves and the need to assert our independence from the attachments of the past—not our parents this time but our previous spouses and lovers—rise up and draw us yet again into the ecstatic state of mind we call being in love.

> **USABLE INSIGHT**
>
> *It's much easier to be alone before you've been in love than after.*

17

Falling Out of Love

To repair the irreparable ravages of time.

—JEAN RACINE

In reality we don't fall out of love. Rather, love falls out of us, like the floors of a building whose foundation crumbles. When we initially bond, it seems as though all the essential ingredients are amazingly strong. The *chemistry* is as natural as two parts hydrogen and one part oxygen combining to form water; *respect* and mutual regard are granted unequivocally; you *enjoy* each other so much you can't stand being apart; you *accept* with great appreciation everything about one another; you *trust* each other with your fears and dreams; you try hard to gain *empathy* for one another's thoughts and feelings. In reality, the relationship is far too new for some of the essential ingredients—trust and respect in particular—to have fully formed, but the thrill of romance and the prospect of a lasting connection is so intoxicating as to make them *seem* perfect. The feeling of perfection is built into early love like the software programs that come pre-loaded with a new computer.

But all honeymoons come to an end. The blinding euphoria and boundless hope of the first stages of love rarely hold up to the reality of being together over time. Soon enough, the effects of everyday pressure and intimate exposure affect the six pillars of love like weather and long-term use affect pillars of stone. In some instances, time polishes and smoothes them until they glisten with an elegant veneer. In others, disappointment, dissatisfaction and frustration chip, crack and wear them down. When that happens, both partners feel wounded and fear

that the intimate connection they always

yearned for will once again slip from their

grasp.

> **USABLE INSIGHT**
>
> *When a relation-ship turns into an arrangement, a home turns into playing house.*

If the deterioration is recognized in

time, the damage can be repaired and the

relationship can not only be saved but

made stronger than ever. Unfortunately,

many couples don't know where to begin.

Denial often creeps in. Or resignation—

the erroneous belief that the decline of intimacy is normal and

nothing can be done about it. This complacency virtually guar-

antees that the relationship will continue to decay. At this point,

friends, family and therapists start to hear remarks like the fol-

lowing:

- "He's changed."
- "She never used to treat me this way."
- "He used to want to be with me all the time, now he squeezes me into his schedule."
- "She used to look up to me, now she treats me with contempt."
- "She used to think I was funny, now she treats me like some silly kid and gets irritated."

Do any of those sound familiar?

Without saying so—sometimes without even acknowledg-

ing it to themselves—each partner secretly hopes that the other

one will do something to stop the decline and solve their prob-

lems. They wish that their mate would finally become the

person they always hoped he or she would be—or return to the wonderful personality they fell in love with. When their wishes don't materialize, their frustration mounts. The person who once made them feel better about their lives now becomes the one who makes them feel worse. Over time, sadness turns to hurt, to blame, to anger, to bitterness and resentment. Now the more unappealing parts of their *own* personalities surge to the forefront. The man tends to get sullen, pouty and withdrawn; the woman tends to criticize, attack and demand. Soon, the former soul mates are cell mates in a prison of negativity.

Sometimes, the silent ache for your partner to respond to your unexpressed needs and desires can go on for months, even years. At some point, however, one of you might feel so desolate and so desperate that you decide to make a unilateral effort to close the widening gap that has opened between you. It's risky to reach across that chasm in hopes that your partner will respond. If he or she does not, you can fall into the abyss. Now humiliation piles onto everything else, and the reality of lost love and shattered dreams can no longer be denied or rationalized. But, if your partner *does* respond well and you can hold hands across the gap, you can begin to rebuild the crumbling structure of your relationship. How successful you are depends on how much the 6 pillars have deteriorated—and how skillful you are at rebuilding them.

Delay and Distraction

For time is the longest distance between two places.

—TENNESSEE WILLIAMS

The longer the initial damage is left unacknowledged and untended to, the faster the erosion and the harder it gets to find the motivation to do the necessary repair work. It's like when you hit your head on a diving board or fall off a bicycle. The longer you wait to dive again or get back on the bike, the harder it is to do.

Typically, however, rather than roll up their sleeves to work on the relationship together, each partner attempts to fill the gap by busying themselves with projects of one kind or another. It could be their careers, it could be recreational activities, it could be building a house—whatever it is, some new focus of energy replaces the passion and intimacy they once shared. If left unchecked, it can grow into a compulsion—an attempt to fill the cracks through which intimacy slips.

If the couple takes on a project together, the common distraction creates the illusion that they are as close as ever, maybe even closer, while all along the ache in their hearts grows and the unacknowledged

> **USABLE INSIGHT**
>
> *By avoiding a difficult task, you turn an anxiety into a phobia.*

feelings continue to fester, leading to everything from stress disorders to temper tantrums. If the replacement activities are *not* shared, the deterioration of the relationship is more rapid and more painfully obvious—especially if one partner's substitute for marital intimacy is the oldest and most hurtful distraction of all, an affair.

In many instances, the attempt to fill the gap takes the form of a child. I often tell clients that despite conventional wisdom, children *do* cause divorce. When the bond between them is strong, of course, a child can bring a loving couple even closer. But if the foundation of the relationship has been weakened, the arrival of a child can hasten the decline of intimacy. Studies show that two-thirds of couples experience a precipitous decline in marital satisfaction after the birth of their first child. Parenthood is much more insidious than careers, hobbies and other distractions because it is so compelling, so challenging and so consuming. It can also be so emotionally rewarding that it makes it easier to ignore the deterioration of the temple of love.

I had seen Todd and Margo for counseling three times when I began to sense that Todd was feeling something he could not reveal to his wife. I asked to see him privately. In that safer setting, Todd confessed to something that was tearing him up inside: He was jealous of his ten-month-old son. It was so hard for him to make that admission that he could not look me in the eye. His voice was barely audible. He explained that Margo was so consumed by being a mother that he felt ignored. Once the center of her attention and the sole focus of her affection, Todd was now displaced, shoved to the periphery of his wife's awareness. He could hardly wrangle a hug out of her, let alone the sustained passion and intimacy he'd come to depend on.

He would see Margo cuddling the child, embracing the child, loving the child with no strings attached, and he too longed to be cuddled, embraced and loved unconditionally. Instead, he was exiled to emotional Siberia. He was mad at Margo for banishing him and being blind to his needs. But worse, far worse, than the pain of rejection and the loss of intimacy was the shame. Todd was convinced that he was the only father in the world who was tormented by such ugly feelings. "What kind of freak am I?" he cried. "Normal men don't get jealous of their babies."

To Todd's great relief, I was not shocked by his admission. I even congratulated him for being able to recognize and acknowledge what a great many new fathers feel but cannot face. It is Freud's Oedipus Complex in reverse: a father wanting to get rid of his child and remarry his wife.

Because of Todd's brave confession, he and Margo were able to nip the problem in the bud before the presence of their child completely destroyed their marriage. Other couples are not so lucky.

When one or both partners becomes so consumed by parenting, careers, projects and other substitutes for intimacy, they don't see the foundation crumbling and the emotional chasm opening wider and wider. They convince themselves that their compulsive activity is necessary and responsible,

> **USABLE INSIGHT**
> *Children* do *cause divorce.*

when in fact much of it is simply an attempt to cover up the sadness and hurt they feel over their disconnection. What was once a union of kindred souls turns into a mere arrangement, with each partner defined by his or her duties; the nuts and bolts of taking care of business create the illusion that they're really close partners. All the while, the six pillars further erode, until one day, to the couple's shock and horror, the entire structure tumbles to the ground.

None of these scenarios is inevitable. Sure, the honeymoon phase can't last, but expecting it to is a naïve delusion, like trying to erect a real cathedral on the papier-mâché columns used on movie sets. The key to mature love is to build strong pillars and constantly reinforce them—not so your relationship can stay the same or return to the halcyon days, but so you can keep on building, adding on extensions, embellishing the decor, always CREATE-ing something new and wonderful and grand at each step of your journey together.

Commitment and Conviction

Whatever you can do, or dream you can, begin it.
Boldness has genius, power and magic in it.
—JOHANN WOLFGANG VON GOETHE

The first step to falling in love again is to make sure you are in agreement with the basic approach of this book. It is extremely hard to make progress if the two partners have vastly different outlooks on the nature of their problems, or if one of them resists working on the relationship. If the approach does not make sense and feel right to both partners, the results are resistance, obstruction and excuse-making.

As mentioned in the introduction, CREATE is a concept you can comfortably share with your lover or spouse. The chances are excellent that he or she will buy into it. It is usually immediately obvious—no convincing required—that when chemistry, respect, enjoyment, acceptance, trust and empathy are strong, the relationship will rest on a solid foundation. For most people, this both feels right and makes sense.

> **USABLE INSIGHT**
>
> *To gain commitment, something has to make sense, feel right and seem doable.*

The first step to using this book with your partner, therefore, is to see if you agree on these three questions:

- Do these six elements play a major role in determining the health of a relationship?
- In your relationship, does the quality of these ingredients need to improve?
- Are you willing to take the necessary steps to rebuild and restore these essentials?

If you can both answer yes to those questions, you will find that any resistance and denial that is present will begin to disappear. What usually follows is a resurgence of optimism and hope. For some couples, it is the first time in years that they've been able to wholeheartedly agree on anything. This makes it possible to join hands in a spirit of cooperation.

Agreeing on a basic strategy provides the essential ingredient of *commitment*. Think of commitment as the granite base on which sturdy pillars rest. Trying to create lasting love without it is like trying to erect a building on sand. Once you're both on the same page, able to talk about your relationship in a common, mutually acceptable language, you'll be able to work as a team, two explorers going forth in search of lost love, ready and willing to put into action the practical tools in this book.

The Keys to Communication

Let us speak, though we show all
our faults and weaknesses.

—HERMAN MELVILLE

Sometimes, people hearing about the six secrets for the first time ask me, "What about communication? Isn't that just as important as the other elements of a healthy relationship?"

The answer is, yes, good communication is vital. There is a chicken-egg relationship between the quality of communication and the strength of the six pillars. It stands to reason that when there is good chemistry between a woman and a man, when they respect, enjoy, accept, trust and empathize with each other, they will be motivated to communicate in a genuinely open and honest manner. At the same time, a high level of communication is crucial for monitoring and maintaining the strength of the pillars—and for repairing and reinforcing them when they've been weakened.

In the chapters to come, you'll be paying attention to the most meaningful aspects of your relationship. Sensitive issues are likely to come up. Delicate feelings may need to be expressed and understood. Important insights and, perhaps, disturbing thoughts may have to be articulated and listened to. The quality of your communication will determine to a large extent how successful you are in repairing and restoring your love. Here are some key principles to follow when working together on the material in this book—and for all your communication as a couple.

1. *It really is better to give than receive.*

Men and women in relationships often become self-centered and lose the sense of "we" and "us." In many ways, this tendency has been made worse by certain self-help approaches, which encourage people to focus on, "What do I want and need?" While it is extremely important to make sure your needs are met and your desires are fulfilled, I have found that when that attitude is taken too far, what should be a collaboration becomes a competition between two self-absorbed, self-centered, unyielding individuals. Selfishness has turned far too many relationships into a zero-sum game, in which one person can win only if the other loses. "Love sought is good," wrote Shakespeare, "but giv'n unsought is better."

> **USABLE INSIGHT**
>
> *Instead of acting entitled, become deserving.*

I have found that the best marriages are those in which the spouses ask first, "What does my partner want and need?" The key, of course, is that *both* partners operate that way, or else one will end up a doormat or a martyr. In my experience, when one person takes a "my partner first" approach rather than a "me first" approach, the other one eventually comes around. When our partners are generous and kind, most of us are naturally inclined to reciprocate. If you allow compassion, consideration and concern to rule your communication, you will earn the right to be treated that way in return.

2. *Put yourself in your partner's place.*

The key to unselfish communication is to always ask yourself this question: "What is it like for my partner right now?"

Most people, caught up in their own frustration and bitterness, never take the time to ask themselves what is going on in the mind and heart of their loved one. But something magical takes place when you walk a mile—or even a step—in someone else's shoes. The shift of attention from me to him or her is both an eye-opener and a heart-opener. No one can contemplate the question "What is it like for my partner?" and at the same time be on the attack. Tension, hostility, defensiveness and blame are quickly replaced by calmness, tenderness, openness and compassion. In addition, you may discover that your partner is not looking for reasons to doubt or reject you, but rather for reasons to trust and accept you.

More effective, but extremely difficult to do, is to extend this question one step further. Ask yourself: "What is likely to be my partner's reaction *after* I say or do what I am about to?" Are you about to say something hurtful? Do you feel the need to unload some pent-up feelings? Pause and ponder what the effect will be. The relief you feel from unloading can blind you to the fact that it might hurt your partner. Is that what will best serve your relationship?

> **USABLE INSIGHT**
>
> *If what you get off your chest lands on your partner's face, you'll just have to face it again.*

Asking "What is it like for my partner right now?" is the essence of one of the six secrets of lasting love, empathy, which will be discussed at length in chapter 7. But the techniques of what I call Empathogenic Therapy have proven to be so powerful in couples counseling that they are used throughout the book.

3. *Listen like you mean it.*

Everyone wants to be understood. But even more important is to know that the other person *wants* to understand and is trying to understand. A sincere attempt to apprehend what another person is trying to communicate demonstrates love, involvement and interest much better than "getting it" does. Learn to listen patiently, with an open mind and an open heart, and convey that you really want to understand what your partner thinks and feels. That effort will do more to cement your bond than the comprehension itself.

Jerry was a sharp young executive who took pride in being a quick study and being able to penetrate swiftly to the bottom line of an issue. This was a big advantage in business, but not at home. One day in therapy, as his wife, Cheryl, struggled to explain what had happened on their first wedding anniversary, Jerry blurted out, "Okay, I get it, you want nicer presents and you like to be surprised. Done." It took an outburst of tears from Cheryl and some prompting from me before he was able to settle down and listen more deeply. Seeing that her husband cared enough to really try to understand had a calming effect on Cheryl. She was able to articulate her thoughts more clearly. Finally, Jerry said, "I think what you're telling me is, you want to know that you're still

> **USABLE INSIGHT**
>
> *Trying to understand is more important than what you understand.*

special to me, because you used to feel that you were the most important thing in my life and lately you don't feel special at all. Is that it?" The difference, in word and demeanor, between that and his previous response was striking. It paved the way for Cheryl and Jerry to work together on the issues that had come between them.

Often, when you come to a quick conclusion about the other person it is satisfying to you but not to them. When someone is in pain or in the grip of intense emotions, the feeling of being all alone with it compounds the suffering. To get away from that awful aloneness, they need to tell their story fully and have it be heard by someone who is truly interested in hearing it. Showing that your partner's pain, confusion, fear and anger are worthy of your total involvement will do wonders to bring the two of you closer. In the early stages of a dialogue, therefore, try to say things like, "I know this is important to you, and I'm struggling to understand. Can you run it by me another way?" It's usually more meaningful than, "I understand."

4. *Dialogue means talking with.*

Communication can take place at four different levels, from least productive to most productive:

- Diatribe—talking *over* each other.
- Debate—talking *at* each other (with no one really listening).
- Discussion—talking *to* each other in a calm, pleasant manner.
- Dialogue—talking *with* each other.

When you're engaged in a *diatribe*, it's as if the other person doesn't exist. It's a monologue. You're ranting or venting, insisting that your view is the right one, the only one, and it's not negotiable. The other person feels invisible.

In a *debate*, you're both trying to prove a point and convince each other of your position. The attitude is, "I'm right, you're wrong."

The atmosphere of a *discussion* is pleasant and calm, but in the context of a love relationship it is often emotionally unsatisfying and somewhat frustrating. It is an intellectual process in which you are communicating head to head.

Dialogue is much more satisfying. It's a heart-to-heart process in which you are connected emotionally as well as mentally. As you move into dialogue, frustration and resentment give way to hope and graciousness. Both partners feel that the other understands where they're coming from and cares how they feel.

As you work together to evaluate, restore and revitalize your relationship, it is vital that you move your communication from the diatribe end of the spectrum to the dialogue end. As a first step to achieving that, I suggest having a conversation with your partner about the differences between the four styles of communication—diatribe, debate, discussion and dialogue—to make sure you're both fully aware of the distinctions. Then, see if you can agree that you will both try never to talk *over* each other or *at* each other, but instead make every effort to talk *with,* or at the very least, *to* each other.

5. *Monitor your communication.*

Try to come up with some ground rules to help your communication stay on the right track. Have a dialogue centered on these questions:

- If one of us has to bring up an issue that might upset the other, what is the best way to do it?
- If either of us starts turning our conversation into a diatribe or a debate, how can we cut it off before it starts to create hostility?
- What should we do to move toward a genuine dialogue?

Your partner's body language will help you monitor your efforts to communicate well. Gestures and expressions say more than words about the effect you are having on another person. Here are the typical signs to look for when you are:

Talking over. The other person tends to look away, as if searching for an exit. Their demeanor will signal irritation, annoyance or anger.

Talking at. People who tend to react to a challenge aggressively will shift the plane of their face upward, sticking out their chin as if to say, "Who the hell do you think you are, talking to me that way?" Those who are easily intimidated will shift the plane of their face downward, tucking in their chin in a submissive reflex, as if to say, "Okay, you win, please don't hurt me."

Talking to. They will knit their brow and narrow their gaze, signaling that they are trying to understand you. They might nod from the neck up, as if to say, "That makes sense," or, "I see your point." They may not agree, but they get what you're saying and their demeanor is not confrontational. You have their mind, but not their heart.

Talking with. They're genuinely taking you in. You may notice that their eyes get more lively and their brow and facial muscles relax. Their shoulders and upper torso will also tend to relax, as if they are letting down their guard and saying, "Good, you understand me, and you accept and respect where I'm coming from. You can tell me anything, and I know I can tell you anything."

The more you are able to talk *with* another person, the more he or she is willing to open up. We should all aspire to this level of communication, not just with our closest intimates but in as many relationships as possible. The only time talking over or talking at is useful is in a do-or-die crisis, where there is no room for emotions and no time for anything but getting the job done.

6. *Always ask, "Am I being fair and reasonable?"*

We all keep score. Even if we're not aware of it, our unconscious scoreboard keeps a strict tally of who's dumping on the other, who's not listening, who's criticizing, who's turning every dialogue into a diatribe and so forth. So try to maintain balance in your communication. If, for instance, one of you has a basic policy of, "I want you to say only nice things to me, but I get to tell you whatever I want," it won't be long before the other's scoreboard starts to blink and whistle and the fireworks go off.

The principle of fair and reasonable applies to the content of your communication as well as the style. The things you ask of one another should be balanced over time. If one constantly demands, manipulates or takes while the other always gives in without receiving equal treatment, the foundation of the relationship will crumble like an old loaf of bread. Of course, there may be times when you want something that is not particularly fair or reasonable. Go ahead and make the request, but both of you should treat it as a favor. If your partner grants it, he or she should be entitled to a fair and reasonable favor in return.

7. *Marriage is presumed dead.*

Presuming to know what your partner is thinking and feeling without checking to see if you're right is not only rude, it's the kiss of death for a relationship. So is presuming that your partner can read your mind and anticipate your needs.

Instead of acting on your assumptions, ask your partner what he or she is actually thinking and feeling. And don't expect him or her to be any better at the presumption game than you are: make sure you communicate your innermost feelings clearly and accurately at all times.

There are many reasons why we hesitate to speak our truth: we don't want to upset or offend the other person; we don't like to admit we need anything; we don't want to risk being refused or rejected; it makes us feel vulnerable. But, while you're waiting for your partner to respond to your unspoken requests, you get more and more frustrated and resentful. If you can't safely bare your neck in your most intimate relationship, something is seriously wrong.

> **USABLE INSIGHT**
>
> *The best way to get what you need is to ask for it.*

8. *Use the six-step pause.*

The biggest regrets in communication occur when we speak impulsively or respond to our partners with a knee-jerk reaction. To guard against saying or doing hurtful things, try to be reflective instead of reflexive. The following steps allow you to insert your rational mind into an overheated loop and consciously choose the right thing to say or do:

STEP 1. Increase physical awareness. Stop and notice what you feel and where you feel it.

STEP 2. Increase emotional awareness. Connect the physical sensation to an emotion. Do you feel tense? Angry? Afraid? Hurt?

STEP 3. Increase impulse awareness. Ask yourself, "What do the feelings I just noticed make me want to say or do?"

STEP 4. Increase consequence awareness: "If I act on that impulse, what might the outcomes be for myself and my partner?" Think both short- and long-term.

STEP 5. Increase solution awareness: "What are my alternatives, and which one is most likely to produce a desirable outcome?"

STEP 6. Increase benefit awareness: "What will be my reward for trying this solution?"

This invervention may seem artificial and intrusive at first. Try to be patient. With persistent practice, you'll be able to do the whole procedure so quickly it will seem like a single step. It takes about thirty days for a change in behavior to become a habit and a minimum of six months for a habit to become a natural part of your personality.

Building the Castle of Love

If you have built castles in the air, your work need
not be lost. That is where they should be. Now put
the foundations under them.
—HENRY DAVID THOREAU

Let's begin the process of falling back in love by evaluating the six basic ingredients of your relationship. On a scale of one to five, one being in desperate trouble and five being perfect, how would you rate each one? (You and your partner should do these exercises separately, without consulting each other.)

	1	2	3	4	5
CHEMISTRY	☐	☐	☐	☐	☐
RESPECT	☐	☐	☐	☐	☐
ENJOYMENT	☐	☐	☐	☐	☐
ACCEPTANCE	☐	☐	☐	☐	☐
TRUST	☐	☐	☐	☐	☐
EMPATHY	☐	☐	☐	☐	☐

Next, think back to when your relationship was at its strongest. How would you have rated the six pillars then? Give each one a retroactive score. If you need to refresh your memory, look at photographs of the two of you when love and fun were in abundance. While sometimes painful, such reminders can be illuminating.

Now, see if you can put yourself in your partner's shoes. Imagine what it's like to be him or her and write down the score you think he or she would ascribe to each pillar. Then, write down the score your partner would have given to each one at the strongest point in your relationship. Don't skimp on this step just because you're not sure how to respond. You know more than you think you do, and it's extremely important to begin the habit of seeing through your partner's eyes.

Assuming you're not in total denial, if you gave every pillar a score of five, you are in the enviable position of being able to emphasize preventive medicine. This book will help you keep your relationship strong by reinforcing what you're already doing well, spotting early signs of weakness and taking immediate steps to fortify areas that need help.

If you scored less than five for any of the categories, you're indicating that your relationship is not where you would like it to be. You have a certain amount of dissatisfaction and disappointment. This book will help you to recognize the reasons why those ingredients are not as strong as they could be and show you how to rebuild them.

What Lies Ahead

Marriage is our last, best chance to grow up.

—JOSEPH BARTH

In the coming chapters, we will be discussing each of the six secrets in the order of CREATE. Every chapter explains why that particular pillar is so vital, what causes it to break down and, most importantly, how you can repair and restore it. At the beginning of each chapter you will find a brief questionnaire that will help you identify how much of a problem that pillar is. Refer back to the questionnaire when doing the exercises later in the chapter.

Your individual circumstances may cause you to place greater emphasis on one area than another. Your specific concerns may even tempt you to skip some chapters. For instance, you might want to go straight to trust because mistrust has eaten away at your love. Strictly speaking, it should not make any difference where you begin; just as all roads once led to Rome, any of the six pathways will put you on the royal road to love. However, I urge you to read the book from start to finish. Because some information in later chapters refers back to earlier parts of the book, reading out of sequence may lead to confusion. I also highly recommend that you work on every pillar, even if you emphasize some more than others. They are as inextricably connected as the legs of a chair. Fortifying the strong ones will help you strengthen those that received low scores.

Before you go on to the next chapter, take a few minutes to reflect on where your relationship is now. Then, imagine what it would be like if you were able to raise the score for each ingredient up to the level of five. What would that feel like? How would you look at your partner, and how would he or she look at you? What would you feel when you're together? What would you do differently? What would having six strong pillars mean to your overall happiness and contentment in life?

This is the destination that lies before you. It is definitely attainable. Keep your eye on the light at the end of the tunnel. That light is *not* from an oncoming train. It is the light of hope— the hope that you can thaw the *hate* between the two of you, heal the *hurt* that neither of you meant to inflict on each other, and CREATE the emotional *home* that both of you are homesick for.

2

Chemistry

Everything You Wanted to
Ask About Sex But Were
Afraid to Know

*Love becomes the ultimate answer to
the ultimate human question.*

—ARCHIBALD MACLEISH

*Love is the answer, but while you are
waiting for the answer, sex raises
some pretty good questions.*

—WOODY ALLEN

How much do the following statements apply to how you think or feel about the chemistry in your relationship?

	Hardly Ever 0	Sometimes 1	Almost Always 2
1. I fantasize about having sex with my partner.	___	___	___
2. Whenever he/she touches me I feel excited or aroused.	___	___	___
3. Touching him/her is irresistible.	___	___	___
4. When we make love, I wish it could go on forever.	___	___	___
5. When we have sex, I'm glad I'm with him/her, not someone else.	___	___	___
6. After sex I feel satisfied and fulfilled.	___	___	___
7. When an evening approaches with the possibility of making love, I look forward to it.	___	___	___
8. When we spend a night away from home, one thing I look forward to is having sex.	___	___	___
9. When we're at a party or in a group, I feel lucky to be with my partner and turned on by the idea of making love later.	___	___	___
10. I love the way my partner looks, dressed and undressed.	___	___	___
TOTAL:	___	___	___

SCORING:

0–6   More like brother and sister than lovers.

7–13   After sex, you think, "We gotta do this more often."

14–20   Make reservations for your next romantic getaway.

It's one of the most wrenching moments in therapy, and unfortunately one of the most common—when a husband or wife confides to me that the spouse who once was irresistible has become unappealing or even repugnant. His passionate princess has become a caustic ice queen who gets headaches whenever he gets close. Her once charming prince has become a couch potato whose idea of romance is to say, "Wanna do it?" as he scratches himself.

"Once upon a time I couldn't wait to see him," a client with tear-filled eyes declared. "I used to hope he'd try to seduce me. Now I dread it. I've tried to bring us back to when it was good, but I couldn't do it, and I'm sick of pretending." The confession usually comes with mixed emotions, such as:

- guilt ("I'm terrible to feel this way")
- fear ("Will the chemistry ever come back?")
- confusion ("Why is this happening?")
- sadness ("It used to be so good")
- frustration ("I can't take it anymore")
- anger ("I hate that bitch/bastard for letting this happen!")

The loss of chemistry in long-term relationships has attracted the attention of both scientists and comedians, and so far the comics are way ahead. When you're dating, sex takes place anywhere in the house, one joke begins. When you get married, it takes place in the bedroom. After you've been married a while, it takes place in the hallway, when you say "Screw you" as you pass each other. Erma Bombeck's quip from two decades ago still rings true for many: "The only reason I would take up jogging is so that I could hear heavy breathing again."

Chances are you know that it's unrealistic to expect the explosive, euphoric, all-consuming animal passion of early love to last as a relationship matures and the partners age. It makes about as much sense as expecting to have the same energy halfway through a marathon as you had at the opening bell. But the chances are also good that you miss that uninhibited lust and would like to get at least some of it back. That's not an unreasonable goal. But you can do even better. You can restore your passion and combine it with the calm wisdom of mature love. For chemistry in the best sense is more than just lust. Let's look more closely at what it means.

The Chemistry Continuum

Men always want to be a woman's first love—
women like to be a man's last romance.

—OSCAR WILDE

Think of chemistry as existing on a continuum of attraction, with oil and water on one end and pure magnetism on the other. On the magnetic end, chemistry usually means a Velcro-like attachment so strong you can hardly tear yourselves apart. You say things like, "I can't wait to see him," and, "I can't keep my hands off her," and, "I get turned on just thinking about our next date." When Velcro chemistry matures, it can be more all-encompassing physically than the combustion of youthful lust. It

42

includes the enjoyment of kissing, touching, fondling and other activities that we often think of as "mere" foreplay but which offer boundless sensual pleasure.

In mature love, chemistry encompasses mental and emotional attraction as well as physical. Time passes slowly when you are waiting for the one you love, and when you're together, hours seem like minutes. At its most intense, chemistry creates a heavenly, euphoric feeling, evoking terms like blissful and ecstatic. It's as though a missing part of you has been found. You feel connected heart to heart, spirit to spirit, and when you have to part it's as though something is being peeled off your skin.

Strong chemistry is not just an overpowering attraction to another person. It is also the feeling that he or she is as powerfully attracted to you. It's when they love to look at you as much as you love to look at them, and to touch you as much as you love to touch them, because that contact creates a wholeness that is more than the sum of both your parts. In every look, touch and kiss there is a sense that both of you are savoring something special, something you can't seem to get enough of. You want to bathe in it and drink it all in. Your partner's presence gives you a sense of enhanced well-being. At its best, good chemistry creates a feeling of unity, physically, emotionally and spiritually, in which, at that moment, all is right in the universe.

> **USABLE INSIGHT**
>
> *Chemistry is as much in the eye of the beheld as the beholder.*

Chemistry has the ability to change from the fiery heat of wanton passion to the warm glow of tender affection. It is only natural for the intensity of early love to dissipate—and beneficial to us, since our bodies could hardly stand up to the perpetual adrenaline rush. But the natural mellowing of age should not be confused with the kind of accommodation that turns many long-term couples into just a higher order of roommates. While lust alone does not constitute chemistry in the best sense of the word, heated passion is crucial or else the chemicals remain lukewarm and never reach the boiling point. Regardless of age, good chemistry consists of both tenderness and strong sexual attraction. Nothing is more inspiring than aging couples who hold hands and cuddle like teenagers and still get goosebumps when they touch.

Unfortunately, a common complaint from partners who have been together a long time is, "We're like brother and sister." They feel comfortable with each other, they have shared values, they love doing things together, they sacrifice for one another, but the sexual energy is gone. That phrase, "like brother and sister," suggests a powerful, positive, unbreakable bond, but it also implies that something important is missing. It announces that they no longer feel what lovers are supposed to feel.

Nevertheless, the peck-on-the-cheek chemistry of a comfortable couple has far greater magnetism than what exists on the oil-and-water end of the continuum. That's where you see the exact opposite of attraction: repulsion. When chemistry is strong, the approach of your lover is like a match; when chemistry is absent, it's like a bucket of water. When chemistry is present, you think, "I'm lucky to be with this person"; when chemistry is gone, it's, "How did I get stuck with that?" With powerful chemistry, you feel a sense of freedom when you're together; without it, you feel trapped.

Better Loving Through Chemistry

Sexual love is undoubtedly one of the chief things in life, and the union of mental and bodily satisfaction in the enjoyment of love is one of its culminating peaks.

—SIGMUND FREUD

Aside from sensual pleasure, the tension-release of orgasm and the emotional satisfaction of intimacy, good chemistry offers a great many benefits. "When approached with love and zest, lovemaking dissolves anxiety, depression, loneliness and despair," writes Felice Dunas, Ph.D., in *Passion Play*. "It elevates the spirit and opens us to joy, enriching our capacity to feel and making life more whole." To put it simply, the chemistry of love makes us feel better, physically and emotionally, casting a warm glow over the entire relationship and our lives.

While our knowledge of the physiology of love is still in its infancy, the evidence strongly suggests that even a simple loving touch produces beneficial physical changes. Research indicates that babies who are touch-deprived tend to suffer severe developmental disorders. Other studies show that the biochemical signs of stress are reduced in adults who are touched. Oxytocin, a hormonelike substance associated with feelings of well-being, soars when a mother breast-feeds. It also rises when loving partners touch each other. In fact, it goes up even when they *anticipate* touching each other, thereby earning a reputation as the bonding hormone. Also, in the intoxication of early love, the body pours adrenaline into the system, producing that feeling of power and excitement we're all familiar with. Endorphins, the body's painkilling chemical, increase as well.

"Romantic love is a mental illness," wrote the humorist Fran Liebowitz. "It's a drug. It distorts reality, and that's the point of it." The point being to make sure we perpetuate the species. But the benefits of chemistry also have a familiar downside. The tendency of lusty love to paint reality with rose-colored glasses, causing us to idealize our partners, can also blind us to their short-comings and carry us into the future on wings of inflated expectations. That's why we're advised not to marry too quickly after meeting someone who seems to be Mr. or Ms. Right. We're also familiar with adrenaline letdown—the depression and despair that comes when our romantic dreams are dashed. We miss the high so much when it's gone that we go to great lengths to get it back. And when we *do* get it back, all is right with the world once more. This can lead to an addiction to the thrill of early love, making it impossible to sustain a mature relationship.

The challenge for long-term chemistry is to combine the excitement of early love with the calm, affectionate qualities of grown-up love.

> **USABLE INSIGHT**
>
> *Focusing only on lust is the surest way to overlook love.*

How Chemistry Spreads

Sex is two plus two making five, rather than four.

—MARTY FELDMAN

Like reinforced concrete, sexual attraction enhances the strength of every one of the other five pillars. Bad chemistry, on the other hand, is like an acid that eats away at them.

That mutual *enjoyment* would be enhanced by good chemistry should be obvious. Passion adds zest to a relationship, and not just in bed. Couples who enjoy each other physically usually find other ways to play together as well. When the attraction is magnetic, it is far easier to find *acceptance* for your loved one. Traits that might otherwise be a nuisance don't seem quite as annoying. They might even seem cute. By contrast, when you are sexually frustrated or turned off to your partner (or your partner is turned off to you), every little imperfection can become an irritant. Good chemistry has the effect of making you want to notice the positive and ignore the negative.

The connection between good chemistry and respect is subtle. Think of it this way: While the heat from a roaring fireplace can permeate all the rooms in a house, a candle will barely warm your hands. Similarly, the heat of a passionate love warms all your perceptions and judgments. When you see your partner's actions in the light of that warmth, you're much more likely to give him or her the benefit of the doubt. That adds up to increased respect.

The link between *bad* chemistry and respect is more obvious. Frustration triggers blame, and it's hard to respect someone you think is depriving you of satisfaction. "No matter how many times I tell him I don't like it, his idea of foreplay is to start groping me," complained one wife. "He comes on like some horny teenager and finishes his business without even thinking about *my* needs." Meanwhile, her husband griped, "You'd think she could lose a little weight and make herself more attractive. It's like she doesn't even care anymore." Those are not just expressions of sexual dissatisfaction, they're signs of disrespect, and it overflowed to other areas of their lives. She saw him as a self-centered adolescent in every way, and he saw her as a slob who let herself go.

Mature chemistry usually carries with it a strong sense of *trust*. When you feel safe to place your sexual needs and desires in your partner's hands, when you know that he or she cares about your satisfaction, that sense of trust tends to carry over to other areas of life. The odds are good that someone who is thoughtful and considerate in bed will be that way out of bed as well. By contrast, bad chemistry can lead to general mistrust. A couple who could not decide whether to get married spoke to me separately. "He's so impatient and careless in bed," said the woman, "it makes me scared he'll be that way with other things too, like our children and our money." Said the man, "She's so timid sexually, I wonder if I can trust her to take chances in life. And I know she lies when I ask her how the sex is for her, so what else will she lie about?"

> ### USABLE INSIGHT
>
> *Good chemistry is a love potion. Bad chemistry is a love poison.*

As for *empathy*, imagine that you're strongly attracted to your lover, you feel great tenderness and warmth toward him or her and you are sexually satisfied. Wouldn't you be inclined to look at things from your partner's point of view? Certainly more so than if you were turned off and frustrated—particularly if you believed that the poor chemistry was your partner's fault. Good chemistry is a terrific motivator. It makes you think, "What does my partner want and need?"—not just during lovemaking but in every area of life.

By contrast, if your relationship is chemistry-challenged, you're likely to be angry, and when you're angry it's hard to be empathic. It's easier to keep feeling victimized than to soften your stance and try to understand the person you hold responsible for your frustration.

Why Chemistry Declines

Love is a fire. But whether it is going to warm your
heart or burn down your house, you can never tell.

    —JOAN CRAWFORD

Chemistry, the mysterious force that initially brings couples together, is often the first ingredient to weaken—although sometimes it only *seems* that way because its decline is more noticeable than that of others. There are a great many reasons why two people who begin as twin flames become, over time, more like icebergs.

Physical Factors

Sometimes, the word chemistry can be taken literally: what is assumed to be an emotional issue or incompatibility is actually caused by an underlying biochemical condition. Sexuality can be affected by a variety of physical factors, including cardiovascular health, endocrine problems such as diabetes and the level of certain hormones and peptides in the body. It is very common for couples to think something is wrong with their marriage when what's really happening are changes in physiology. This is especially true in middle age, when the predictable decline of sex hormones can be quite disconcerting.

Depression and anxiety also have a crippling effect on sexuality. While both conditions can be emotional in origin, they have increasingly well-known biochemical causes that can be effectively treated with medication (the combination of medicine and psychotherapy is the most effective approach). Unfortunately, what begins as an undetected physical problem can quickly snowball into emotional and interpersonal turmoil. Frustrated individuals start to blame themselves or each other, causing a quick descent into self-doubt and strife. In a vicious cycle, they become so anxious and self-conscious that they can't relax in bed and their sexual chemistry is further eroded.

It is beyond the scope of this book to discuss medical factors in detail. If you suspect that the chemistry of your relationship may be compromised by a physical condition, I urge you to discuss it with your physician.

The physical component of chemistry also includes the ravages of time on our bodies. At forty, we don't respond sexually the same way we did at twenty. This is not necessarily a bad thing. There are different pleasures to be had with middle-aged bodies if you understand what's going on and adapt to your new biology. Men often become more skillful lovers, more inclined to slow down and enjoy the foreplay they used to get out of the way as quickly as possible in their drive for gratification. Women tend to become more adventurous, confident and aggressive about their sexuality. These factors, along with the growth of affection and tenderness that comes with long-term intimacy, can make for *better* chemistry in middle age. Unfortunately, many couples insist on comparing themselves to the hot young lovers they once were—and see in the media—and conclude that their chemistry is in critical condition.

We also don't *look* the same at forty as we do at twenty. Few of us are Sean Connery or Susan Sarandon, growing sexier with age. It may be a sad commentary on human beings, but the sight of beer bellies, double chins and sagging erogenous zones does not excite us the way slim, firm bodies do. Actually, in many cases, an aging body is more of an obstacle to the person looking in the mirror than it is to his or her partner. Love, and all the emotional factors that contribute to chemistry, can override a person's esthetic preferences, but the self-image of someone who sees him- or herself as ugly, fat or otherwise unappealing can snuff out passion before it even ignites.

> **USABLE INSIGHT**
>
> *Constantly asking your partner to tell you you're attractive is unattractive.*

The High Cost of Stress

The pressures of work, money, parenting and having too much to do and too little time can wreak havoc on chemistry. Part of it is purely physical: stress can increase the level of substances that reduce sexual desire and performance. It can also exhaust the body, and fatigue is not compatible with passion. Sometimes, the tension that builds up under prolonged stress can make a person feel exceptionally aroused, as the body cries out for the relief of sexual climax. But that too can interfere with a couple's chemistry if the impassioned partner is out of sync with his or her mate. A common complaint from women is stressed-out husbands who crave sexual release and abandon all traces of subtlety to get what they want. Few things turn off a woman like a clumsy come-on.

The psychological and emotional impact of stress only adds to the problem. When tension is high, things that normally evoke tenderness and affection may instead breed aggravation and hostility. This is especially true when you perceive—accurately or not—that your partner is the cause of your stress.

Stress is particularly damaging when it prompts a dip in self-esteem. If you're worried about losing your job, for instance, you might start to feel inadequate—a terrible blow to a couple's chemistry. Men whose self-image is measured by achievement or money are especially vulnerable to this. Claude was a forty-seven-year-old real estate developer whose business had suffered a major setback. Unable to provide for his family in the manner he was accustomed to, he became increasingly despondent. The prospect of having to sell his home and move to a smaller one and sending his children to public school instead of the expensive private school they were attending, made him feel like a failure. Convinced that his wife, Sandra, saw him as something less than a real man, he withdrew into a sulking silence. In truth, Sandra still thought the world of her husband and loved him as much as the day they married. But Claude's self-worth had gone the way of his income. In his mind he was unworthy, and he projected those feelings onto his wife. Subconsciously, he felt, "Why would she want to make love to a loser like me?"

When, in therapy, Claude was able to reveal his shame and self-doubt, Sandra burst into tears. "You're still the sexiest man I've ever known," she told him. That night, they made love for the first time in months, and Claude's self-defeating thought pattern was thrown into reverse: the restoration of chemistry provided a major boost for his self-esteem and he started on the road to rebuilding his business.

Familiarity Breeds Monotony

Beauty soon grows familiar to the lover,
Fades in his eye, and palls upon the sense.

—JOSEPH ADDISON

In animal experiments, researchers place a male and female (in heat) in a cage together and measure the amount of time it takes for the male to attempt to copulate. They also measure the time between ejaculation and the next sexual engagement. This interval, called the refraction period, grows increasingly longer after each copulation, until the male eventually reaches exhaustion and stops trying. That much would no doubt sound familiar to any human. But here's the rub: if a new female is introduced, the weary male quickly responds, reinvigorated by the prospect of a different mate. The refraction period reverts to what it had been earlier.

This phenomenon, called the Coolidge Effect, seems to have a parallel among humans. In one of the jokes that surfaced when Viagra was first introduced, a middle-aged man asks his doctor for medication so he can at last make love to his wife again. The doctor tells him to take the pill and drive home, by which time the drug will have taken effect and he'll be ready to go. He arrives, eager to get on with it, only to find that his wife is not home. In a panic, he calls the doctor and asks what to do. The doctor slyly suggests that the impassioned man might want to find a substitute for his wife. "Is the maid home?" he asks. To which the man replies: "Doc, if I wanted to screw the maid I wouldn't need a pill."

A large number of anguished husbands—and a smaller, but significant number of wives—have confided similar feelings to me in therapy. "I look at other women and fantasize about them," said one confused forty-year-old man who was struggling to stay faithful after fourteen years of marriage. "Objectively, most of them are less attractive than my wife, with less appealing personalities, yet they turn me on. I think to myself, 'I wish I didn't know my wife, because she's exactly the kind of woman I'd find sexy if she were a stranger.'"

One cause for a decline in chemistry, therefore, is simply familiarity and sameness. The memory of highly charged eroticism with an exciting new lover is something most long-term relationships, with their sexual monotony and romantic routine, can't measure up to. The honeymoon period is more unreal than the rest of life, but unfortunately we allow it to become the standard instead of seeing it as the exception—a high-voltage adventure that is duplicated only in rare moments.

> **USABLE INSIGHT**
>
> *Variety is the spice of love.*

We then feel disappointed, sometimes blaming our partners for spoiling the fun, and we fail to appreciate the calmer, more tender kind of chemistry that comes with mature love.

The solution to this particular cause of declining chemistry is *not* to find other partners. As we'll see later in this chapter, the problem can be solved with a little imagination.

Emotional Wear and Tear

In the early stages of romance, when the flames of passion burn strong, you squeeze your life into your relationship. Nothing matters as much as the thrill of being with your lover—except maybe the thrill of knowing that nothing matters more to your lover than being with you. Over time, as everyday responsibilities reassume their importance, the equation shifts: you begin to squeeze your relationship into your life. Each person begins to feel diminished in the eyes of the other. I can't count the number of times I have heard a spouse complain: "He used to juggle everything in his life in order to see me. Now he juggles me so that I don't get in the way of a football game or his business schedule." (Of course, when the man complains, it's not football but social obligations, children or career pressure that take the woman's attention away.) Feeling less important to your partner can have a dampening effect on chemistry.

In addition, all the little flaws you readily overlook in the early stages can start to get in the way as time goes by. At first, your lover's annoying habits—the too-rough way he touches you or the way she moves (or doesn't move) while making love—are like the sounds of a city outside the window: you don't hear them when the stereo is on, but they drive you crazy when the music stops. Then there is the emotional baggage that piles up in the course of a long-term relationship. Nothing kills chemistry like the buildup of resentment and criticism.

Performance Anxiety

Whether it's a woman who is afraid of not exciting her lover or a man who's afraid to lose his erection, fear is a chemistry killer. And it doesn't take much for a vicious cycle to start rolling. One or two painful or embarrassing instances—which could be triggered by any of the factors we just described—can lead to anxiety about what might happen next time. That anxiety makes a recurrence even more likely, as the fear of failing again becomes a self-fulfilling prophecy.

The vicious cycle continues when the partner reacts. Suppose a man has an instance of premature ejaculation or erectile dysfunction. His partner may be compassionate, but sometimes the more she tries to reassure him, the more pathetic he feels. This further increases his anxiety, which only makes him less appealing, since most women find a confident man sexy and a fearful one a turn-off. Before long, both partners are thinking and worrying instead of abandoning themselves to pleasure.

> **USABLE INSIGHT**
>
> *Performance anxiety puts the worry into getting close.*

The more that sex becomes associated with tension, the more the overall chemistry of the relationship becomes polluted. Avoidance is sure to follow, and what used to be fun becomes work. The couple might even be afraid to get aroused because it puts them on the spot and opens the door to frustration.

Other Chemistry Killers

Anything that diminishes respect, enjoyment, acceptance, trust or empathy is going to affect chemistry. Let's look at an example for each:

RESPECT. When Randy and Marilyn first got together, they admired each other tremendously. But, over the course of a six-year marriage, Marilyn had watched the bold young man she fell in love with turn to a battered shell who was constantly taken advantage of and verbally abused by his boss. For his part, Randy had seen his vivacious wife turn moody and mean under the spell of alcohol. Eventually, they lost respect for each other, and their mutual disrespect turned their bedroom from an erotic playpen to a cold-war zone. "Sometimes I come home feeling like I want to make love," said Randy, "but then I see that boozy look in her eyes and want to fondle the remote instead of her." Marilyn said simply, "Wimps turn me off."

ENJOYMENT. When they were dating, Steve and Betsy used to have enormous fun together, and their enjoyment flowed naturally into the bedroom. But the pressures of parenting and high-powered careers had worn them out. They had also developed new interests they did not share with each other. What little time they had for recreation was pursued separately. Privately, each spouse told me the same thing: the relationship had stopped being fun, and lovemaking had become another chore. Naturally, each of them thought it was the other one's fault. Once upon a time, laughter had been an aphrodisiac to Betsy and Steve. Now they hardly laughed at all—and they made love even less often.

ACCEPTANCE. So much hostility had built up between Justine and Roger that it was impossible for them to find something nice to say about each other. They both had a list of their partner's traits that they just could not accept. Their sex drives were still functional, and they occasionally found each other sexy enough to set the lovemaking process in motion. But they could never set aside their criticism long enough to get aroused. No sooner did their body temperature rise than one would do or say something that triggered some unexpressed irritation from earlier in the day, or a week before, and bickering would replace foreplay. Instead of falling asleep satisfied in each other's arms, they would count sheep—or more likely, grudges—with their backs to each other.

TRUST. For Kathy and Paul, mistrust had doused the fires of love. In the throes of passion, Paul had a tendency to get careless with his wife's body. "It's like he forgets I'm a flesh and blood woman," said Kathy. "He throws me around like I'm some kind of blow-up doll or something." When they first fell in love, she found Paul's wildness exciting. A year later, she was tempted to break off their engagement because she was afraid she might get hurt. In the meantime, Paul himself had started to avoid sex because of a trust issue of another kind: "She blabbed to her friends about how I am in bed," he said. "I'm not sure I can trust her anymore."

EMPATHY. Resentment over a thousand little hurts had brought Jordan and Connie to therapy to see if they could fend off divorce. "We haven't made love for about three years," said Jordan. "We have sex sometimes, but we don't make love." What he meant was, sex had become routine, something they engaged in out of habit and the need to release tension. "We used to be tuned to each other like a pair of violins," lamented Connie. "We wanted to please each other and we knew exactly how." But anger had made them selfish and vindictive instead of empathic. They could not bring themselves to think, "What will please my lover now? What would he or she want me to do?" Instead of focusing on giving their partner pleasure, they thought only of their own gratification, and the result was not very gratifying for either of them.

In each of these examples, the couple had to identify the pillar whose weakness had destroyed their sex lives. Before they could revive their chemistry, they had to repair the damage.

Spotting the Early Warning Signs

The will is infinite and the execution confined . . .
the desire is boundless and the act a slave to limit.

—WILLIAM SHAKESPEARE

"Josh and I have become like brother and sister," Dana confided to me. "We have the same values, we care deeply about each other, and we're a great team when it comes to getting things done. But something is missing." What was missing was sex. Dana and Josh had become affectionate friends who treated each other with the consideration of close family members. But lovemaking had become a thing of the past since the birth of their third child, who was autistic.

Having quit her job to care for the kids, Dana was so drained of energy at the end of the day she could barely brush her teeth, let alone make love. On a couple of occasions, she yielded to Josh out of a sense of obligation, but it was not very satisfying for either of them. Josh, who was under tremendous pressure to make ends meet, grew weary of being told "I'm too tired" every time he wanted sex, even though he knew it was the truth. He just stopped trying. The couple not only avoided sex, they avoided any contact that might lead to arousal, fearing it would end in frustration.

As mentioned earlier, if you avoid something potentially unpleasant long enough, it begins to turn into a phobia. That's what happened to Josh and Dana's sex life, a pattern that is all too common among long-term partners. I suggested that they go away to some peaceful, romantic hideaway to try and rekindle the spark of love. The strategy usually works wonders with couples whose chemistry has been consumed by everyday burdens. But things had gone too far for Dana and Josh. For two straight nights, over lovely dinners at a country inn, they drank so much that lovemaking was impossible. Neither of them was much of a drinker, but they indulged that weekend to dispel the anxiety of having to perform sexually.

They had also begun to display other signs of lost chemistry. Misplaced jealousy, for instance. Josh found himself being nasty toward the family dog, and he couldn't figure out why. When we discussed it in therapy, he realized what had happened: "Watching Dana get all coochy-coo with the dog made me feel even more deprived."

Compulsive behavior also surfaced. To fill the hole where the pain gets in, people often become obsessed with some activity that provides momentary pleasure or a distraction from thoughts and feelings they can't bear to face. Josh started gambling. Dana went shopping constantly, dragging her kids to every sale in town.

Josh and Dana were plummeting toward the basement end of the chemistry continuum. Fortunately, they had not slid so far as to be hopeless. Like someone who spots the early warning signs of cardiac disease in time to prevent a heart attack, they were able to halt the deterioration and gradually restore their chemistry. Other couples are not so lucky. They hit bottom, where the direct opposite of chemical attraction dominates their relationship: they find each other repulsive.

At its worst, when the chemistry is totally gone, what comes to mind are thoughts like, "Get away from me," "Don't come near me" and "Don't you dare touch me." The repulsion is not just sexual, but an overall aversion. Almost everything your partner says or does hits you like fingernails on a chalkboard. Whereas you used to eagerly anticipate your lover's return from work or a trip, you find yourself hoping he or she stays away longer. That aversion to someone you once found irresistible can be so painful and scary that you try to distract yourself by doing something else, whether it's work, the Internet, the children or food. That's how obsessions and compulsions are born.

You also find yourself avoiding every type of intimacy, not just the overtly sexual kind. When chemistry is strong, you can't keep your hands off each other; when it's gone, you stop doing the little affectionate things, like hugging when you greet each other, or holding hands on a walk, or resting your hand on each other's legs while watching TV. You might even stop kissing on the lips. There is a good reason that prostitutes say they never kiss their clients on the lips—in many ways it's a more intimate act than having intercourse. I have counseled dozens of couples who air-kiss or exchange quick pecks on the cheek when they say good-bye, but have not really kissed on the lips in ages—in some cases, not even when having sex, which they engage in strictly for tension release.

As with cholesterol tests, blood pressure exams or mammograms, the sooner you spot the early warning signs of chemistry loss, the better your chances of reversing the decline. Don't wait for it to reach the extreme of mutual aversion. Reflect on your relationship and see if any of these warning signs are present:

- You don't look forward to seeing each other at the end of the day or after some time apart.
- You find fault with each other for little things.
- You don't like looking at each other.
- You don't hug, touch or kiss on the lips much.
- You avoid intimacy.
- You often feel disgusted or repelled by each other.
- You're using compulsive behavior to compensate for the lack of passion.
- You drink or use drugs to numb the pain.
- You fantasize a lot about having sex with other partners.
- You're masturbating more than before.

Speaking of Sex

Sex is a conversation carried out by other means. If
you get on well out of bed, half the problems of bed
are solved.

—PETER USTINOV

The first step to restoring the pillar of chemistry is to sit down in a
relaxed setting and have an honest, open dialogue. Before you
begin, each of you should reread the guidelines for good communication on page 26. Make sure you apply those principles
diligently, so you have a genuine dialogue and not a debate. You are
going to be discussing sensitive issues. At times it might be difficult
or even painful. I assure you that if you work through those
moments in a spirit of love, respect and true consideration, you will
emerge with far greater understanding than you now think possible. The end result will be a resurgence of tenderness, a renewed
commitment to make things better and a stronger conviction that
together you can accomplish your goal. Perhaps most important,
through deep communication, you will create a powerful *emotional*
chemistry—the crucial ingredient that enables mature love to tran-
scend the purely physical aspects of sexual passion.

Deep, intimate dialogue allows each of you the opportunity
to be listened to. If lingering hurt, resentment and blame stand as
impediments to working on your chemistry, it is vital that those
feelings be expressed and resolved. The understanding and compassion fostered by good dialogue reduces the You vs. Me attitude that stands in the way of intimacy, and replaces it with a
renewed sense of *We*. That We may have been lost as each of you

struggled to get your needs met. The dialogue process will help you feel once again that *we* are in this together, that *we* have created some problems that *we* have to solve and *we* can succeed if *we* work as a team. Instead of "If my partner would only change, our chemistry can get better," it can become, "We can make our chemistry better than ever."

So, roll up your sleeves, take a deep breath and prepare yourselves to once and for all shake off the demons that have come between you and your dream of lasting passion. The following steps have proven extremely effective for a dialogue on chemistry. For the best results, stick as closely as possible to these guidelines.

Write It Down

Instead of jumping right into a conversation, take some time to think about your sexual history privately. Each of you should complete the following sentences without editing or censoring yourselves (if a sentence doesn't apply to your relationship, simply skip it):

1. What I liked most about our sex life early in our relationship was

   _____.

2. The first time I felt nervous about our sex life was _____

   _____.

3. The first time I felt turned off was _____.

4. Initially, what upset me was _____.

5. What scared me was _____.

6. What made me angry was _____.

7. What disappointed me was _____.

8. Later on, my worst fears were _____.

9. It made me feel _____.

10. It reminded me of _____.

11. What still lingers is _____.

12. When we are about to have sex I feel _____.

13. What worries me when we are about to have sex is _____

_____.

14. When we're having sex, what I like most is _____.

15. When we're having sex, what bothers me most is _____.

16. After sex, what I like most is _____.

17. After sex, what bothers me most is _____.

18. I hope that when my partner reads this _____.

19. I'm afraid that when my partner reads this _____.

20. I have contributed to our chemistry problems by _____

_____.

21. Now that I have finally gotten these things off my chest, what I would like us to do next is _____.

(Many people find it easier to relax and express themselves more fluidly by speaking into a tape recorder instead of writing. This method also allows for greater spontaneity and the expression of subtle nuances of meaning through voice tone, emphasis and other vocal cues. The same suggestion applies everywhere in the book that a written exercise is presented.)

Read and React

The next step is to read and re-read what you have just written (or listen back to the tape). Your words may trigger strong emotions. You may feel sadness, anger, shame, fear or pure pain. Whatever feelings come up, let yourself experience them. The negative feelings coming out are just the pus in the abscess that has infected your love life. It's time it was drained. If you are moved to tears, let them flow. They are long overdue. As an ancient saying goes, tears are to the soul what soap is to the body. Let the painful feelings motivate you to make the changes necessary to get your chemistry back. You haven't lost it forever as you had feared; you simply misplaced it.

Exchange Your Responses

You're now going to read or listen to each other's thoughts and feelings about your chemistry. Before you make the exchange, each of you should make sure that you have expressed exactly what you want your partner to hear, no more, no less. Edit or rewrite if necessary.

Just as you wrote down your answers without editing or censoring them, read your partner's words without analyzing them or reacting emotionally. Try to imagine your partner as a little child who has been carrying awful secrets around for years, too afraid to tell anyone but too unhappy to keep the feelings inside any longer.

After you have read your partner's responses once, read them again, slowly and carefully. Try to imagine what it must have felt like to be holding those feelings in. If you are moved to cry, that's fine. In all likelihood your tears contain a mix of feelings, including compassion for your partner's pain and guilt for having contributed to it (knowingly or unknowingly). If, on the other hand, you find yourself becoming angry, pause and remind yourself that what you are reading is not an attack. Your task in this exercise is not to defend yourself or convince your partner of anything. It is to understand what he or she is thinking and feeling. Try not to take anything personally. Ask yourself what would best serve your relationship, holding on to that anger or harnessing its energy to motivate you to do what's necessary to repair your chemistry.

Set the Stage

Now that you've read each other's statements, it's time to begin your conversation. Set aside at least an hour where you won't be disturbed. Make sure the atmosphere is quiet and comfortable; schedule this discussion for a time when you're both well rested and not preoccupied with other matters. A certain amount of awkwardness and apprehension is perfectly normal. Don't let it stop you from proceeding, unless you are so nervous that good two-way communication is impossible. Some couples—especially those who have never explored their emotions in a deep, vulnerable way—find it difficult to share their feelings about something as sensitive as sexuality. It can also be extremely hard to admit to feelings that might upset your partner or reveal your own fear, shame or pain. If you find it impossible to have this conversation on your own, I strongly urge you to seek the help of a qualified counselor who can guide you through it in a supportive, nonthreatening manner.

You might also try this: using the principles of good communication, talk about why it's difficult to talk to each other. This will not only break the ice but reveal any hidden fears and anxieties that may be standing in the way of honest communication. Eric and Alice, for example, were a reserved couple who grew up in well-to-do families that valued stoicism and keeping emotions to yourself. In eight years of marriage, they had never dipped beneath the surface of feelings. But when a layer of emotional frost covered their bedroom and threatened to ice their sex lives into a permanent deep freeze, they came to see me.

After several unsuccessful attempts to get them to open up, I finally asked them to talk about why they couldn't talk to each other more honestly. "I'd like to be able to speak openly with him," said Alice. "I know it would be good for us to express our feelings and all that. But I never really learned how." Then she added the *real* reason: "I guess I'm afraid that if I do open up, he wouldn't understand, and he'd get so upset that things would just get worse."

I could sense Eric's heart melting during that display of vulnerability. With some prodding, he was able to follow Alice's lead and let himself be somewhat vulnerable as well. "Emotions are like a foreign language to me," he admitted. "I don't know how to talk about feelings, let alone 'get in touch' with them, whatever that means." Then he showed that he could, indeed, speak the language of emotion. Turning to Alice, he said, "I guess I'm afraid you'll think less of me if I show you what I feel."

That brief, simple exchange was just the catalyst they needed to begin a deeper, more meaningful dialogue about the issues that had come between them.

Remember When the Chemistry Was Good

God gave us memory so that we might
have roses in December.

—J. M. BARRIE

Once you've done whatever is needed for both of you to feel safe, it's time to begin your dialogue. Begin by elaborating on your responses to the first sentence fragment; "What I liked most about our sex life early in our relationship was _____." I have found over and over again that no matter how disappointed two partners are, or how pessimistic they are about ever getting their chemistry back, if they let themselves recall the times when things were good, everything changes.

With a couple named Barbara and Chuck, for example, all I heard for the first twenty minutes was, "She's a bitch," and, "He's a jerk," "It's all her fault," and, "He'll never change," "He's a control freak," and, "All she does is criticize me." Partners in a public relations firm, they had been living and working together for six years, and the only time they'd had sex in the previous two was when they drank enough to get past their antagonism.

After they had vented for a few minutes, I asked them to tell me how they met. The mood immediately lightened as they recounted how they were both disappointed on their blind date because of the extravagant buildup their friends had given them. I then guided the conversation to what it was like when they first made love, the most passionate experiences they had when they were dating, and the funny and romantic things that happened on their honeymoon and their life together as newlyweds. It wasn't just the X-rated scenes they reminisced about. Chuck grew wistful describing how Barbara used to rub his back when he came home from a hard day at work, and how, when she was feeling amorous, she would gently kiss his neck and shoulders as she massaged. Barbara remembered the confident young man who would sweep her in his arms and dance her around the living room, then carry her to the bedroom. By the end of the session, they were holding hands.

Too much water had passed under the bridge for a complete restoration of their sex life. But the memories did inspire Barbara and Chuck to get serious about the emotional issues that had polluted their chemistry. Once they resolved their conflicts and healed the pain they had caused one another, they were able to be intimate without the need for alcohol. As of the last time I saw them, the high-voltage electricity of their early chemistry had not been duplicated, but they didn't care. They were thrilled to have rediscovered their attraction for each other, and to have added the sweetness of forgiveness.

Sometimes you need to go back to when it started and recall what brought you together in the first place. You need to remember when you couldn't wait to see each other and couldn't take your hands off each other. You need to relive the times when sex was good. It may make you sad at first to remember what you no longer have. But if you take it a step further and look beneath the wrinkles and the layers of fat and delve deep beneath the emotional baggage you've piled up along the way, you may realize that within each of you there is still a man and woman who wanted to be together and couldn't bear to be apart.

So share your fondest memories. Go into detail. Your old stories may delight you or sadden you. Treat whatever comes up with the respect it deserves. When you talk about the good times, don't fall into the "Yeah, but . . ." trap. Just remind each other of the details—what turned you on, what it felt like when you touched, why you liked to kiss, how you felt after you made love. Just knowing it was once good can inspire you to get it back. But it's very important not to expect to duplicate the excitement of the good old days. They cannot be resurrected because you're older and different. Your bodies are not the same and your personalities are not the same. You can, however, create a new and exciting chemistry once again, if you take the elements of the past that can be recaptured and mix them with the maturity and wisdom you now bring to the table—or the bedroom.

Remember When the Chemistry Went Bad

Something there is that doesn't love a wall.
And wants it down.

—ROBERT FROST

You're about to turn to less pleasant memories. Take turns speaking and listening, with no interruptions, as each of you describes when and how the chemistry went bad. This will probably be uncomfortable. You may be tempted to quit while you're ahead and call it a night. I urge you to stick it out. There is a saying in India; "It takes a thorn to remove a thorn." Discussing when things went bad is a thorn, but the bigger thorn is what's eating away at you over the loss of chemistry. Getting it out is not only cleansing but illuminating. Sometimes you have to face some difficult truths in order to heal the past and move into a new future.

Jessica and Bill were married only six months when they came to see me. "Something's wrong with our sex life," said Bill. "It's just not fun anymore. It's like work." He said that he feels resistance from Jessica and that it takes a lot more effort to arouse her than it did before. "It never gets wild and crazy anymore," he moaned.

"You mean it used to be wild and crazy?" I asked.

"Hell, yeah," exclaimed Bill. I asked when things had changed. As far as Bill could recall, it was around the time of their wedding. Before that, their sex had been unrestrained. He did not have a clue as to why it had changed.

All this time, Jessica hardly said a word. The more we talked about the past, the more she shifted position and fidgeted with her bracelet. Clearly, she was holding something back. After a while, she saw that we could not get anywhere unless she spoke up. She knew exactly what had precipitated the change in their sex life and exactly when it happened.

It was their first night as a married couple. Bill had been a nervous wreck the entire day. A somewhat shy man, he had hoped for a small, intimate wedding. But Jessica's family insisted on an extravaganza. To keep himself calm amidst the menagerie of rowdy guests, Bill drank more than he was accustomed to. Even with the help of alcohol, though, he was so tense that he flubbed his lines in the ceremony and was uptight throughout the entire reception. When, in the hotel room, he was finally alone with his bride, he let it rip. It was full speed ahead to the release he needed, and rules of the road be damned. Then he passed out. Naturally, Jessica had hoped for something more romantic. But it wasn't just the disappointment that had made her less responsive sexually. In his drunken frenzy, Bill had drooled and slobbered on her, and she ended up with a bruised chest and an inflammation in her vagina. Ever since, fear would rise up in her whenever they began to make love. That was the resistance that Bill was feeling.

"Why didn't you tell me?" was Bill's response. He had no memory of what had happened.

"It was extremely upsetting," said Jessica, "and I was afraid that bringing it up would make it worse. I hoped it would just go away." Bill was still incredulous. Then Jessica added something that affected him deeply. "I didn't think you would care."

He cared all right. He started crying and apologizing as if it had happened the day before. As shocking as Jessica's revelation was to Bill, the fact that he had absolutely no memory of the incident was just as shocking to Jessica. She thought the absence of an apology meant that Bill was indifferent to the pain he had caused her. That is precisely why the conversation was so important to them—and why yours will be to you and your partner. When Bill promised he would never do such a thing again, it was easy for Jessica to believe him. It was also easy for her to drop her defenses the next time they made love.

Like Jessica, you may be afraid that talking about events that were upsetting in the past will make the present *more* upsetting. In fact, it usually makes things better; clearing the air gets you unstuck. Anything from personal hygiene to jealousy, from bad technique to injured feelings, might have contributed to the cooling of chemistry. It is crucial that you talk about everything that may have caused your lovemaking to go from turn-on to turnoff. If you don't get it off your chest, it will stand between you like a wall.

When it's your turn to speak, tell your truth gently and with compassion for the one who is hearing unpleasant news. When it's your turn to listen, remember that your partner is not throwing bricks, he or she is trying to break down the wall between you. Resist the urge to argue or debate. Rather, seek to understand your partner as thoroughly as possible. Also resist the urge to get it over with quickly. In fact, do the opposite. Ask questions that encourage further reflection and deeper insight.

For instance, a client named Frank told his wife, Andrea, that the first time he felt nervous about their sex life was when she didn't have an orgasm and he felt that he was unable to satisfy her. Andrea asked, "How did it make you feel?"

"Like a failure," said Frank.

"How did it affect you the next time we made love?" she asked. "Did you worry about being inadequate?"

When it was Andrea's turn to speak, she revealed that the first time she felt turned off by Frank was on a trip to San Francisco, when he wanted sex so badly that he kept whining and insisting until she gave in. "I did it even though I was exhausted," she said, "but I was totally uninvolved, and you didn't seem to care."

"How did it make you feel?" asked Frank.

"Used and dirty," said Andrea.

> **USABLE INSIGHT**
>
> *What you don't talk through grows into a wall you can't break through.*

"You must have been angry as hell. Why didn't you say something?"

"I didn't want to spoil our trip. I tried to just forget about it, but I couldn't."

"How did it affect your attitude toward sex afterward?" Frank continued.

You get the idea. By helping your partner unfold the complete story, you add to your understanding and chip away more of the wall between you.

Apologize and Forgive

Don't ruin the hallowed ground you have just created by arguing over details, making accusations or defending your past actions. The first item on your agenda should be for each of you to apologize for the pain or frustration you have caused in the past, and for not understanding just how badly the other person felt. A good way to begin is to share how you misinterpreted each other.

This is what Andrea told Frank: "I thought you weren't attracted to me anymore. I didn't realize that you were nervous about having to bring me to orgasm every time. I'm so sorry I didn't understand how you felt."

When it was Frank's turn, he said, "I thought you stopped liking sex, but what was really happening is that you were turned off by the way I approached you. I'm really sorry I upset you. I wish I'd done a better job of understanding what was really going on."

Then you may need to forgive each other. Like all couples, you've accumulated a good deal of baggage—everything from serious betrayals to minor letdowns. It may not be easy to do, but unless you're willing to at least try to forgive, your hearts won't open to the warmth that a chemical reaction needs.

The first step to forgiveness is to stop seeing yourselves as victims. Very rarely is the loss of chemistry one person's fault. As long as you are in a victim's mindset, you will feel that something is owed to you, and that feeling sets up a zero-sum game in which you think, "I'm not going to reach out until he/she reaches out." Take two people in that frame of mind and you have an emotional stalemate in which nothing can change. Each of you has to be willing to look at how you contributed to the decline of chemistry and take responsibility for making it better.

Josie and Aaron had always been more than hot lovers. Every since they met, when she was in law school and he was getting his MBA, they had served each other as best friend, chief defender and one-person booster squad. By the time I met them, in the eighth year of their marriage, they had gone from being loving mates to checkmate to stalemate. They were stagnant, stuck, too bitter over real and imagined hurts to make anything in their lives better. Including sex. When they talked about their history together, it quickly became clear that their passion was mired in the quicksand of blame.

Aaron was an investment banker whose intellectual brilliance was matched only by his ambition. Painfully shy about emotional matters, he was immediately smitten by Josie's effervescence and social charm. She was a nonstop talker with a bawdy sense of humor, who could captivate any group. Aaron went to parties he would normally avoid, just to watch Josie in action and bask in the glow of her charm. She made him feel alive. His rapid rise up the corporate ladder, he felt, was due as much to his wife's social graces as to his own skills. Without her, he could never have played the networking game.

Josie made Aaron come alive sexually too. Until she introduced him to practices he'd only read about, his bedroom experience had been as bland and predictable as his Brooks Brothers suits.

For her part, Josie appreciated Aaron's humility and steadfast confidence, his gentle kindness, his generosity and many other qualities. She saw their differences as complementary. Aaron steadied her. His soft-spoken common sense and sharp advice tempered her impulsivity and kept her on an even keel as she worked her way up in the district attorney's office.

But their differences could not stand the pressure of their hectic lives. When Aaron moved to a new company with a stodgy corporate culture, Josie's life-of-the-party nature was not only out of step but a detriment. To make matters worse, she had started drinking heavily after a courtroom mistake of hers enabled a killer to go free. They became increasingly critical of one another. Josie berated Aaron for being unemotional and boring. He called her vulgar and crude. The animosity was so thick they began to sleep in separate rooms. But, while the venom was mutual, Josie's style was in-your-face, take-no-prisoners candor while Aaron's was don't-make-waves restraint.

Those roles were evident in the first few minutes of our initial session. Josie was the aggressor, bluntly stating her case against her husband. When Aaron finally spoke up, it was to portray himself as a put-upon victim. "She's so unforgiving," he said. "She can't let anything go. I'm always wrong." With a hangdog expression, he described how Josie, the one-time sexual adventurer who introduced him to erotic delights, rejected his advances with demeaning put-downs until he just gave up.

With typical frankness, Josie admitted to everything Aaron accused her of. Then, like the skilled prosecutor she was, she told the other side. In her portrait, Aaron's quiet, courteous personality was a mask. Whereas she was brutally honest, Aaron was sly. His insults and faultfinding were sneaky; he disguised them as polite suggestions. And, she said, in recent months, *she* had tried to initiate sex and Aaron always found an excuse.

Soon it became clear that Aaron was just as unforgiving, just as critical and just as vengeful as his wife. Rejecting Josie's advances was his way of getting revenge on her for rejecting him. "Too little, too late, baby," was the hidden message. "Now it's your turn to squirm."

> **USABLE INSIGHT**
>
> *When you hate hating more than you hate your partner, it's time to forgive.*

As our hour drew to a close, the basic decency of both partners, and their aching desire to get their marriage back on track, began to shine through their animosity. Now they were more sad than angry. It was Aaron, the passive-aggressive one, who broke the ice. "You're right," he said to Josie. "I've been holding grudges as long as you have. I'm just more of a sneak, that's all." Struggling to hold back tears, he added a comment I've never forgotten: "The only thing I hate more than you is hating you."

He was tired of the anger and all that it had done to them. "What do you want to do now?" I asked.

"I don't know," said Aaron.

Josie leaped into the breach. "I think we need to start by forgiving each other," she said.

Without that breakthrough the productive dialogues they had in our subsequent sessions would not have been possible. It was the first and most necessary step in restoring their chemistry.

Let's Get Practical

Now is the time to look ahead. Share your thoughts about how to get your chemistry from where it is to where you would like it to be. A good way to begin is for each of you to ask the other,

"What can I do to make it better for you?" and "What would you like me to do from now on?" This will encourage you to think about one another's needs, not just your own.

After you exchange responses, see if there is room for further exploration. Ask your partner, "Is there anything you've left out that would really make a difference but that you're hesitant to tell me?" In this solution-oriented part of the conversation, there is no place for rebuttal, refusal or argument. Simply accept that whatever is said, no matter how unrealistic it may seem, is the expression of a genuine desire to light a fire under your sex life. In fact, if your imaginations happen to kick into gear, open the throttle wide. You may surprise yourselves with some great ideas.

> **USABLE INSIGHT**
> *One of the greatest turn-ons is removing a turnoff.*

Make a Chemistry Vow

Commit yourselves to stop doing the things that cooled your chemistry in the past and to doing the things that will keep it warm. Don't leave it to chance. Make a date for sometime in the next two weeks. Get a baby-sitter. Reserve a room in a hotel. Make whatever arrangements you need to have an atmosphere conducive to intimacy.

End your conversation with a deep, long hug, and seal it with a kiss. But stop it at that. If you start to feel sexy, save it for the date you just made. Remember when you were young and couldn't wait for the weekend to see your girlfriend or boyfriend? Part of chemistry is the eager anticipation of pleasure.

(A note of caution: Don't expect perfection on that date.

Not only are you likely to be apprehensive, but it takes time to break old habits and solidify new ones. Just relax and enjoy yourselves. See the section "Make Time for Making Time" later in this chapter for additional suggestions.)

Come on Baby, Light My Fire

There is no greater nor keener pleasure
than that of bodily love.

—PLATO

You have explored the reasons your chemistry deteriorated. You have bravely revealed your feelings to one another. You have made a commitment to making things better. You have discussed practical ways to make that happen. To supplement the work you've done so far, here are some suggestions that have had a powerful chemistry-enhancing effect on hundreds of my clients who have been through the dialogue process.

Cherish and Admire

In my twenty-five years in private practice, one of the few things that has remained a constant is that most women want to be cherished and most men want to be admired. Everyone wants both, of course, and there are always exceptions, but by and large the distinction holds true.

Unfortunately, over the course of a long-term relationship, we not only find reasons to cherish less and admire less, we get sloppy about showing our partners how much we still cherish and admire them. Making the effort to do so can thaw out a frigid emotional atmosphere, bringing the kind of warmth that leads to good chemistry. We'll return to this topic in greater detail in a later chapter. Here, I want to give you one simple technique that can work wonders to restore your chemistry. Quite possibly, it will lead to one of the most intimate conversations you've ever had.

Wait for a quiet time in your day, when the cares and chores of your lives are put to rest. Take your partner aside. Sit down someplace, take his or her hand in yours, look lovingly in his or her eyes and speak from your heart.

Men, tell your woman: "Have I ever made you feel that you are not worth listening to?" She will probably be startled. She may respond with a sarcastic remark, or crack a joke, or get suspicious, or even crtiticize you by saying, for example, "Yeah, you're a rotten listener and you make me feel like you couldn't care less about what I have to say." Whatever her response, maintain your equanimity and continue to speak sincerely: "I'm bringing it up because I know I'm not the best listener in the world. Sometimes I'm preocuppied or I get impatient. I know it must make you feel awful. I just want you to know that you *are* worth listening to. Don't let anyone, including me, make you feel that you're not. If I ever made you feel otherwise, I'm sorry."

In my experience, no woman has ever failed to soften when her man has said that. Many break into tears. You have just surprised her with your tenderness, caring and compassion. She not only wasn't sure that you knew you had hurt her feelings in the past, she thought you didn't care if you had. As for chemistry, the warming effect can be quite spectacular. As one woman said when she told me that her husband had carried out this assignment, "He got lucky that night."

Now, for you women. Take your man aside and say to him, "Have I ever made you feel that I don't admire and respect you more today than when we first fell in love?" In all likelihood his jaw will drop and he'll be at a loss for words. Just look him in the eye and continue: "Just because I sometimes take out my stress on you doesn't mean that I don't think I'm lucky to have you in my life. If I've failed to let you know that, I've really been remiss. I'm sorry. You're the best man I've ever known."

If his heart doesn't warm up on hearing that, he's hopeless. How do men usually feel when their wives or girlfriends say that to them? As one man put it, "Like I died and went to heaven."

There are many other ways to let your partner know he is admired or she is cherished. Finding them on a regular basis will cement the pillar of chemistry and keep it rock solid as long as you're together.

One way to do it is to put yourself in your partner's shoes and ask yourself this question: What would he/she want me to do that would make him/her feel special right now? Here is an example of a simple thing a client named Carl did. Carl's wife loved to take walks at night, but Carl did not. Since he always refused when Sharon asked him to join her, she eventually stopped asking. One night, when Sharon was in the dumps and feeling overwhelmed by parenting and career responsibilities, Carl went to her and said, "Let's go for a walk." Sharon was astonished. "We're going for a walk," said Carl with a gentle smile, "and the only choice you have is whether to wear a jacket or a sweater."

Sharon couldn't believe her ears. "You hate walks," she said.

"But you love them," Carl responded, "and right now a walk would do you a world of good. Come on, let's go."

Dumbfounded and clearly touched, Sharon could only say, "I think I'll wear a sweater."

Sharon needed no instructions from me to reciprocate. Feeling cherished by her husband was enough of a cue. On their walk, she was moved to tell him something she had neglected to say earlier: "I really admire you for standing up to your partners when they bent the rules in order to land that client."

That night, cherished Sharon and admired Carl made love for the first time in five months.

Use Your Imagination

Imagination is the voice of daring.

—HENRY MILLER

Remember the animal experiments we mentioned earlier, in which familiarity breeds disinterest in the male of the species? Well, it seems that the bored male perks up not only when a new female is introduced but when the appearance or scent of the *old* female is changed. This is not necessarily an inducement to purchase perfume or a chiffon nightie—although anything that might enhance chemistry should be considered—but rather an insight into the importance of freshness. Your chemistry may have waned simply from the monotony of long-term mating. The way we humans are built, it doesn't take much to turn each other on at first. But as time goes by, the same old strokes and kisses, or the mere sight of our partner undressing, is just not enough. But sexual malaise is not inevitable if you allow your-selves to be creative. Why be a prisoner of routine? Give your imagination free reign.

Ask yourself how your partner might like to be seduced. Which new words or gestures might excite him or her? What have you always wanted to do in bed but haven't done? What kind of foreplay practices haven't you tried? Which romantic activities might stir the old passion and bring back your sense of adventure? If you need help, there are plenty of books and videos available to stimulate your thinking and get your juices flowing. The point is, you don't listen to the same music every day or give each other the same gifts every Christmas, so why play the love game the same way every time? Take the risk of surprising your partner with something fresh and different. Some of your attempts will succeed and some will fail, but the effort alone can boost your chemistry because your partner will know you find him or her important enough to try.

To stimulate your imagination, take the lead of people who are cheating on their husbands or wives—but without the cheat-ing. When someone is having an affair, they start to do odd things—which is one of the reasons they get caught. A guy who's a couch potato might go on a diet or start an exercise routine to lose his potbelly. A woman who has let her appearance slide is now getting makeovers and shopping for new outfits like a teenager with a crush. And behind the scenes, they're flirting, sending cards and flowers, composing cute E-mail messages and shopping for just the right gifts. So, pretend you have a secret and treat your partner as though you were having an affair with him or her. Be romantic. Be sensual. Be generous. Be your lover's fantasy.

A client of mine named Irene did exactly that. After a few days in which she looked exceptionally stunning and giggled quite a bit, her husband jokingly said, "Are you having an affair or something?"

"Not yet," she said, "but I'd like to. I really have the hots for someone."

Her husband was flabbergasted. Losing the battle to keep his composure, he roared, "Okay, who is this guy?"

"You," said Irene.

It was a turning point in the revival of a marriage that had been wallowing in the doldrums of stale chemistry.

What is the best way to suggest something new and sexy to your partner? Which approach is most likely to get an enthusiastic response rather than rejection? The answer is simple: express what you want in the form of a wish. Not a suggestion. Not a request. Not a recommendation. That would only put uneccessary pressure on the other person. Just

> **USABLE INSIGHT**
>
> *Cheat on your marriage by having an affair with your spouse.*

say, "I wish we did more _____," or "I wish we could _____." People will often resist anything that sounds like a demand, but they love to fulfill wishes.

Make Time for Making Time

Many of us think that lovemaking should always be spontaneous. It is one of many erroneous assumptions that limits our sex lives. Especially if your chemistry has been weakened and avoidance has entered the equation, it would be foolish to hope that in the midst of all the demands of everyday life, spontaneous combustion is going to take place. You have to set aside time for it. Planned intimacy may sound unromantic, but, just as a great business idea won't get off the ground without a plan, your chemistry won't be restored just because it's a good idea and a grand hope.

Think of it as arranging a special date. You had no problem planning to be together when you were single, and there was nothing unromantic about those occasions just because they were prearranged. Quite the contrary, in fact. Sometimes, the expression, "Where there's a will, there's a way" needs to be reversed: where there's a way, there's a will. Create the way with forethought and intelligence, and the will just may follow. As they said in *Field of Dreams*, "Build it and they will come."

> **USABLE INSIGHT**
>
> *Where there's a way, there's a will.*

Make a commitment to set aside time for just the two of you, with no distractions—no kids, no chores, no answering the telephone. Make any discussion of practical household matters strictly prohibited. It could be an evening or a weekend or a longer vacation. It could be home alone or a night on the town or a romantic escape. Think of it as a time for intimacy—and not just sexual intimacy. Leave the door open for lovemaking, of course, but don't make sex a necessary part of your time together. That could put too much pressure on you, especially if performance anxiety or the fear of frustration has entered the picture. Your date should be a time to share fun and warmth. The important thing is to re-establish your connection and remind yourselves of why you fell in love in the first place. Mature sexual intimacy begins with emotional intimacy.

During your date, make an effort to show your affection and appreciation for one another. If difficult issues arise unavoidably, take special care to conscientiously apply the principles of good communication that we discussed earlier. Don't spoil the evening by arguing, debating or accusing. Express your feelings on another occasion.

If you can, I highly recommend going away—for a night, a weekend, or longer—to a place neither of you have been to before. The absence of familiarity can add a sense of adventure, and the shared excitement is often a catalyst for sexual chemistry. It also has a way of bringing you closer; in a new and different environment, the one thing you have most in common is each other. Alternatively, you might consider going someplace that holds fond memories for both of you. Be careful though: choosing a sentimental location might heighten your awareness of what you've lost.

One couple, for example, went to the resort where they'd spent their honeymoon having hot sex day and night. But that was twelve years earlier, and the impossible dream of recapturing that heat only set them up for a colossal letdown. They came home more depressed than they'd been before, and more pessimistic about their future. It took a good deal of effort to convince them that the goal is not to duplicate the chemistry of old but to create a new, mature chemistry that suits the people they have become.

Even if all you can squeeze into your schedule is one evening, spend it doing something new and different. Don't go to your favorite restaurant, but one you've both been meaning to try. If you stay home, don't rent a movie if that's what you usually do. Dance together, or read poetry, or play a game you've never played before. Anything that breaks the routine, whether it's a destination, an activity or the clothes you wear, has a better chance of lighting a spark.

If it seems natural and mutually desirable, by all means make love. But don't do it just because you think you should. Sometimes, before real chemistry can be restored, it's necessary to re-establish a sense of comfort, affection and safety. That might take a while. It's not always wise to hop into bed on your first "date."

End the Goal Orientation

Most of us have been conditioned to think of lovemaking as a means to an end. We think that orgasm is the be-all and end-all of sex, and that if it is not achieved all is for naught. That attitude diminishes everything else that is pleasurable and beautiful about human sexuality. We disparagingly reduce kissing, licking, stroking, snuggling and other joys to the status of second-rate comedians who warm up the audience before the real show. The emphasis on intercourse and orgasm not only deprives us of sensual pleasures and emotional bonding, but it can also place tremendous pressure on both partners.

Your preconceptions of what "good sex" means may have contributed to the decline of chemistry in the first place. Allow it to mean whatever feels right and good to both of you at any given time. Take the pressure off by giving yourselves permission to bask in each other's sexuality without thinking about how much, how many or how often. In fact, if your chemistry has been marred by anxiety, frustration, or avoidance, go a step further and agree *not* to have intercourse the next time you get intimate. Spend some time just touching each other. Many couples touch sensually only when they're trying to get aroused. But touching and being touched is not only pleasurable, it is an essential human need.

Returning for a while to the simpler, less complicated aspects of sexuality can be a great way to restore tenderness and, eventually, igniting the passion you seek.

Smile!

If you have only one smile in you, give it
to the people you love.

—MAYA ANGELOU

The next recommendation is so simple you will probably dismiss it as absurd. Give it a try anyway.

Here's the suggestion: when you first see each other at the end of the day, no matter how stressful a day it was, no matter how irritable or worried you feel, the first thing each of you should do is smile. That's all. Just smile. Act like you're glad to see each other even if it's not entirely true. As they say in twelve-step programs, fake it till you feel it.

Most of the couples I recommend this to think it's silly. The ones who agree to do it anyway usually come to their next therapy session ticked off—not because it didn't work but because it worked extremely well. They report feeling more tenderness for each other. They say they are less likely to argue or fight now that they greet each other with a smile. They thank me for the suggestion, but they're also annoyed. Why? Because they like to see themselves as way too sophisticated and complex for such a simple remedy.

Research shows that simply moving your mouth into the position of a smile, even if it's purely mechanical, makes you feel better. Sure we smile when we're happy, but the opposite is also true: we're happier when we smile. It does something to the biochemistry of the brain itself. And it works wonders on the person we smile at. Try it and see.

Women! Let Your Man Use You for Sex

Did that heading get your attention? Did it make you mad? Or, did it excite you? I know it's a controversial statement, but before you dismiss me as a sexist pig, please hear me out.

Feminism has, for very good reasons, put an end to the days when men could use women as sex objects with impunity and it was a woman's duty to service her man (lie back and do it for England, as a proper British lady once said). Men and women alike are better off now that it's no longer a man's right to have his way whenever he pleases.

But let's face it, having an orgasm is often the best way to relieve tension. There are times when the buildup of stress has to be unloaded, and jogging or hitting a punching bag or talking about your troubles just won't do the trick. This seems to be especially true for men. They never asked for this to be so, nature just made them that way. And when men can't fulfill their need for sexual release with the woman they love, they have a choice: bury the urge and have the tension build up even further, or find another outlet—a quick affair, a prostitute, or, increasingly, masturbation. James Joyce once marveled at "the amazing availability" of masturbation. With the Internet, it's more amazingly available than ever before, which is one reason it's become a virtual epidemic among married men. When you need to release tension, it is a lot less complicated than negotiating for sex with a partner with whom you share emotional baggage.

In the context of a loving relationship between equals, allowing a man the release he needs is not necessarily degrading or demeaning. If done in the right manner, it can actually serve the needs of both partners and help restore the connection we call chemistry.

The first key is to approach it with dignity and respect. Men, when you feel the need for tension-relieving sex, don't be a sneak, and don't be piggish. Don't demand it or insist on it. Don't start groping and grabbing. Don't impose yourself on your partner. And above all, never use force or coercion. In other words, don't do anything that can be construed as invasive or demeaning, or that will diminish your lover's trust in you. Instead, request it plainly and nicely: "Honey, I had a really nerve-wracking day. The pressure was intense. I know sex is mainly about being intimate with one another, but right now I just need to release this tension. I was wondering if we could have sex tonight."

Approached in such a way, most women will understand. She might still have a good reason to say no, but she is likely to do so in a spirit of love and compassion, not annoyance.

Women, there is no need to be a martyr. Don't let yourself do anything sexually that might be physically damaging or emotionally depleting. There are many ways to help a man achieve the stress-relieving orgasm he needs. And if the timing is absolutely wrong for you, don't feel obligated to comply. But turn him down gently, without whining or complaining or acting as though you resent the proposition. The best way to let him down easy is to offer a rain check: "I'd love to give you what you need, honey, but I'm really exhausted and I promised the kids I'd help them with their homework. Let's make a date for Friday, okay?"

Men, if you get such a response, be grateful. Don't pout, don't groan, don't sulk. Just accept the rain check and make Friday night a lovely occasion for your partner as well.

The second key to making this work is even more important than the first: *reciprocation*. This is not a one-way street, guys. You have to give something in return for getting what you need. One possibility is to let *her* use *you* for sex when she needs it. While the hard-wiring of the male and female bodies makes it less likely that a woman will seek sex strictly for stress release, it is by no means uncommon. And, despite the macho mythology, men are not always ready and willing. Still, the gander has to be willing to give the goose what's good for her too. That could mean a quickie to release her tension. But most women would rather have something else: a promise to make love the way *she* likes it next time—slow, calm, sensual and gentle, even if it goes against your natural inclination.

There is another way to give a woman something she needs. Just as men seek sex when they're under stress, the instinct of most women is to blow off steam verbally. So, men, let your woman use you for venting—about work, the kids, her mother, whatever. Let her speak her mind and heart. Let her rant and rage. You don't have to do anything, solve anything, fix anything. Just be there and listen.

Women, when you need to vent, don't just dump the cares of your day on him the minute he walks in the door. Don't launch into a tirade and expect him to drop everything and give you his full attention. Give him advance notice, even if it's just a couple of minutes. If possible, call him during the day and say something like this: "Sweetheart, I'm having a horrible day. My boss is making impossible demands, and my mother is driving me crazy. I feel like I'm about to explode. Would you mind giving me about ten minutes tonight and just let me get it off my chest?"

Asked that way, most men will say, "Sure, take as much time as you need."

Allowing yourself to be used for stress release is not demeaning if you think of it as a gift to someone you love. In fact, even better than *allowing* it is to invite it. When your partner is stressed, offer him or her the opportunity for release, whether through sex or other means. It won't, by itself, bring ideal lovemaking back to your relationship. But the honesty and compassion of loving reciprocity can bring you closer emotionally—and that can make a big difference as you rebuild the pillar of chemistry.

> **USABLE INSIGHT**
>
> *You can't be used if you invite them to use you.*

If CREATE did not begin with a C, I would have been forced to not use the acronym. Chemistry has to be the first pillar discussed and worked upon. The reason for that is that chemistry is the biggest concern of most couples and the most complicated of the six secrets of a lasting love (it's no accident that this is the longest chapter in the book). It is also the area about which couples become most pessimistic when it starts to go south. They fear that their sex lives can never be fixed. Working on chemistry first, even if the improvement is slow, helps to restore their optimism about their relationship in general.

You may already be seeing some improvements in your chemistry, just from reading this chapter and starting to apply the recommendations. You will continue to see improvement as you work your way through the remaining chapters. Chemistry heats up dramatically when the other five essentials are strengthened.

3

Respect

Find Out What It
Means to You

> For you in my respect are all the
> world:
> Then how can it be said I am alone,
> When all the world is here to look on
> me?
>
> —WILLIAM SHAKESPEARE

How much do the following statements apply to how you think or feel about respect in your relationship?

	Hardly Ever 0	Sometimes 1	Almost Always 2
1. I listen to my partner and hear him/her out.	___	___	___
2. My partner listens to and hears me out.	___	___	___
3. I consider my partner's suggestions instead of quickly rejecting them.	___	___	___
4. My partner considers my suggestions instead of quickly rejecting them.	___	___	___
5. I don't second-guess my partner's decisions.	___	___	___
6. My partner doesn't second-guess my decisions.	___	___	___
7. I stand up for my partner in public.	___	___	___
8. My partner stands up for me in public.	___	___	___
9. I am neither crude nor rude to my partner.	___	___	___
10. My partner is neither crude nor rude to me.	___	___	___
TOTAL:	___	___	___

SCORING:

0–6	With all due respect, you need to work on this.
7–13	A respectable score.
14–20	Not only respectable, but admirable.

On an Internet chat room where I work with couples, the following exchange took place. In one form or another, it has been repeated countless times, whether from a keyboard in the anonymous regions of cyberspace or spoken in the intimate confines of my office.

Dr. Mark: Look at your husband now, and ask him this question: "What would I have to do for you to take me more seriously?"

Wife: He said, "Don't get so emotional over everything."

Dr. Mark (to husband): Look at your wife and ask her: "When was the last time I did anything right?"

Husband: She said I do a lot of things right, but she gets really frustrated with the stupid stuff I do, so she focuses on that.

Dr. Mark: What do you both want to do right now?

Wife: Feel better about each other.

Husband: Agreed.

Dr. Mark: What would be a good first step?

Wife: I should probably apologize for not respecting all the good things about him.

Husband: That goes double for me.

R-E-S-P-E-C-T: all we're asking for is a little of it when we come home. Sometimes we want it more than a good meal, or a smile, or even sex. Respect is defined in the *American Heritage Dictionary* as "a feeling of appreciative, often deferential regard; esteem," and "willingness to show consideration or appreciation."

The reason audiences could relate so well to Rodney "Can't get no respect" Dangerfield is because the respect of others is so vital to our sense of well-being—and the lack of it is such an awful blow. Respect is one of the six pillars of love because, without it, a relationship is doomed to either end quickly, coast along in denial and suppressed contempt until it explodes or wallow forever in a quagmire of sneers, put-downs and wise-cracks.

If you doubt the importance of respect, imagine how you'd feel if your partner were to look you in the eye and say, "I have no respect for you." How devastating would that be? Worse than being told you're ugly? Worse than being told you're stupid? Most people would say so. And losing respect *for* your spouse or lover is no better. It can be worse than disagreeing on important issues or no longer finding him or her physically attractive. A severe loss of respect in either direction can turn a heavenly bond into hell on earth.

It is hard to say which is worse, feeling that your partner doesn't respect you or not respecting your partner. Either one can spell disaster. "The moment I knew the marriage was in big trouble was when I realized I had lost respect for my husband and couldn't get it back," a client told me. "I can say all kinds of things to him. I'm brutally honest. But I just can't bring myself to tell him I don't respect him. I feel like a horrible person for even thinking it."

She didn't have to tell him; he felt it. "The most painful thing in my life," her husband said, "is knowing that the person who thinks the least of me is the one I love the most. She used to look up to me. Now she holds me in disdain." It was one of those heart-wrenching moments in therapy where raw hurt needs to come out before healing can take place.

We all need to feel esteemed by our mates. We want to be looked up to and made to feel that we're special. We want to know that our partners think of us as a good catch, and that when they speak about us to others it is with the highest regard. We thrive on the knowledge that we measure up to their standards, that they believe in us and admire us. We want them to be proud of us. And we want to feel pride and admiration for them.

One reason why respect is so important is that it makes both partners feel better about themselves. Feeling respected enhances our *self*-respect—especially when the respect comes from someone whom we hold in high regard. It works the other way as well: Having respect for our mates makes us feel good about ourselves because we must be pretty special to deserve someone so worthy of admiration. In this way, respect and self-respect feed on each other and in turn enhance all of the other pillars.

Of course, the opposite occurs when respect wanes. How long can you respect yourself when you tolerate the disrespect of your partner? Being disrespected resonates with your own deepest criticism of yourself, and you come to internalize your partner's lack of respect. And it cuts both ways: You also lose self-esteem when your respect for your partner diminishes. After a while, you can't help but think, "I must be pretty unworthy to be with someone who doesn't deserve respect."

Disrespecting yourself for disrespecting your partner is something to which women are especially prone. When Anne married Ted she was well aware of his shortcomings, but his admirable qualities more than made up for them. As time went on, however, the equation changed. To her dismay, Anne found that her husband's flaws came to dominate her awareness. They made her feel distant and cold more than Ted's good traits made her feel close and warm. A nurse practitioner, Anne was increasingly put off by the polite deference that she'd found so appealing when she and Ted were dating. What she thought was flexibility and consideration came to be seen as wishy-washy indecisiveness. "Does he always have to ask what *I* want to do and where *I* want to eat?" she complained. "Can't he just take charge once in a while?"

Even worse in her eyes was Ted's lack of ambition. A historian, he felt most at home in the library. Once he received tenure at the university where he taught, his striving was limited to getting accolades from his colleagues for his research. Once upon a time Anne had adored his high-minded lack of materialism and stood firm when her parents raised doubts about the wisdom of marrying such a man. But as she approached forty and her two children entered their teens, she found herself wishing Ted were different. It started to bother her that she earned more money than he did. While far from materialistic, she nevertheless found herself wanting certain things they could not afford and worrying about the quality of education they'd be able to provide for their kids. When the chairman of Ted's department retired and recommended that Ted take his place, Anne's hopes were lifted; the promotion would mean an increase in income and could become a stepping-stone to a dean's position. But Ted declined. Administrative work would cut into his research.

That was a turning point for Anne. While her love for her man remained undiminished, her respect was plummeting rapidly. She kept it to herself, assuming correctly that absentminded Ted would be oblivious to what she was feeling. She only wished that *she* could be oblivious. Instead, she was tormented by hatred—not for Ted, but for herself. "What's wrong with me?" she cried. "He's the sweetest, kindest man I've ever known. He's responsible, he's brilliant, he's wonderful with the kids . . . I mean, it's not like he lied to me or misled me or anything. He's who he is. It's me! I've become a heartless, selfish bitch."

She hadn't become any such thing, of course. She was just afraid that she had. For most women, it is extremely important to know that deep down they are basically warm, tender souls. When, instead, they feel icy and callous inside, they feel less like a true woman. As Anne discovered, it's hard to feel warmth toward someone you don't respect, even if you love him. And that lack of warmth makes women feel awful about themselves.

> **USABLE INSIGHT**
>
> *A woman without warmth doesn't feel like a woman; a man without courage doesn't feel like a man.*

Once disrespect starts chipping away at each partner's self-esteem, the relationship can quickly descend into a spiral of loathing and self-loathing. Having lost respect for yourself, you reinforce your partner's disrespect for you; he or she is now even more convinced that you don't deserve respect. They'll show it, and you'll feel it. And, because part of you feels that you don't deserve to be treated any better, you don't stand up for yourself—which is, of course, further reason to disrespect you.

In many cases, the vicious cycle is intensified by a buildup of rage and resentment. When you lose respect for the person you live with, you begin to resent more and more about them. You might even blame your partner for trapping you in a relationship with someone so unworthy. And consider what happens when you're the one who's not respected: you'll soon turn the tables. It's only human to think, "Who are *you* to disrespect *me*? You're not so hot yourself!" That reaction can easily lead to a desire for revenge.

It hurts to be disrespected, and hurt usually turns to anger. "How dare you think so poorly of me!" Each put-down or disapproving smirk triggers retaliation, and before you know it, the score-keeping, win-at-all-costs, tit-for-tat behavior becomes standard operating procedure. When retaliation becomes a way of life, resolution is nearly impossible. No one wins, because if you win today your partner will try to get even and you will lose tomorrow.

The simmering rage that builds within when you're being disrespected can be terrifying—especially for men. It makes them feel as though they might lose control at any moment, and nothing is scarier than thinking you could actually do something horrible to someone you love. Many decent men have confessed to me that they were thinking of leaving their wives because their anger was so intense they were afraid they might go over the edge. "What kind of monster am I?" said one man on the brink of walking out on his family. "I caught myself clenching my fist last night, I was so pissed off. She has no right to treat me with such disrespect, but for God's sake, anyone who even *thinks* about hitting his wife is beneath contempt. I'm scared of myself, Doc. If I ever laid a hand on her, I'd kill myself."

This was an emergency—not just because he might lose control and harm his wife, but also because his guilt and self-hatred were driving him crazy. It would inevitably make him behave in such a way as to lose even more respect. We were able to avoid disaster only because he and his wife were willing to discuss the issue of respect openly and honestly in therapy.

In sum, disrespect brings out the worst in people, creating a vicious cycle of hurt, anger, retaliation and loss of self-esteem. Because it is so difficult to face, we tend to make excuses and rationalize away the signs of lost respect. But the denial cannot be sustained; respect is far too crucial to remain hidden. At some point, something has to give. One partner or the other is bound to let loose the pent-up feelings or simply throw up their hands and shout, "I can't take this anymore!" If steps are not taken to rebuild the pillar of respect, the emotional tone of the relationship goes either north or south: ice cold or hot-headed.

Extramarital Respect

Every man wants a woman to appeal to his better side, his nobler instincts and his higher nature— and another woman to help him forget them.

—HELEN ROWLAND

One of the great dangers of loss of respect is that it can lead to infidelity. The hunger to be respected—and to be with someone whom you respect—is so great that it is only natural to turn elsewhere for it. Here are four typical examples:

A forty-five-year-old musician, Rob ran into a streak of hard luck and was having difficulty finding work. His wife, Lynn, who had been through many financial ups and downs over twenty years of marriage, was worried about feeding her three children. She kept bugging Rob to get "a real job." While she tried to keep it under wraps, her declining respect for her husband was leaking more and more to the surface. With his own self-esteem at an all-time low, Rob was highly vulnerable. Shortly after he did what his wife demanded and got a job in a music store, he started sleeping with another employee—a young, starry-eyed music student who thought Rob was a genius and worshipped him as though he were John Lennon.

Sally was the trophy wife of a powerful trial lawyer. Although she had a college degree, she may as well have been illiterate for all the respect her husband showed for her intelligence. He belittled her opinions, constantly interrupted her in midsentence and in general made her feel like a bimbo whose only value was to parade before his associates in sexy outfits. After three years of this, Sally's lavish lifestyle could no longer compensate for the lack of respect that was destroying her self-esteem. When the professor who moved in next door paid as much attention to what she had to say as how she looked, it was too seductive to resist.

When Doug married Colleen, he cherished her goodness, her integrity and her resourcefulness. Then Doug's Internet business took off. Colleen quit her nursing job, saying it was too stressful to continue now that they didn't need her income. But she did not replace her career with something productive. She did not go back to school or pursue enriching hobbies or devote time to a worthy cause. And she did not want to have a child. She spent her time shopping, eating (with corresponding weight gain), and compulsively redecorating the house. Eventually, Doug's admiration turned to disgust. He had nothing to talk to his wife about and was ashamed to be seen with her. Before long, he was having an affair with the curator of an art museum.

Annette had always been attracted to ambitious, strong-willed men with an edge of toughness about them. But a series of failed relationships in which she felt controlled and unappreciated had convinced her that what she really needed was a sensitive man. She found one in a sweet and gentle business colleague named David. The relationship was a big relief to Annette. David was kind, fair and attentive—qualities her previous lovers had sorely lacked. After a while, though, his agreeable nature began to disturb her. David was content with his present position in life and would rather get along than get ahead. In Annette's eyes, he was being pushed around by his boss, manipulative coworkers, members of his family and even Annette herself. She had no respect for men like that. By contrast, the macho assertiveness of her no-nonsense fitness trainer was irresistible.

> **USABLE INSIGHT**
>
> *Many affairs begin when people search for the respect their partners once gave them.*

Disrespect creates a need for someone to admire and be admired by—to cherish and be cherished by. It makes us vulnerable to temptation. By contrast, mutual regard heightens our sense of loyalty and amplifies the voice of conscience, whispering, "No!" when we're tempted to stray. One of my clients expressed this memorably when he told me why he turned his back on an opportunity to sleep with a seductive stranger on a business trip: "Why would I want anyone in the world to think that I had such little respect for my wife?"

For more complicated reasons, the respect factor can lead to the classic affair between a successful man and a younger and less accomplished, less educated or less intelligent woman. Men who have a strong drive for achievement usually have a strong sex drive as well. They are also very goal oriented; they see their objectives clearly and remove all obstacles in their way. That goes for sex as well as power or profits or touchdowns. When men like that fall in love with their equals—women who command respect for their talent, brains and accomplishments—they learn not to treat them as sex objects, not just because the women won't stand for it, but also because the men know instinctively that it's wrong to use someone you respect to gratify your basic instincts. And yet, many of those men still desire a pure sex object—someone who won't say no and does not have to be taken seriously; someone for whom being attractive to a powerful man gives her all the respect she needs. The fact that their mistresses look at them with wide-eyed admiration and make them feel like heroes—whereas the wives see through them and call them on their shortcomings—is even more reason for the liaison.

Think of it this way: around the time Monica was flashing her thong, Bill Clinton had nothing but respect for Hillary.

Why Respect Deteriorates

No memory of having starred
Atones for later disregard,
Or keeps the end from being hard.
—ROBERT FROST

Isn't it amazing that when we're on vacation, or riding on a plane, or chatting at a cocktail party, we are highly respectful of the people we meet? We are polite, we mind our manners, we listen with a minimum of judgment, and if we think the other person is foolish or stupid or self-centered, we certainly don't let them know we feel that way. Isn't it amazing that we often get more respect from—and give more respect to—strangers than the people we love and live with?

Actually, it shouldn't amaze us at all. Familiarity *does* breed contempt.

For one thing, the comfort and security of a committed relationship causes us to slack off on how we present ourselves. In the early days of a love affair, we're on our best behavior for obvious reasons: we're trying to impress the other person and not give them any reason to turn away. As time goes by, and we come to take them for granted, we relax. We might even get a little careless. The not-so-lovable traits that we kept under wraps begin to creep into view, like weeds between rose bushes. As our flaws start to show, the pedestal we were placed on begins to get shaky.

Another factor is how we evaluate our partners. In the early days of a relationship, we want to see them as near-perfect. It could be said that we *need* to view them with the utmost respect, for otherwise the bonding process would be less complete and less cementing. We project onto our new love all that we need, all that we wish for, all that we've dreamed Mr. or Ms. Right would be. Then, as our dreamboat becomes a real person, we almost always experience a letdown; they are not quite as worthy of unconditional respect as we thought. The greater the fantasy, the bigger the letdown and the more drastic the plunge to disrespect.

Deserving Respect

Sometimes, the loss of respect is a rational outcome: one or both of you may be behaving in a way that is unworthy of admiration.

The drop-off in esteem can result from a single instance—a major act of cowardice or betrayal, for example—or from a steady accumulation of revealing actions. It may result from a violation of moral or ethical principles that the offended partner holds dear, or from a failure to live up to standards of behavior he or she considers appropriate and necessary in a mate. Here is a list of typical behaviors that erode respect. See if any of these has damaged your respect for your mate or your mate's respect for you:

- betraying a sacred vow
- breaking promises
- dishonesty in business or personal affairs
- manipulating others for personal gain
- letting others take advantage of you
- arrogance
- lack of courage
- lack of integrity
- inability or unwillingness to change harmful behavior
- lack of ambition
- giving up too easily
- self-indulgent behavior
- selfishness or lack of concern for others
- avoiding challenges or difficult issues
- cynicism
- sarcasm
- having to be right at all costs
- gloating in victory, bitter in defeat
- bullying or abusive behavior

- self-pity, helplessness or defeatism
- not doing what you say you'll do
- neediness or dependency
- crude, rude or vulgar behavior
- blaming others when things go wrong
- childishness or immaturity
- incompetence
- self-deception
- complaining without trying to solve the problem

Just how badly the relationship is damaged depends on a number of factors, such as how consistent the negative behavior is, how many of those traits the person displays and the severity of the problems they cause.

The presence of admirable qualities can compensate for traits we disrespect, however. If our eyes are open, time and familiarity can reveal more and more of what is noble and worthy about the other person, balancing the ever-changing ledger sheet of our partner's assets and liabilities that we all keep. Such was the case of an entrepeneur named Sam and his schoolteacher wife, Mindy. In his business dealings, Sam could be ruthless, greedy and arrogant. When Mindy learned about some of the things her husband did to defeat his competition, she was appalled, and when one of his actions resulted in a heavy fine and public embarrassment, she was enraged. But the loss of respect she felt was offset by the loving and attentive way Sam treated his children and stepchildren, his tireless philanthropic work and the sure knowledge that he would lay down his life for the wife he openly worshipped. Sam's self-deprecating honesty also helped: he acknowledged his flaws, and when he made mistakes he was always contrite and willing to accept the consequences.

Self-awareness and self-honesty go a long way toward ameliorating traits that diminish respect in the

eyes of others, particularly when it is combined with kindness. Joan, a veteran of two marriages and a series of failed relationships, had done enough introspection to know that she was emotionally needy. That tendency, which stemmed in large part from the loss of her parents in early childhood, would rise to the surface the minute she started a promising relationship. Her insecurity sent many a man scurrying for cover and contributed mightily to her two divorces.

When she started to fall for Ken, Joan was afraid she'd be unable to hide her neediness and would scare him away. After discussing the situation in therapy, she decided to take a different tack. As soon as things reached the level of intimacy that normally triggered clingy, possessive behavior, she said to Ken: "In the past, when I opened my heart to a man, I've acted very needy. I'm telling you now so that if it happens you won't be surprised. If you lose respect for me and walk away, I'll understand. But I respect you too much to try to hide who I really am." Ken admired Joan's self-awareness, honesty and presence of mind so much that it was easy for him to maintain respect for her even when she displayed the very behavior she warned him about.

Respect Is in the Eyes of the Beholder

Tell me who admires you and loves you
and I will tell you who you are.

—CHARLES-AUGUSTIN SAINTE-BEUVE

In a great many cases, lack of positive regard says more about the person who loses respect for another than the one who is disrespected. We all give respect and take it away according to the values and standards we hold dear. Qualities you find unworthy may be water off a duck's back to someone else, and vice versa. On one recent day, for instance, I counseled two couples where respect was a major issue, but for exactly the opposite reasons. In one case, a husband had lost respect for his wife, a corporate vice president, because she did not stand up for principle when her company betrayed her ethical standards to swing a major deal that would net shareholders (including the couple) a bundle of money. In the other case, a wife lost respect for her husband because he blew the whistle on his company's violations of environmental laws, risking his job in the process. One spouse considered personal integrity more important than financial security; the other felt that providing for one's family was a higher responsibility than standing up for principle.

In my years as a couples therapist, I have seen partners lose respect for each other over what many would consider trivial reasons. I've heard men put down their wives for not being able to make up their minds at a restaurant, or for gossiping on the phone or for being overly concerned with their appearance. I've seen many wives lose respect for husbands because their moods were drastically affected by the ups and downs of their jobs or even of their favorite sports teams, or because they leered at supermodels on TV or made crude remarks in public.

Such behavior may seem too insignificant to cause a major breach in respect. But look again. These apparently minor traits add up to something far more crucial: immaturity. Everyone wants their partner to be a mature, responsible grown-up. We want them to be high-minded, to have an adult sense of values and rise above trivial matters. Having such a mate makes us feel more secure—and better about ourselves. If you or your partner is losing respect for the other over what seem to be insignificant traits, examine them more deeply and see what larger issues they represent. It might be immaturity, or it might be selfishness, arrogance, cowardice or other qualities that represent a threat to your well-being.

> **USABLE INSIGHT**
>
> *Maturity is doing the right thing even when you feel like doing the wrong thing.*

You should also examine your own self-respect. Groucho Marx once joked that he would not join a club that would have him as a member. If you don't respect yourself, can you respect a lover who would have you as a mate? One solution is to join a club that's beneath you. At first, such a relationship offers a certain amount of relief; the disrespect you feel toward your partner takes some of the heat off your own self-contempt. But it always backfires. Pretty soon, everything you can't stand about your lover reminds you of everything you despise about yourself.

The other common solution to low self-esteem—hooking

up with someone you see as more worthy than you—also back-fires quickly. At first, it boosts your self-image to be with someone of such superior quality. But self-esteem that's linked to someone other than yourself is too flimsy to last. Pretty soon you get paranoid. Deep inside you don't feel good enough to be with that person and you live in fear that they'll wake up one day and realize they've bought a lemon.

The only solution is to abandon the hope of gaining self-respect through your choice of a mate. Find ways to develop it from within and marry for love.

Another major cause of disrespect is the tendency to measure our mates according to unrealistic standards. You would be surprised, for example, how many people have adopted the images they see in the media as models of how their partners should behave. In one therapy session, I heard the following exchange. "Maybe if I had a bunch of writers scripting my lines for me, I *would* be as decisive as the guy on *Law and Order,*" the husband protested. "Yeah," said his wife, "and if I had a personal trainer and tons of money, maybe I'd be built like Madonna."

Even more than public figures and fictitious characters on screen, we compare our partners to the impossible standard of our parent of the opposite sex. A great many marriages have been ruined because a spouse lost respect for a husband or wife who could not measure up to the sainted image of a dead father or mother. Here are some of the remarks I've heard in couples counseling:

"My mother didn't waste *her* time reading fashion magazines."

"My father never complained, and he held down *two* jobs."

"My mother had *four* kids and she *still* kept the house clean."

"My father considered it an honor to give my mother what she wanted."

"My mother wouldn't whine, she'd roll up her sleeves and *do* something about it."

"My father never dressed like a slob, and he couldn't even afford to buy a suit."

"My mother would *die* before she would betray a friend."

"My father would *never* let someone get away with that."

You get the idea. Very often, we lose respect for our mates for not living up to the best qualities of our parents—whether those qualities were real or imagined.

Parents only die to more effectively meddle in
their children's affairs.

—CARL WHITTAKER

The changing roles of men and women has made the issue of respect more complicated than ever. For example, many men who take pride in being providers and insist that they don't want their wives to work outside the home later lose respect for their spouses because they don't have interesting careers like the women they meet through their jobs. By the same token, women no longer regard with awe what their husbands do for a living. The mystique has been shattered now that women see firsthand the reality of the workaday world, and in many cases do the very jobs that their mothers and grandmothers could only imagine—and revere—from a distance. Another unprecedented phenomenon is female earning power. I've counseled a number of women who said they wanted equality in their marriages and that it would be perfectly fine if their husbands were to earn less than they do—only to lose respect for their mates when that actually happened.

The Warning Signs of Disrespect

The impact of declining respect on a relationship depends in large part on how it is handled. The first reaction is usually disappointment, sometimes accompanied by shock: "This is not the person I fell in love with." Your partner may have actually changed for the worse, or you may have been in denial about his or her less admirable traits all along, or you may have had unrealistic expectations about life in a committed relationship—whatever the reason for the letdown, it is real and it hurts.

That pain can quickly turn to anger and bitterness. You may suppress those emotions, either because you fear retaliation or do not want to hurt the other person. But the feelings won't just die. They may leak out in the form of put-downs. They may erupt in sudden tantrums or inexplicable acts of defiance. Or they may fester inside, leading to chronic depression or a steady diet of sadness, loss and regret. Whatever happens to the anger, you can count on this: it will create a poisonous atmosphere for your relationship.

Wherever the decline of respect begins, whatever its cause and however it is expressed, it will ultimately rebound. The disrespected partner will eventually lose respect for his or her mate.

At that point, the pillar of respect can start to crumble rapidly, jeopardizing the entire structure of the relationship.

An excellent example of this pattern was on the final episode of the sitcom *Mad About You*. The show portrays Jamie (Helen Hunt) and Paul (Paul Reiser) in the future, having been divorced. We see Jamie telling a girlfriend that she had always been the dissatisfied one, the one who thought the marriage couldn't work. Paul was the optimist. He always calmed her down and reassured her. Then, ironically, he was the one who left. She says this with pain on her face, as though thinking that she may have had it coming.

In the next scene we see the future Paul with a friend. Through most of the marriage, he says, he was trying to win his wife's respect. Then he realized that he was so busy trying not to disappoint her that he couldn't see that *she* was disappointing *him*. Finally, he couldn't take it anymore and left.

The story was poignant because it resonates with the truth of many couples' experience. The longer you go on feeling that your partner is disappointed in you, the more you have to struggle to maintain your self-respect. Ultimately, you will turn against your accuser. This being the finale of a beloved TV series, Jamie and Paul naturally get back together. In real life, it doesn't always work that way. The key is to spot the early warning signs of disrespect and stop the deterioration in its tracks.

> **USABLE INSIGHT**
>
> *If you can't get respect from them, you begin to lose respect for them.*

One sign of waning respect is speaking ill of your partner behind his or her back. Another is put-downs and snide remarks, often dressed up to seem like innocent jokes. Yet another is rudeness: as your respect for someone declines, you are less willing to put in the effort to be sensitive and considerate. Your fantasy life can also provide clues. Do you find yourself wishing your partner was like the men or women you *do* respect, or lovers from the past whom you glorify in memory?

Another clue is how you feel about being with your partner in the company of people who matter to you. When you respect someone, you are eager to be seen with them. They make you feel proud. They enhance your standing in the world. But when your respect has diminished you feel embarrassed to be with them. You get nervous before social events because you're afraid they'll say or do something that will put you in a bad light. You find yourself making excuses all the time: "Oh, she didn't mean that, she's just been under a lot of stress lately," "He's really not much of a drinker, I don't know what got into him," "Ha ha, she's quite the kidder, isn't she?" "He just likes to tease," "Oh, no, he had a very nice time, he's just kind of quiet." Meanwhile, you're so mortified you want to run away and hide, and you're sure that everyone thinks you're a real loser for being with such a person.

One of the most vivid signs of declining respect can be seen in the way partners listen to one another. There are four distinct levels of listening: removed, reactive, responsive and receptive. Each level represents a higher level of respect for the speaker.

With *removed* listening, the person is in the room but not really present. You might see signs of impatience or facial gestures that suggest that the speaker is boring, stupid or otherwise not worth listening to.

Reactive listeners hear what you say but take issue with everything, often in a combative or condescending manner.

Responsive listeners hear you out and respond appropriately and respectfully to the content.

With *receptive* listeners, direct eye contact and the absence of fidgeting, interruptions and other signs of impatience extend a genuine welcome mat.

People who respect you the most listen receptively; they care about what you have to say and consider your thoughts and feelings worthy of their attention. They may not agree with you, but they'll take what you say seriously. In the absence of respect, you'll find removed listeners, who communicate exactly the opposite: what you say is not worth their time.

Look for the signs and be prepared to take action, or the disrespect will only grow bigger and uglier, like a malignant cancer cell. You don't want to reach the point of no return, as a client of mine named Sonia did. "If only I knew then what I know now," she lamented, "I never would have married him. Now I'm trapped." She felt cornered, with no way out, because at age forty-seven, "Who would have me?" That she might be better off alone than feeling trapped never occurred to her because eighteen years of marriage to a man she did not respect had so destroyed her self-esteem that she didn't think she could bear her own company.

Overcoming Your Resistance

The first step in restoring the pillar of respect is to see if either you or your partner is resisting it. Does one of you, for example, have a need to look down on the other because it makes you feel big by comparison? Do you need to have the upper hand? Do you need to feel superior? Does disrespect give you a sense of power and control? Is one of you putting up with more disrespect than you deserve because it confirms your innermost feelings of inferiority or unworthiness? Are you afraid you'll lose your partner if you take a stand? Those are all common reasons why people resist taking the necessary steps to restore respect.

Perhaps the *most* common source of resistance is that we are reluctant to give up that which is familiar, even if it is not in our best interest. Are you feeling disrespect for your partner, or tolerating disrespect *from* your partner, out of habit? Are you repeating a pattern you experienced before? Are you reliving what you observed in your childhood home?

Sal was married to a spoiled woman who seemed to take pleasure in finding ways to let him know he didn't measure up. He took her criticism, sarcasm and other signs of disrespect without complaining or striking back because, he said, "I didn't want to be like my father." He had grown up in an explosive environment in which his father bullied everyone in the family. When he wasn't battering his wife or smacking one of the kids, he was threatening to do it. An ex-boxer who now toiled on construction sites, Sal's father had a legendary temper. Fear was the background music of their lives because everyone knew that the old man could detonate at any moment.

Sal swore that no one he loved would ever be afraid of him. He never imagined that he would lose their respect in the bargain. The more his wife berated him, the more respect she lost for him because he did not stand up to her.

Sal is an example of how what we observe in our parents as

we grow up determines how we act in our love relationships. In his case, he got into trouble because he was determined not to act out what he saw growing up. Other people do the opposite: repeat exactly what they witnessed as children.

Since our parents are our first and most important models of how men and women relate to one another, it stands to reason that we would internalize their behavior. I can't count the number of people who have said something like, "I vowed never to be like my father/mother, but as soon as I get into a relationship I become just like him/her." Many people are critical and disrespectful of their mates because that's the way their mothers or fathers treated the other parent. And many victims of disrespect accept it without protest because they saw their fathers or mothers do the same; the situation is so familiar they think it's normal. Sal's sister was one of those people; she married an abusive man and let him bully her, just as her mother did with her father.

Look for signs that either you or your partner is resisting the changes that have to be made to regain respect. Resist the resistance by examining it carefully and eliminating the source.

Learning to Respect Your Partner

Disappointment should always be taken as a
stimulant, and never viewed as a discouragement.

—C. B. NEWCOMB

If you are having trouble respecting your partner, you may very well be justified. On the other hand, at least part of the problem may be your own inability to respect another human being. We have such an enormous emotional investment in our love relationships that it is easy to focus exclusively on the areas where we feel disappointed. Feeling wounded by our partners' flaws, we lose sight of the qualities that make them worthy of respect.

Needless to say, you may feel that certain behavior is so despicable that forgiveness is impossible. You may find certain traits so dishonorable or immoral that they blind you to the person's better qualities. In such cases, respect may be unattainable and pretending otherwise would only lead to severe discontent. If your lack of respect for your partner has reached that level, for the sake of your *self*-respect—and perhaps your overall well-being—you may have no acceptable alternative but to end the relationship.

But the likelihood is strong that the damage is neither total nor irreversible. You owe it to yourself to ask whether your partner is truly unworthy of respect or whether you are being too demanding and unforgiving. Are your standards realistic? Could *anyone* earn your respect—anyone you live with and know intimately, that is? Are you capable of recognizing what is most worthy of admiration and cutting people enough slack to make mistakes and expose their human frailties?

With that thought in mind, ask yourself, "What can I do to increase my capacity to respect my partner?"

At the same time, it's appropriate to ask what your partner can do to earn your respect. What changes in attitude and behavior would enhance his or her esteem in your mind? Make a list of what you would like your partner to work on in the future. When you're finished, arrange your list in order of priority, from "absolutely essential" on one end to "it would be nice, but I can live without it" on the other.

Earn Your Own Respect

*Experience is a hard teacher because she gives
the test first, the lesson afterwards.*

—VERNON LAW

Let's face it, if your partner has lost respect for you, it may not be entirely undeserved. Part of the solution may be to take a good,

> **USABLE INSIGHT**
>
> *Earn your own
> respect and
> you'll earn your
> partner's too.*

honest look at yourself and see if there are aspects of your personality or behavior that attract disrespect. Are there things about yourself that *you* don't respect? Traits you would like to eliminate or improve upon? Qualities you admire in others and wish you could emulate? Chances are, your partner has noticed the same things. If you look for ways to earn your own self-respect, you will probably enhance your respect in the eyes of others—including your partner—at the same time.

A key in this regard is to be true to yourself and act with the highest possible integrity at all times. That point was driven home to me at a convention a few years ago. The person who had invited me to do a workshop urged me to think of some attention-grabbing techniques to entertain the crowd. My usual style is pretty direct and sincere, but I gave in and came up with some flashy gimmicks I thought would wow the audience. The 300 people who attended my workshop seemed to respond well to the material, but I felt unnatural and awkward throughout the session. Afterward, I felt awful because I had given far less than my best.

122

One of the reasons the experience was so painful is that I had just seen how a speaker can command the attention of an audience without jokes or gimmicks. The main keynote address for the convention had been given by General Colin Powell. In his sincere, understated manner, Powell held about 7,000 people in the palm of his hand. After a quietly moving speech, delivered with humility and dignity, Powell asked for questions. One man made a rude and pointless query about the fact, recently revealed in the press, that the general's wife had received treatment for depression. Unshaken but clearly outraged, Powell stared at the questioner for a moment, then said something like this: "Let me see if I understand you correctly. Someone you love is in misery, and there is something you can do to help her, and you have a problem with that?"

If there was anyone in the room who did not already respect the general, there were surely none after that exchange.

That night, as I reflected on the day, I found myself feeling as low as my respect for General Powell was high. The next morning I made an announcement apologizing to everyone in my audience and offering a refund to anyone who had bought a tape of my presentation. For the benefit of my self-respect as well as the people in attendance, I scheduled another session on the same topic. This time I showed up as myself.

Handle Disrespect with Dignity

By indignities men come to dignities.

—FRANCIS BACON

Are you the one who's being disrespected? If so, you may be making the problem worse by the way you're dealing with the situation. If you respond with pouting, whining or other child-ish behavior, your partner's respect will only diminish further. Ditto for becoming hostile or lashing out in retaliation. Ditto again for stuffing your feelings inside and becoming sullen or pretending you don't know you're being disrespected. One of the keys to getting back the respect you've lost, therefore, is to start dealing with that very lack of regard in a way that commands respect. We tend to admire people who face up to unpleasant realities, who handle adversity with dignity, integrity and assertiveness—even when that means standing up to us.

For the entire therapy session, Linda talked about her hus-band, Roy, with obvious scorn. At first, he just sat there, taking it in, saying nothing, looking down at his shoes like a sad child who's been scolded many times for the same offense. As his wife continued to vent her discontent in the most emasculating way, Roy's body language started to shift. He moved from embarrass-ment to irritation to anger to resolve. Then Linda turned to him for her final summation. "You're just a wimp, Roy," she said. "If you keep letting people walk all over you, your life is never going to get any better."

Slowly, Roy raised his head and looked her in the eye for the first time. "You're right," he said. "I have to stand up for myself more. And the first place it starts is with *you*."

Linda was flabbergasted. You could practically see her mind doing flip-flops: "I didn't mean me, I meant everyone else. I know what's best for you." But as Roy kept his gaze firmly on her eyes, revealing a steely resolve she hadn't seen before, Linda became the sheepish one. Fidgeting, she began to backtrack: "You know I exaggerate. I was just trying to make a point."

It was the beginning of an important change in their relationship; Roy's action elevated him in his wife's eyes and placed the issue of respect squarely on the table.

Examine Yourself

Of all knowledge the wise and good seek
most to know themselves.

—WILLIAM SHAKESPEARE

To help you identify possible areas of improvement, ask yourself what character flaws have already cost you significantly in your life. Which aspects of your personality and behavior have led to pain, failure, despair, humiliation or loss? What parts of yourself are you afraid will never change and might, at the end of your life, cause you to look back with regret?

I suggest that you list the ways you might improve your self-respect. These common responses may help you identify them:

- say what you mean and mean what you say
- stop fooling yourself and deceiving others
- start standing up for yourself
- don't give up when things get difficult
- do more for others
- become more reliable
- stop complaining about the same old things
- take charge

- show more courage
- be more decisive
- stop blaming things on other people
- control your anger
- own up to your feelings
- give more and take less

By all means don't limit yourself to this list, and be sure to make your own list specific to your circumstances.

Needless to say, there is not always an exact correlation between how you see yourself and how your spouse or lover sees you. So, another important exercise is to make a second list. Write down what you think your *partner* would say if asked how you could earn his or her respect. Don't stop to analyze or debate each item, just write down everything you think your partner would include.

When you're finished, look at the lists side by side. The items that appear in both places are likely to be areas you will benefit most from working on.

The next step is to circle the items that appear on your partner's list but not your own. How do you feel about them? Do you think your partner is right about you? Do you think it is fair and reasonable to expect you to change in those ways? Do you think improvement in those areas is possible without getting a complete personality transplant? Are you willing to work on those aspects of yourself without resenting your partner?

A client named Yvonne, an executive assistant at a radio station, filled out her lists this way:

How I Can Respect Myself More

1. Stop being late for things.
2. Finish my masters degree.
3. Control my temper.

What Michael [her boyfriend] Needs from Me to Respect Me More

1. Stop second-guessing everything he does.
2. Learn how to be on time.
3. Stop flying off the handle.

It was the second-guessing that would be the hardest for Yvonne to work on. She knew it would rank high on her boyfriend's list, but she wasn't entirely sure it was her problem and not his for being oversensitive to her "suggestions." But she was open to discussing it with Michael, and she was willing to consider working on it if it meant that much to him.

Thinking About Respect

To prepare for a dialogue on respect, each of you should take some time to think about your history. Complete the following sentences without editing or censoring yourselves:

1. What I admired most about my partner in the early stages of our relationship was _____.
2. The first time I remember losing some respect for my partner was _____.

3. When that happened it made me feel _____.

4. And it made me think_____.

5. Other instances where I lost respect include _____.

6. What keeps me from regaining the respect I once had for my
   partner is _____.

7. What I still respect and admire about my partner is _____
   _____.

8. What would help me regain respect for my partner would be
   _____.

9. The first time I felt my partner begin to lose respect for me was.
   _____

10. The way my partner showed the loss of respect was_____
    _____.

11. I think what would help my partner respect me more would be
    _____.

Opening the Dialogue

It may not be easy and it may not always be pleasant, but a heart-to-heart conversation on the issue of respect will bring enormous relief to both you and your partner. If you follow the principles of good communication in chapter 1, you will not only set the stage for a resurgence of respect, you might very well experience a major breakthrough in intimacy.

Because of its capacity to hurt, the subject of lost respect must be approached gently and compassionately. It's important to address the situation head-on, without evasion or denial. But it is equally important to express your feelings without hostility, always remembering to ask, "What is it like for my partner right now?"

If you need to initiate the conversation and draw your partner into it, an excellent approach is to do what Yvonne did: After she made her two lists, she showed them to Michael and said, "Did I leave anything out? Is there something you would add to that list?" By baring your neck first, you have a far greater chance of creating a genuine dialogue than if you start out by telling your partner why you don't respect him or her—a surefire recipe for an argument.

Yvonne's approach worked wonders. Michael had an aversion to therapy and had resisted all of Yvonne's attempts to get him to discuss their issues openly. When she showed him her lists and asked for his comments, Michael's resistance melted immediately. He was so moved by Yvonne's effort to figure out what was causing the tension between them, and to look at it from his point of view, that he offered to reciprocate. "I guess we need to discuss this," he said. "Why don't I make two lists of my own, and then we'll talk." It was the beginning of their first sustained conversation about how to improve their relationship.

Another respect-preserving technique is to talk in terms of your own struggle and your own pain. This is how Astrid, a forty-two-year-old airline executive, opened the door to communicating with her husband. She had lost respect for Bruce when he began drinking and moping around the house despondently after his business went bankrupt. "What bothers me most about your behavior is what it's done to the way I feel about you," said Astrid. "I wish I had the patience and understanding of a saint, but I don't. I have to admit that I'm losing respect for you, and it hurts me terribly."

She then offered to make a trade: "I don't think it's fair to ask you to change if I'm not willing to work on myself just as much. So I'd like you to tell me some of the things that you don't respect about me." The combination of honesty, compassion, humility and fairness was hard for Bruce to resist.

A similar approach can be taken when you're the one who is being disrespected. As a full-time homemaker, Martina had raised three children, a job she'd approached with such devotion and skill that her husband, Wayne, was in awe for twenty-two years. Then their middle child went off to college and the youngest got a scholarship to a boarding school. Martina's nest was suddenly empty. Wayne had warned her that this day would come and encouraged her to think about how she could fill her time productively. She didn't listen, and now she was bouncing off the walls of her hollow house without the faintest idea of what to do with herself.

As he watched his wife kill time with unsatisfying activities, Wayne grew increasingly disappointed. He would not say so, but he broadcast his disrespect in a thousand unspoken messages, and Martina picked up on it. After discussing the situation in therapy, she decided to raise the issue herself. "I feel that you've lost respect for me," she told Wayne. "You may not be telling me because you don't want to hurt my feelings, but I think it's true. I want you to know that I don't think it's entirely undeserved. I know I have shortcomings, and I'm not happy with how I've been acting. What would I have to do differently to regain your respect?"

By demonstrating the courage to face their problem openly and honestly, and by stating their feelings with dignity and fairness, both Martina and Astrid immediately strengthened the pillar of respect. In each case, their statements opened the door to a long overdue dialogue.

The Heart of the Conversation

In my experience, the most fruitful respect dialogues follow four distinct steps.

STEP 1. The best and safest place to begin is with each person making the two lists we just described—How I Can Respect Myself More and What My Partner Needs from Me to Respect Me More. Share them and welcome one another's comments. Limit your remarks to no more than three minutes, avoiding the temptation to lecture or blame. The listener should pay close attention without responding. Accept your partner's comments as valid expressions of his or her feelings. This is not the time to defend yourself or explain your past behavior. It is not the time to debate what is true and what is not, or what is doable and what is not. Above all, refrain from launching a retaliation, as in, "Yeah, but you do that too!" or "I wouldn't act that way if you didn't . . ."

Remember, you are working together to fortify the pillar of respect, so don't disrespect your relationship. If at any time one of you starts to get defensive or retaliatory, immediately call a time out. Go off by yourselves and re-read the principles of good communication. When you're ready to follow them, come back together and resume your conversation.

STEP 2. Take three to five minutes each to describe when, where, how and why the loss of respect began. Which incidents first made you feel that you were losing respect for your partner? What changes in attitude, demeanor or behavior caused your respect to diminish? What changes in *you* may have led you to respect your partner less?

Take care to express your thoughts in a considerate manner. One key is to identify the principles and values that underlie the loss of respect. Consider this statement: "I lost respect for you when I found out you lied to your brother, because I consider honesty and integrity to be nearly sacred." Now consider this one: "You're a liar, and liars are the scum of the earth." Which one do you think would foster a meaningful discussion?

STEP 3. Once each of you has described the origins of your declining respect, move the discussion into the future. Referring to the lists you made earlier, take turns naming the changes you think are essential to restoring respect. It is crucial that both of you get to state your wishes without interruption. Accept that what each person says is a true representation of his or her needs.

After you have each expressed your wish list, it is time to discuss what you are willing to do. Which expectations do you think are realistic? What tradeoffs do you think should be made? It is very important to enter this phase of the dialogue in a spirit of mutual give and take.

STEP 4. Getting your negative thoughts and feelings out in the open was painful but necessary. So was discussing what you need to do to restore respect. You may feel a bit raw after that difficult work. Give each other all the comfort and reassurance you need. Then, to end the discussion on an upbeat note, take some time to accentuate the positive.

Separately, take a piece of paper and divide it into two columns. Head one column What I Respect Most About Myself, and the other What I Respect Most About My Partner. Then write down the top items in each category. When you finish, share your lists. Think of it as giving one another your favorite dessert. You deserve a treat.

It Can Be Done

Hope is the thing with feathers
That perches in the soul . . .
—EMILY DICKINSON

If your respect for one another has diminished significantly, you may think it's hopeless to expect conditions to improve. I can state with confidence that if you are both willing to do the exercises in this chapter in good faith your chances of restoring mutual respect are excellent. Here is an example of one couple who achieved that goal:

Sandy and Edward were attorneys who shared a dedication to both the legal profession and the finer things in life. They had season tickets to the ballet and the theater. They had interesting friends with whom they shared an interest in art, literature and travel. Having a son did not slow them down a bit. Then they had a daughter, and shortly afterward their son developed behavioral problems. Since they didn't need her income, Sandy took a leave from her practice to stay home for a while. A while became a year, and Sandy's sabbatical became early retirement. That she could do without practicing law was understandable to Edward. What was not acceptable was her lack of interest in everything else they used to enjoy. Losing his companion made Edward moody and sullen. The atmosphere at home became tense.

"If I were to ask your husband what he is having the most trouble with in your relationship, what do you think he would say?" I asked Sandy in their first therapy session. After contemplating the unexpected question for a few moments, she replied, "I think he has a very low opinion of me. I think he feels I've become some kind of boring 1950s housewife who's obsessed with her children."

Edward confirmed her diagnosis. "We used to have stimulating conversations," he said. "Now all she talks about is the kids. We don't see our friends anymore. We don't do anything interesting. She's become a worrisome, fearful mother and a one-dimensional human being."

I then asked Edward what he thought Sandy would say if I were to ask her to name her biggest difficulty in the relationship. This was hard for him to do; he had never thought of their marriage from his wife's point of view before. "She'd probably say I don't appreciate how hard it is to be a mother," he finally muttered. "She probably also thinks I've become moody and petulant."

Sandy added that she was losing respect for Edward because he was not living up to his responsibilities as a father. Seeking fun and companionship elsewhere, he accepted only the bare minimum of parental duties.

At one point, Sandy snapped at Edward: "You don't have the faintest idea what my life is like."

"What's to know?" retorted Edward in a condescending tone.

Later, I took him aside and made a recommendation, using legal terms he'd understand. "Your wife thinks you've rushed to judgment," I said. "Why don't you gather some evidence before you make your case?" I suggested that he take a day off and stay home, just to see firsthand if Sandy's life was really unworthy of his respect. Somewhat reluctantly, he went along with the plan. Telling Sandy he needed to catch up on some reading, he hung around the house on a typical weekday, trying to be unobtrusive. But the kids made that impossible.

He found himself drawn in by the innocent playfulness of the youngest child and the melodrama of the difficult child. He watched as Sandy juggled all the details of mothering, carpooling, after-school

> **USABLE INSIGHT**
>
> *Seeing is respecting.*

activities and household chores. He overheard a series of phone conversations in which Sandy had to coordinate a group of parents involved with a school fund-raiser, at one point calming an angry mother and at another point rearranging all the schedules because someone got sick. He watched as she helped their son with an art project he was anxious about, combining the patience of a saint with the skill of a Montessori teacher.

That evening, instead of going to the lecture series he attended once a month, Edward chose to stay home and help Sandy with the kids. "It looks like you have your hands full," he said. "Are you kidding?" Sandy replied. "This was an *easy* day!" He stayed home anyway because he found himself more intrigued by his son's project than the topic of the lecture. By bedtime, Edward was frazzled, but also strangely exhilarated. His attitude toward Sandy's life had gone from belittling to awe. Being a full-time parent, he realized, was not one-dimensional but multidimensional. The rebirth of respect led directly to a rebirth of romance.

Try it yourself if you can. There's no better way to gain respect for others than to witness a day in their life.

4

Enjoyment

Eat, Drink and Be Merry

All animals, except man, know that the principal business of life is to enjoy it.

—SAMUEL BUTLER

How much do the following statements apply to how you think or feel about enjoyment in your relationship?

	Hardly Ever 0	Sometimes 1	Almost Always 2
1. I usually smile when I think about my partner.	___	___	___
2. I look forward to seeing my partner at the end of the day.	___	___	___
3. My partner looks forward to seeing me at the end of the day.	___	___	___
4. We enjoy each other's company when we do something by ourselves.	___	___	___
5. I'm happy to do things that my partner enjoys more than I do.	___	___	___
6. My partner is happy to do things I enjoy more than he/she does.	___	___	___
7. I would rather have lunch with my partner than anyone else.	___	___	___
8. My partner would rather have lunch with me than anyone else.	___	___	___
9. I make my partner laugh.	___	___	___
10. My partner makes me laugh.	___	___	___
TOTAL:	___	___	___

SCORING:

  0–6   You're avoiding each other, not enjoying each other.
  7–13   You tolerate each other.
  14–20 You like each other, you really like each other!

Enjoy: "To enter into a state of rejoicing." Compare to endure: "To carry on through, despite hardships; to bear with tolerance; to suffer patiently without yielding." When you're enduring something, time passes slowly; when you're enjoying it, hours seem like minutes and weeks go by in a blink of an eye. Without enjoyment, a relationship is more like an endurance contest; every minute is torturous, whereas fifty years of an enjoyable marriage pass all too quickly.

Do you enjoy your relationship, or do you merely endure it?

Enjoyment means taking delight in the other person—the twists and turns of their mind, their quirky ways, the things they do for fun, their conversation, their silly jokes, the way they walk. Couples who enjoy each other tend to smile a lot, over little or nothing. They can't wait to see each other, and they're gladdened when they do. When they hear the other's footsteps outside the door, or the car pulling into the driveway, their hearts lift. For couples who *don't* enjoy each other, the same sounds may as well be coming from a bill collector or a blabbermouth neighbor.

Where enjoyment is strong, the two partners take pleasure in doing things together, whether it's partying with friends or sitting in the living room, quietly reading. They plan to do things together, not because it's expected or because they have to, but because they know the experience will be richer and more pleasurable if they share it. When they're enjoying themselves *apart,* they say "Wish you were here" and really mean it, and they can't wait to describe their experience when they get home. Couples who basically enjoy each other even find enjoyment in doing things they're *not* particularly interested in—just because they're together. They also enjoy activities that excite only one of them. "I couldn't care less about baseball, but I go to games because I love seeing my husband having fun," one wife told me. "The truth is, I'm not really into ballroom dancing," said a husband. "I go to classes just to see the joy on my wife's face."

Where enjoyment is missing, people might attend the same social functions, or go to movies or concerts with one another, but they don't enjoy the *sharing* aspect. They don't talk with each other or exchange the silent looks and gestures that unite people in a common experience. Many try to avoid being alone together. They include other couples or bring their kids along to take the edge off the fact that they've stopped enjoying each other.

An advertising executive named Amanda told me about the moment she knew her nine-year marriage was in trouble: "One of the things that first drew me to George was that he was a great conversationalist. He was witty, insightful and a master story-teller. I couldn't wait for him to come home and tell me about his day. About a year ago, I realized that he'd changed. I'd say, 'What happened today?' and he'd say, 'The usual,' and pour himself a drink and turn on CNN. We'd go weeks without having a real conversation, when we used to have long talks practically every day.

"I figured he was burned out from working so hard," she continued. "Maybe things had become less interesting at work. Plus, we had a couple of kids by then, one of whom was waking us up at night, so there were lots of excuses. Then one night, when we were having dinner with another couple, the man asked George how things were going at work. George launched into a nonstop fifteen-minute show, telling stories about the funny things that went on at the office, and his lunch meeting and what happened on his last business trip. I couldn't believe my ears! I'm sitting there thinking, 'The usual?' That's when I knew that the air had gone out of our tires."

It must be emphasized that enjoyment also means taking pleasure in sharing everyday routines, whether it's making a meal together, playing with the kids, going shopping or just doing nothing. You could be raking leaves, washing dishes or even paying bills, but the presence of your mate adds luster to the commonplace and takes the sting out of drudgery. The simple joy of a partner's company reveals a subtle but important reason why enjoyment is one of the six pillars of a lasting relationship. Being loved is simply not enough; we want to be *liked* as well. We want the warm, cozy feeling that the person we love finds us enjoyable and is glad that we're around.

> **USABLE INSIGHT**
>
> *Ask not what you can enjoy about your partner; ask what your partner can enjoy about you.*

Laughing and Kvelling

*The sound of laughter is like the vaulted
dome of a temple of happiness.*

—MILAN KUNDERA

What greater pleasure is there than the sound of a loved one laughing? In surveys of what women look for in men, sense of humor always ranks at or near the top of the list, and "He makes me laugh" is one of the most frequently heard statements from women in love. The reason for that is not just the obvious pleasure we get from goofing around and sharing jokes and funny stories. Humor is a wonderful—and highly cost-effective—form of giving: saying something funny is a gift, and laughing at another person's humor is an immediate and generous way to reciprocate. Lifting your lover's spirits with well-timed humor can be as rewarding as satisfying him or her in bed. It makes the giver feel competent and effective, and it makes the receiver feel treasured. One of the sadder signs of a marriage in trouble is when someone whose humor used to bring delight is seen as a ridiculous clown whose feeble jokes make his or her spouse grimace.

When two people thoroughly enjoy (and respect) each other, they can even make jokes at one another's expense and draw a laugh. A telltale sign of the *absence* of enjoyment is when teasing and personal jibes have a snide, taunting or sarcastic edge. Even more telltale is when those jokes are greeted by icy sneers and dagger-filled glances, or immediate, not-so-funny retorts. That's when onlookers find themselves fidgeting in their seats thinking, "Get me outta here!"

The quality of enjoyment can be seen vividly in the way partners talk about each other to outsiders. Consider two of my favorite Yiddish words, *kvell* and *kvetch*. Kvetch means to complain or gripe. Kvell, according to Leo Rosten's *The Joys of Yiddish,* means, "To beam with immense pride and pleasure." The most common form of kvelling is that of a parent or grandparent over the glorious attributes of a child, but the word applies to everything that makes us want to sing its praises. People who feel like kvelling over the men or women they love are proud of them and find joy in being with them (even though they usually kvell with more restraint than they display for their kids). We all hunger to be with someone that makes us want to kvell—and who kvells over us.

Do you kvell over your mate, or do you kvetch about your mate?

Terms of Enjoyment

There are two things to aim at in life; first, to get
what you want; and after that, to enjoy it.
Only the wisest of mankind achieve the second.

—LOGAN PEARSALL SMITH

Of the six pillars, enjoyment is the most self-sufficient. It is less influenced by the other five and affects them less in return. Certainly, it's easier to enjoy someone if the other essentials are strong. But two people can thoroughly enjoy each other's company even in the absence of chemistry; they can have fun together and share mutual interests even if they don't entirely respect or trust each other, or accept most things about each other, and they can certainly have a good time without any empathy for each other outside of the activities they both enjoy. But, if enjoyment is the only strong ingredient, what you usually have is a friendship, not a romantic bond, and not a very intimate friendship at that.

More common is to have five relatively strong pillars but not a whole lot of enjoyment. I have seen this numerous times with couples who come to me for counseling. Almost without exception, they are people who enjoyed one another a great deal in the past and still have a lot going for them, but they've become bored within the context of their marriage, and they're upset—often to the point of despair—over their lack of enjoyment. The problem can usually be traced to one or more of these factors:

• One or both has lost interest in the things they once enjoyed together.
• They have developed new interests that they don't share.
• They have failed to make room for enjoyment in the midst of busy, duty-filled lives.
• One or both has lost the capacity for enjoyment.
• Unacknowledged anger, guilt or other emotions are festering between them.

Enjoyment exists on a continuum, ranging from consistently pure delight on one end to abject boredom, discomfort and misery on the other. A couple with zero enjoyment is one of the saddest things to observe. You may have witnessed it in restaurants, where a husband and wife sit across from each other at a table for two, saying nothing beyond "Pass the salt." They look everywhere but in their partner's eyes, searching the room for something—anything—to spark their interest and divert their attention. Friends and relatives find it unbearable to visit the homes of such couples; they often try to spend time with one of the spouses alone rather than having to endure the sorry spectacle of two people who bring each other down.

One common variation that I see in therapy is when one person is miserable over the relationship's lack of enjoyment while the other is totally oblivious to it. A joke someone once told me captures this arrangement well. "What happened to our sense of adventure?" exclaims the wife. "Where did the fun go? Where is the romance?" To which the husband replies, "How do I know where you put things? I can't even find my shirt."

At its best, enjoyment is spontaneous, uncalculated, natural and innocent. It is not something you have to think about, work for or earn. Whereas trust and respect are given or taken away depending on how someone measures up to your standards, enjoyment has fewer conditions attached to it. It either happens or it doesn't happen. But that does not mean it has to be left to chance. As we'll see, there are many ways to create the proper conditions for enjoyment to flourish, and it is vital that you do so.

Baby, Baby, Where Did Our Fun Go?

There are countless reasons why love relationships slide down the continuum from ecstatically enjoyable to barely endurable. They fall into three basic categories: outer circumstances, emotional baggage between the partners and the individual capacity to enjoy.

The Weight of the World

If a man insisted always on being serious, and never
allowed himself a bit of fun and relaxation, he would
go mad or become unstable without knowing it.
—HERODOTUS

When the bloom of early love settles into the ripe fruit of maturity, many couples get infected with somberitis—an excess of seriousness. We often forget that the human need to goof off and fool around does not disappear when we become adults. We let ourselves become excessively busy, filling our lives with goal-driven exertion. Not only do we forget to stop and smell the roses, we don't stop to do *anything* that thrills or delights us.

To many couples, having fun is seen as frivolous, and they're afraid that if they get *too* frivolous something won't get done. Enjoyment gets squeezed out, put aside for another day, when they finish this or accomplish that. But that day keeps getting postponed. Meanwhile, the simple pleasures get overwhelmed by duties. When you think that everything has to be purposeful and every action must be directed toward achieving a goal, it's hard to enjoy yourself because true enjoyment is something that happens, not something you accomplish.

Apart from everyday pressure, unusually stressful situations can have a severe dampening effect on enjoyment. A problem with a child, an illness in the family, a financial setback, the loss of a loved one—these and other challenging circumstances can darken the spirit and cripple the capacity to gain pleasure from things you normally enjoy. In most cases, the impact is temporary. Sometimes, sadly, the conditions that destroy enjoyment are more tragic and lasting.

Following the murder of their son, the Corbetts' household was transformed from a castle of joy to a dungeon of gloom. The couple's love, previously an engine of pleasure, was now directed toward helping one another survive the trauma. Certainly, enjoyment following such a devastating loss would be unlikely, even unseemly, for quite some time. But the Corbetts imposed upon themselves additional austerity.

Even after three years had passed, the couple felt that if they laughed or fooled around or acted silly, it would in some way dishonor the memory of their son. The moment the natural instinct for enjoyment swelled up in them, they felt guilty and squashed it like a bug. This went on for another two years, until they realized that they were actually dishonoring their fun-loving child by shuffling through life in a shroud of despair. It was difficult at first; the Corbetts found that their old sources of enjoyment failed to amuse or enchant them the way they used to. They had changed. They were not the same people they were before their son's death, and a major part of that change was that they had grown used to relating to each other as fellow victims struggling to make sense of their loss and get through another day. It took quite some time to redefine themselves and learn to enjoy each other in a new way.

The Corbetts' story illustrates a crucial point about the effect of outer circumstances on enjoyment. Couples who basically enjoy one another's company may not laugh and frolic during difficult times, but they find a different kind of pleasure in being together—the quiet relief and tender contentment of knowing that they're in this mess together. It's not enjoyment in the usual sense, but a reassuring hug or a hand that reaches out for yours at just the right time are joys of a high order. Such couples emerge from life's upheavals with the pillar of enjoyment intact, sometimes even enhanced.

It is usually much too simplistic to blame the loss of enjoyment on outer stress. It's a good bet that some of the other pillars had been weak to begin with. Statements like "We're too busy," or, "How can we enjoy ourselves with all this going on?" may be perfectly true, but they're seldom the entire story, especially when enjoyment does not bounce back after circumstances change. In most cases, something deeper has taken a toll on the relationship. In fact, the busyness itself could be a *symptom,* not a cause; to compensate for the pain of lost enjoyment, couples often throw themselves full force into other interests or goal-attainment to keep from being alone together.

Outer circumstances can certainly destroy enjoyment in the short run, but it's up to us not to let temporary conditions become permanent joy-killers. We may not be able to control everything that happens to us, but we can control the way we respond, and when the dust settles, loving partners find a way to enjoy each other once again.

The Buildup of Baggage

Love is an ideal thing; marriage is a real thing.
A confusion of the real with the ideal never
goes unpunished.

—JOHANN WOLFGANG VON GOETHE

Nothing cramps enjoyment like the accumulation of anger, resentment and other negative feelings between partners. Obviously, overt hostility will utterly destroy enjoyment, unless you happen to enjoy fighting. It's hard to find pleasure in being with someone who has done something to enrage you—or is seething with animosity toward you. But it's not just the anger we wear on our sleeves that ruins enjoyment; the unexpressed, unacknowledged kind can be just as toxic. Usually rooted in the long-term pileup of minor hurts, irritations, annoyances and disappointments—as opposed to a single painful incident—resentment, like all suppressed emotions, festers inside until it either causes physical illness or erupts in destructive actions.

Unresolved resentment often bubbles to the surface in behavior that sabotages enjoyment. The subconscious mind whispers, "He/she made me unhappy, so I'm going to get revenge by making sure he/she is unhappy too." Then you retaliate for previous hurts by ruining your partner's pleasure. "I just can't have a good time without her spoiling it," complained a client named Steve. His wife, Rebecca, was harboring a deep sense of disappointment in the relationship as a whole; it had just not measured up to her expectations, and Steve had become, in her words, "an old fart before his time." More specifically, Rebecca was still simmering because Steve spoiled the first vacation they had taken since their honeymoon, making business calls from Hawaii and cutting the trip short to get back to the office.

Ever since that incident, three years earlier, Rebecca had found a way to spoil every activity that Steve looked forward to—including coming home from work. If they were supposed to do something together, she would get mysterious headaches, find excuses to be late, act unsociable or make critical comments that punctured her husband's enthusiasm. Out of sheer spite, she would ruin his fun by refusing to enjoy herself. Her subconscious mind was thinking, "I'm going to have a bad time just to spoil it for him." She would sigh or yawn conspicuously, mutter complaints and basically act as though she'd rather be someplace else. She even lied on occasion. "Great movie!" Steve would declare. "It was terrible," Rebecca would counter, even if she liked it.

She found ways to ruin Steve's enjoyment even when he was doing something on his own or with friends. She would phone him with some problem that could easily have waited, belittle him for playing poker or watching ball games with his buddies and tune him out when he tried to talk about what he did.

Often, when one partner starts spoiling the party, the other quickly follows suit and a vicious cycle sets in. That's what happened to Steve and Rebecca. At first, Steve tried to come up with ways to restore the enjoyment to his marriage. The more he tried, though, the more Rebecca sabotaged his efforts. After a while, he started to feel like a colossal failure. Naturally, that made *him* resentful. Enter the vicious cycle. Steve grew so discouraged he not only gave up trying to create mutual enjoyment, he started ruining Rebecca's *private* enjoyment. By the time they came to see me, they were intent on making each other miserable.

Rebecca and Steve were unaware of their anger-driven behavior until it was exposed in counseling. It was only when they realized that they were destroying their *own* enjoyment and poisoning their marriage in the bargain that they found the motivation to look at themselves honestly.

How do you know if your enjoyment has eroded due to a buildup of emotional baggage? The best clue is whether you're enjoying yourselves outside of the relationship. It can be very disheartening to realize that you're cheerful with your friends and a drag when you're with your partner, but it's a clear indication that something has gone seriously wrong between you. In this regard, the lament of a client named Lynn is typical: "I can't seem to get any pleasure out of anything my husband and I do together. When we go out, I feel like I'm just going through the motions. But when I'm with my girlfriends from work, I'm suddenly the life of the party. Why can't I be that way with my husband?"

Why? Because years of disappointment and irritation had grown into a big lump of resentment in her gut. It was vital that Lynn own up to her negative feelings toward her husband before she could begin to rebuild the pillars of their marriage.

The Capacity to Enjoy

If your capacity to acquire has outstripped your
capacity to enjoy, you are on the way to
the scrap heap.
—GLEN BUCK

In many cases, lack of enjoyment is not a symptom of a diseased marriage. Rather, it's rooted in the internal state of one or both of the partners.

The ability to enjoy life is made up of some mysterious combination of energy, sensory alertness, mental sharpness and positive attitude. Obviously, the capacity varies from one person to the next; put two people in the same exact situation and one might get annoyed or scared while the other is cracking jokes. In fact, from one day to the next, the same person might respond in diametrically opposite ways to the same outer conditions. "Everyone is familiar with the phenomenon of feeling more or less alive on different days," wrote the pioneering psychologist William James early in the last century. "Everyone knows on any given day there are energies in him which the incitement of the day do not call forth . . . Our fires are damped, our drafts are checked."

If you or your partner has lost the ability to find pleasure in everyday circumstances, it will act like a lead weight on your relationship. If you're worn out or not getting enough sleep, for instance, you're probably not enjoying much of *anything*. It's important, therefore, to see the situation for what it is and not make the mistake of thinking it's your partner's fault and you'd really enjoy life if only he or she wasn't there to bring you down. It's precisely at such times when we're vulnerable to thoughts such as, "Things would be different if I was with that fascinating person at the office . . ."

Anhedonia, the inability to experience pleasure, can have a number of causes, among them fatigue, physical illness or clinical depression; sudden disruptions in your way of life; anxiety, worry, guilt or fear; and loss of confidence or self-esteem. One of the most common factors in our culture is the tendency to get hooked on the trappings of material success. We want more and more, and we think we can't be happy until we get enough—and there's never enough. There is always one more carrot dangling before us, and we fool ourselves into thinking we'll enjoy ourselves once we have it. Sometimes we do, but only for a little while. Then the craving for something new begins.

Anxiety over getting older can also drag someone into anhedonia. Because of society's misbegotten emphasis on youth, people as young as forty start to feel over-the-hill and vital men and women in their seventies feel unneeded. Internalizing these erroneous attitudes can sap the fun out of life. Women who see their hips expand and their faces wrinkle and men who see their sexual capacity and physical stamina diminish often lose their capacity for joy because their self-image depends on the outer signs of womanliness or manliness. For others, it's not the physical decline of middle age but a longing for the glory days of youth, which they've lost and can't recapture.

The approach of his fiftieth birthday threw Lou into a tailspin that lasted over a year, driving his wife, Judy, to the brink of leaving him. Twelve years younger than Lou, she never saw the age difference as a deterrent because in many ways she was more mature than he was. She wondered, in fact, if he would ever be "ready" for marriage or grow up enough to want children. A sometime writer, sometime housepainter, Lou had little ambition and scorned his compatriots who strove for material success. All of which would have been fine with Judy if Lou was happy. But he wasn't. And turning fifty made him even less so.

Lou made a desperate attempt to recapture the only time in his life when he really enjoyed himself. Out came the Jefferson Airplane and Janis Joplin albums. Out came the newspaper clippings about the Summer of Love and the photos of him at antiwar demonstrations. He started using '60s slang. He tracked down his old hippy buddies, most of whom were now living "straight" lives and did not want to be dragged back to a romanticized past. He went looking for a radical cause to get behind. If he'd had any hair left, he'd have grown it long. Worst of all for Judy was the drugs. Lou had always smoked the occasional joint, but now he was stoned much of the time in a desperate attempt to get back the "Oh, wow!" state of mind that had made him feel alive thirty years earlier.

It took a bad LSD trip for Lou to wake up and realize it was

time to find more appropriate sources of satisfaction and enjoyment.

Even age and disability can't dampen the spirits of those whose
basic attitude is one of appreciation. For them, the capacity to
enjoy shines through at all times. This was
driven home to me one day early in my
career by two women I met while doing
rounds in a hospital. The first woman had a
sour frown on her face despite the smooth,
tight skin of someone who'd had more
cosmetic surgery than she needed. In her
mid-seventies, she was bemoaning the fact
that she was in the early stages of arthritis.
It was hard to tell what bothered her more,
that her fingers were stiff in the morning or that the swelling in her
hands meant she'd have to get her rings resized.

> **USABLE INSIGHT**
>
> *You can be grateful
> and end up a
> better person,
> or ungrateful
> and end up a
> bitter person.*

A few hours later I saw a slightly older woman whose face
had every line that a lifetime of sorrow and joy, love and loss had
etched into it. Her arthritis was quite advanced. She walked
unsteadily, hunched over a cane without which she could not
take three steps. But her smile was radiant and her eyes twinkled
with amusement. I asked her why she was smiling. I'll never forget her answer: "I was just thinking how great this cane is going
to seem five years from now when I'm using a walker."

This woman had probably enjoyed herself her whole life,
throughout her many ups and downs, and she probably will enjoy
herself to the end. The first woman may have been enjoyment-
deprived her whole adult life, and if she doesn't wake up soon,
her remaining years will be intolerable.

The Vicious Cycle of Depression

*Mysteriously and in ways that are totally remote
from natural experience, the gray drizzle of horror
induced by depression takes on the quality of
physical pain.*

—WILLIAM STYRON

Losing the enjoyment in your relationship can be depressing. But the opposite is also true: The biochemical imbalances in the brain that cause depression cripple the capacity to enjoy.

The typical signs of chronic depression include the following, according to the National Institutes of Mental Health:

- persistent sad or "empty" mood
- loss of interest or pleasure in ordinary activities, including sex
- fatigue and lack of energy
- sleep disturbances
- eating disturbances (loss of appetite and weight, or weight gain)
- difficulty concentrating, remembering, making decisions
- feelings of guilt, worthlessness, helplessness
- thoughts of death or suicide, suicide attempts
- irritability
- excessive crying
- alcohol or drug abuse

Depression can be so severe that you become virtually disabled. More common is the condition known as dysthymia, a persistent, low-grade depression that can be so subtle as to go undiagnosed for years, even as it robs you of passion, optimism and pleasure. You can shuffle through life with a bland "Who cares? What's the use?" attitude, with a constant flow of gloom and doom running through your mind, thinking all the while that it's the normal human condition.

Within a relationship, chronic depression can act like a contagious disease. If one partner develops the condition, his or her negative moods will eventually darken the outlook of the other. At first, a loyal mate might try to cheer up the depressed person. But clinically depressed people can't be cheered for long; the very chemistry of their brains can't sustain it. Usually, instead of the depressed partner being uplifted, he or she drags the other one down. The negativity and despair become magnified and pretty soon you have two people who have lost the ability to enjoy.

It's important to understand that depression is not caused by faulty character or lack of strength. It is a debilitating illness like any other, and it is highly treatable. If you think you may be clinically depressed, speak to your physician or therapist.

The Warning Signs

In the early days of a relationship, enjoyment is so effortless that it takes you by surprise. Just getting to know each other is more enjoyable than any sport you've played, any show you've seen, any trip you've taken. You find yourself having a blast doing nothing.

The *loss* of enjoyment comes as a surprise too. It seldom disappears overnight. Instead, it gradually fades away, like the sound of music as you drive away from a party. To some extent this is inevitable; as with chemistry, it is unreasonable to expect the glee that you derive from each other's company to stay the same as the months and years wear on. A common lament from couples is, "Our relationship isn't fun anymore. It's work."

While it's naïve to expect the spontaneous delight of early love to last forever, it's tragic to let enjoyment slip so far away that it can't be retrieved. One danger is settling for a drab, lifeless marriage. Another is the temptation to find enjoyable companionship elsewhere. Say you meet someone new through your work. He or she shares your interests, listens eagerly to your stories and laughs at your jokes—just as your partner once did. You look forward to seeing that person, whereas you *don't* look forward to going home. You tell yourself that he or she is just a friend. No way you'll get romantically involved. You're much too honorable for that. You're just having some fun.

> **USABLE INSIGHT**
>
> *When your worst day at work is better than your best day with your partner, it's time to work at getting the fun back.*

Look out. Enjoyment can be a Bunsen burner that heats up a chemical reaction. As the friendship warms up, it's easy to trick yourself into believing that it could be like this all the time. You can't possibly project what being with your new "friend" would really be like once you start sharing everyday duties, arguing over money and dealing with each other's mood swings, irritating habits and other fantasy killers. Meanwhile, as the chemistry heats up, you've neglected your mate so much that life at home has all the fun of a textbook.

You can stop the deterioration of enjoyment by spotting the symptoms early and taking action before it's too late. These are some of the warning signs to look for:

- You enjoy the company of friends and coworkers, particularly the opposite sex, more than your partner. Watch out for thoughts like, "I wish it could be like this with the person I love."
- You see your partner enjoying him- or herself with others, and making plans with them instead of you. When you find yourself saying, "How can you waste your time doing such and such?" or, "Why would you want to hang out with so and so?" you're starting to feel resentful, and maybe jealous.
- The two of you have to make major plans in order to have a good time, and even then you don't always succeed. The simple pleasures have lost their charm, and just being together doesn't cut it anymore.
- One or both of you complains to friends, saying things like, "He's no fun anymore," and "She spoils everything."
- One or both of you disparages the other's interests.
- One or both of you consistently refuses to do things that the other one suggests.
- Increasingly, you'd rather be alone.

As the pillar of enjoyment slowly rots, you typically go through a stage where you feel indifferent, bored, stuck, and frustrated. During this phase, you're likely to make excuses—job stress, parenting, lack of time, and so forth—or lie to yourselves that the loss of enjoyment is not as bad as it really is. That is when steps must be taken. If you don't act in a timely manner, you might suddenly cross into the zone of true misery. Sadly, it's usually a short ride from there to the point of no return.

Do something about it quickly. As an old song goes, enjoy yourself, it's later than you think.

A Dialogue on Enjoyment

A deep conversation about lagging or absent enjoyment is a crucial step to restoring it. When you begin the discussion, be sure not to do it in an accusatory or complaining manner. "You're no fun anymore" is not a good opening. Nor is, "Our life is a total bore." Even if you could find a polite way to say such things, you will only trigger defensiveness. Instead, share your own struggle. Lead with a question that invites your partner to join in a conversation. For example, "Do you ever wonder where the fun has gone?" or, "Does it scare you like it scares me that we don't enjoy ourselves the way we used to?"

Before you begin the conversation, complete the following sentences:

- What we enjoyed most when we first fell in love was _____
_____.

- What I miss most about those days and wish we could have back
is _____.

- The enjoyment in our relationship started to diminish when

  _____.

- The last time I enjoyed my partner's company without being engaged in some activity was _____.

- My partner is hurting our ability to enjoy each other because

  _____.

- What I enjoy most about my partner is _____.

Now, try answering the same questions from your *partner's* point of view:

- What my partner probably enjoyed most when we first fell in love was _____.

- What I think my partner misses most about those days is _____

  _____.

- My partner probably thinks the enjoyment in our relationship started to diminish when _____.

- The last time I think my partner enjoyed my company without being engaged in some activity was _____.

- My partner probably thinks I'm hurting our ability to enjoy each other because _____.

- What I think my partner enjoys most about me is _____.

It's a good idea to begin your dialogue by talking about the good times together in the past. As you reminisce, be specific. "We really enjoyed that trip to Spain" is not as evocative as, "Remember the time we got lost in Madrid and the drunken bullfighter drove us home?" To refresh your memories and add flavor to the experience, you might want to take out your old photos.

Recalling memorable moments in detail helps you to re-experience positive feelings and remember what is possible. It can lighten your mood instantly. But be aware that it can also make you wistful or sad; what you once had can highlight what you don't have now. While this may be a bit painful, starting with the good times establishes a closeness that makes talking about the problem areas easier.

Sharing positive memories can also set the stage for constructive solutions. Many couples report that the simple act of reminiscing is the first truly enjoyable thing they've done together in a long time. The laughter and warmth triggered by good memories is a potent signal that you can still find enjoyment together. This is especially true if you pay attention to what you enjoyed about *each other* during those good times. Surely those qualities haven't all faded away with the passing years.

When you're finished reminiscing, let your conversation proceed along the lines of the questions you just answered separately. Now you'll be entering the tricky terrain of what went wrong. Remember what we said in previous chapters about the principles of good communication and the importance of always asking yourself, "What is it like for my partner right now?"

Listen to each other's responses to the questions carefully, without arguing or contradicting. Then discuss how each of you is contributing to the lack of enjoyment and what you can do about it. How do each of you spoil the fun? Do you make cynical or disparaging comments? Are you rigid, refusing to try anything new? Do you talk too much or too little? Are you a fussbudget? Look at the traits that diminish the other's ability to enjoy and determine which ones you're willing to put an end to.

See if you can cut a deal to make an equal effort to make your-selves more enjoyable.

When you've both had your chance to express yourselves, conclude on a positive note by sharing your answers to the last question, "What do you enjoy most about your partner?"

Now, with your enthusiasm for each other rekindled and your memories of past enjoyment fresh in your mind, it's time to discuss how to enhance your enjoyment from now on.

Creating Space for Enjoyment

My advice to you is not to inquire why or whither,
but just enjoy your ice cream while it's on your plate.

—THORNTON WILDER

In a perfect world, enjoyment would be spontaneous, natural and effortless. But if your world was perfect you would not be reading this book. You might have to set aside time

> **USABLE INSIGHT**
>
> *The firmer*
> *your resolve to*
> *enjoy, the less*
> *you need to*
> *resolve.*

and do some planning to restore the habit of enjoying each other. Most couples find that if they hit the bull's-eye on some planned activities, the enjoyment carries over to ordinary circumstances and the simple, innocent pleasure of each other's company begins to come back.

"How can we make plans to enjoy our-selves when we have all this emotional baggage?" some people ask. "Don't we have to work out our issues first?" Yes and no. It's true that resentment and unresolved conflicts are major barriers to enjoyment. But the reverse is also true. Shared delight can break through those barriers, like sunlight penetrates even the darkest clouds, and when it does it can make the emotional atmosphere much more conducive to resolving your difficult issues. In short, you don't have to wait for all the obstacles to be removed before you start working on the pillar of enjoyment. But you do have to think clearly about which steps to take and the best way to take them.

Brainstorm Enjoyable Activities

One good way to come up with things to do together is for each of you to write down all the activities that make you feel good while doing them, and those which leave you with a feeling of satisfaction when they're completed. This could include things you do specifically for the sake of enjoyment, and things you do because they're necessary and just happen to put you in a good mood; activities that take a lot of effort and those that are easy and natural; things that create thrills and things that lead to quiet contentment.

Once you have your list, try to identify the themes that run through them. For example, one theme might be pushing yourself to the limit physically. Another might be activities that focus your intellect, such as reading or solving puzzles. Passive entertainment might be another (and within that, the theme might be comedy or music). Maybe a particular source of pleasure crops up in different places—nature, for instance, or beauty. Identifying themes will give you more insight into what you *really* like about the activities you enjoy.

When you've both completed your lists, compare notes.

Look for areas of commonality and themes that appear on both your lists. By using your individual pleasures as a launching pad for generating ideas, you may come up with fresh things to do together. Don't even think about the effort it would take to do them, or how to fit them into your busy lives. Just ask yourselves what would result in enjoyment.

This process alone can be revealing. Wouldn't it be great if you found that you enjoy just hanging out together and thinking up great things to do? If, on the other hand, you end up squabbling, take it as a sign that there are deeper issues that must be addressed before you can rebuild the pillar of enjoyment.

Assuming all goes well, go ahead and make some plans. I suggest starting out with something mutually agreeable and easily doable. Build up to activities that need planning or schedule shuffling, and save for later anything that requires one of you to make sacrifices.

Approach these activities with realistic expectations. It is not reasonable, for example, to expect one enjoyable evening to end all your emotional conflicts. Expecting too much creates anxiety. You could put so much pressure on yourselves to have fun that you end up forcing it and ruining any hope of spontaneous pleasure. Furthermore, if you anticipate ecstasy and merely have a terrific time, you'll end up disappointed when in fact you should be encouraged.

> **USABLE INSIGHT**
>
> *Wistful thinking about the past and wishful thinking about the future can cause you to miss out on the present.*

One mistake many couples make is to try to recapture the past. Clea and Martin, for example, had been married for nine years and hadn't really enjoyed themselves for the last five or so. Desperate to end the tedium, Clea arranged a trip to Eugene, Oregon, where the couple had met during their college years. They visited the nightspots they used to haunt, saw some former classmates, went to a football game and did the outdoorsy things they used to love doing together, like rock climbing. They came home feeling miserable. "It's hopeless," Clea moaned. "We're just not compatible anymore."

A more accurate statement would have been, "We're not the same people anymore." They were more than a decade older. Their tastes had changed. Their habits had changed. It was foolish to expect that they would enjoy the same exact things they once did—especially when the basis of comparison was their carefree college years. Thinking back to those days was a good idea, but they needed to extract some insights from the past and apply them to the people they had become.

Follow Through

"How did your weekend go?" I asked Randy and Tina. In counseling, a week earlier, they had agreed that they would both leave work early on Friday and get away for the weekend. It had been a long time since they'd really enjoyed themselves, and a few days at a beach resort seemed like just what the doctor ordered to break the rut.

"We didn't go," said Tina. "We'll have to do it some other time."

They looked like kids who had not turned in their homework. It seemed that neither of them could find the time to make the necessary arrangements. They considered just hopping into the car and driving up the coast until they found a place they liked, but when Friday rolled around there was too much to be done and they both ended up working late. They worked on Saturday too.

Clearly, our discussion about the importance of making time for enjoyment had not hit home. I had to do something more drastic. "Imagine it's ten years from now," I said. "You've continued to live just the way you're living now. Then one of you gets cancer. When you look back, do you think you'll have any regrets?"

They spent the next weekend in Santa Barbara.

That's one way to follow through: make a commitment to make room for enjoyment and stick to it. But that's not enough.

By Thursday, Tina and Randy were bickering again. "It's the same old same old," said Tina. "Too bad we can't go away every weekend."

Getting away once was not a panacea. It reminded them of how enjoyable their life together had once been, but it was not enough. They needed booster shots.

That brings us to another level of follow-through. Once you *do* find a way to enjoy yourselves, capitalize on the momentum right away. Don't settle for "That was great, we should do this more often," and then go back to your old ways. Immediately, before the glow wears off, plan to do it again or schedule something different. Block out the time. Make a reservation. Buy tickets. Line up a baby-sitter. Whatever you have to do, commit to another occasion right away—and soon—so you don't procrastinate or wait for the other person to take the initiative. This is extremely important. On the heels of their first good time in quite a while, far too many couples fool themselves into thinking they've solved the problem. Months later, they're wondering why they're back in the doldrums, and this time it hurts even more.

But there is yet another way to follow through. Randy and Tina could not carry the lesson of their weekend away into their everyday life. That takes a different kind of effort. It was time to dig deeper and talk about the emotional issues that had been eating away at their enjoyment. That's the most important follow-up of all.

When You Enjoy Different Things

You like potatoes and I like potahtoes . . .

—IRA GERSHWIN

No two people have all the same interests or enjoy all the same things. That may sound obvious, but you'd be surprised how many men try to get women to watch football or go bowling, and how many women expect their macho men to love the ballet or art museums as much as they do. On the subject of clashing tastes, compromise, understanding and generosity of spirit are vital.

When your partner enjoys something you don't, you have a wide range of options. On one end of the spectrum is contempt, which can be expressed overtly in the form of snide comments or covertly through sneers, smirks and rolled eyeballs. Needless to say, contempt is poisonous to a relationship. A more constructive attitude is tolerance. But even that can subvert a relationship if the feeling conveyed is, "I think what you're doing is moronic, but I'll tolerate it without complaining." Far better is to appreciate that your partner enjoys certain things and graciously grant him or her the time and resources to do them. Remember how it felt when you were a child and you ran home to your parents to tell them how much fun you had? And how great it felt when they smiled because your happiness delighted them? That's how your mate feels when you enjoy his or her enjoyment. The key is to switch your frame of reference from "What's in it for me?" to "What's the experience like for them?"

Try to shift your attitude toward your partner's interests from disapproval to tolerance to encouragement. Don't just give them permission to do something they like. Actively encourage it. If you merely give your blessing, your partner may still feel, "Yeah, but he/she really doesn't like me doing this. If it was up to him/her, I not only wouldn't do it, I wouldn't even *want* to." So, don't just say, "Yeah, go ahead, but don't get home late," or, "Sure, have a good time, but don't spend too much money." Instead, say, "I'm really glad you're doing this." Even better, suggest it from your side: "You haven't played golf in a long time. Why don't you go enjoy a round with your friends"; "It would give me pleasure to see you take painting classes again. You used to enjoy that so much."

But why not take it one step further? Are there things your partner enjoys that you can participate in? This won't work for everything, of course, but there are often ways to find enjoyment together even when the activity is mainly one person's thing. Sometimes a simple compromise does the trick. For example, when two of my clients, Tanya and Richard, decided to make the effort to share more in each other's lives, she said, "I'll go to the auto show with you. Then I'd like us to stop at the antique mart on the way home." Tanya was not into cars, but she went with a positive attitude. She had no idea what Richard was talking about when he explained the fine points of automotive design, but she got a kick out of his un-bridled excitement. On the way home, Richard returned the favor. Instead of pacing impatiently as Tanya admired antiques, he tagged along and let her share her enthusiasm, enhancing her enjoyment by being curious and asking questions about some of the strange objects they saw.

> **USABLE INSIGHT**
>
> *Sometimes the best way to get along is to go along.*

He even bought something—a cigar humidor from the 1930s.

Like Richard and Tanya, if you approach outings with an open mind and a spirit of adventure, you might find something to enjoy where you least expect it. The key is to look for aspects of the activity that would make it enjoyable to you. Encouragement and willing participation usually have the welcome effect of inviting reciprocity. Unless your partner is hopelessly self-centered, he or she will feel grateful and will look for ways to return the favor. Don't be surprised if one day, when you're about to do something your partner never does, you hear, "Can I join you?"

One client shocked his wife by offering to help her weed the garden. "What? You *hate* gardening!" she said.

"That's true," he confessed, "but we haven't spent much time together lately, and I was thinking about how much we used to enjoy just hanging out. So, yeah, I don't like gardening, but what I like even less is the big empty desert between us."

When she stopped crying, his wife took his hand and walked with him to the garden.

Enhance Your Capacity for Enjoyment

A good and wholesome thing is a little harmless fun
in this world; it tones a body up and keeps him
human and prevents him from souring.

—MARK TWAIN

Are you enjoying your own life? Are you depending on your partner too much? Are you blaming your relationship for your own lack of pleasure? Chances are you won't find enjoyment with your mate if you can't find it with yourself. Take a good look inside and see if your personal rut is too deep for another person to enter. If you take full responsibility for your own lack of enjoyment, you stand a far better chance of enjoying life with your partner. Here are some suggestions for getting your joy back:

TAKE CARE OF YOURSELF. As mentioned earlier, fatigue, tension and bad moods can destroy enjoyment. Therefore, not just your health but the pillars of your relationship depend on good lifestyle choices. Be mindful of the generally accepted standards: watch your weight, eat a low-fat, high-fiber diet; learn to reduce and manage stress; drink in moderation; don't overdo the caffeine; make sure you get enough sleep; exercise regularly. None of this is impossible to do, no matter how busy you are. If you can't find time to jog or get to a gym, take frequent breaks to stretch and move around the workplace, and take every opportunity to walk—use the steps instead of the elevator, park at the far end of the lot, get off the subway a stop early. The endorphins that course through your body when you exercise are pleasure producing.

TREAT DEPRESSION. In this day and age, there is no reason to wallow in chronic depression without seeking treatment. You might not think it's treatable when you're in the grip of despair and everything seems hopeless, but the condition can be overcome, and there is no more shame in getting help than in trying to cure persistent headaches or control diabetes. Today's antidepressant medications are highly effective and generally have few side effects when monitored properly by a physician. Natural remedies such as St. John's Wort have also shown promise. Research indicates that medication in conjunction with psychotherapy produces the fastest, best and most lasting results.

CULTIVATE APPRECIATION. The people who enjoy life most are those who are capable of appreciating all of life's little gifts. Otherwise, enjoyment is limited to only the most exciting and extraordinary moments, which don't come around that often. Try not to be what I call a high-maintenance person: easy to disappoint and tough to please. Instead, learn to be low maintenance: easy to please and hard to disappoint. Remember the two old women with arthritis? Which one would you rather be like?

UNLOAD YOUR BAGGAGE. Search your soul and identify any unprocessed negative feelings that might be preventing you from fully enjoying your life. Do you harbor shame or self-loathing from the way you were treated when you were younger? Are you holding onto anger and bitterness toward someone—not necessarily your partner, but a parent, sibling, friend, boss or former spouse? These emotional demons can sap your vitality and cast a dark shadow over everything life presents to you. What about unresolved grief? Is the loss of a loved one or a bitter divorce ruining your capacity for joy? "There are basically three stages of recovery from loss," says Harold Bloom-field, M.D., author of *Making Peace with Your Past*. "If you get stuck in the first phase, denial, or in the second stage—anger, fear and sadness—you can't complete the grieving process and move on. This can lead to emotional numbness, chronic sadness and other debilitating symptoms."

One powerful way to work through long-buried feelings is to write them out. Scientific research has demonstrated the value of this simple practice. Patients who wrote about their past trau-mas healed faster, visited their doctors less often and had stronger immune systems. Sit down with some paper or a word processor and get out the feelings of pain and rage that have been festering inside you. Don't hold back. Don't censor yourself. Pay no atten-tion to spelling, grammar or coherence. Just let loose. No one has to read what you write, not even you.

Writing out your feelings can help a great deal, but it is not always easy to resolve deep-seated emotions on your own. You may benefit from seeing a qualified psychiatrist or psychothera-pist (see chapter 8 for guidelines).

Some Final Tips

Variety is the mother of Enjoyment.

—BENJAMIN DISRAELI

By now you should have a wealth of ideas for restoring the enjoyment to your relationship. But just in case, here are some tips from clients of mine who have done this work already:

- Do something unpredictable and creative.
- Avoid ruts. Use your imagination.
- Go to an amusement park without your kids.
- Call in sick and goof off.
- Remember, "because it's fun" is a good reason to do something.
- Finger paint.
- Get messy.
- Paint each other's toenails.
- Have a pillow fight.
- Dance. If you can't get to a club, turn on the stereo and boogie in the living room.
- Take adult education classes together.
- Learn a foreign language.
- Play sports but don't keep score.
- Paint a mural on a wall.
- Go hiking or biking.
- Clean the house together. Seriously!
- Go ice skating in the summer and swimming in the winter.
- Build sand castles.
- Do a jigsaw puzzle together.
- Go to a comedy club.
- Go to the zoo.
- Lighten up.

That last suggestion may be the best of all. As G. K. Chesterton said, "Angels can fly because they take themselves so lightly."

5

Acceptance

You're OK, I'm OK

> The greatest happiness of life is the conviction that we are loved—loved for ourselves, or rather, in spite of ourselves.
>
> —VICTOR HUGO

How much do the following statements apply to how you think or feel about acceptance in your relationship?

	Hardly Ever 0	Sometimes 1	Almost Always 2
1. We can be ourselves with each other.	____	____	____
2. I feel accepted by my partner more than I feel disapproved of.	____	____	____
3. My partner feels accepted by me more than he/she feels disapproved of.	____	____	____
4. I notice what my partner does right more than what he/she does wrong.	____	____	____
5. My partner acknowledges what I do right more than what I do wrong.	____	____	____
6. I am more likely to accept my partner's point of view than take issue with it.	____	____	____
7. My partner is more likely to accept my point of view than take issue with it.	____	____	____
8. There is more about each other that we would like to stay the same than we would like to change.	____	____	____
9. We can listen to constructive criticism from each other without feeling attacked.	____	____	____
10. If my partner never changes the things I don't like, I'll still be glad we're together.	____	____	____
TOTAL:	____	____	____

SCORING:

0–6   You very much want each other to change.

7–13   An acceptable and accepting score.

14–20 You're exceptional at acceptance.

In his Family Research Laboratory at the University of Washington, psychologist John Gottman has been studying married couples for more than twenty years. He has found that the most destructive qualities in a relationship—what he calls the Four Horsemen of the Apocalypse—are criticism, contempt, defensiveness and stonewalling. The first two traits suggest that one partner has a lot of trouble accepting the other one; the second two are typical reactions to feeling unaccepted. The importance of acceptance has also been documented by other researchers. Neil Jacobson and Andrew Christensen, cited in *Newsweek,* found that "an inability to accept differences" was the leading predictor of failure of couples in traditional therapy.

The root of the word *accept* is the Latin term for receive. That's what we do when we accept someone: we receive them. We take them in. I like to think of it in terms of this analogy: Your doorbell rings. You open the door to find a small, frightened child, soaking wet, looking for shelter from a terrible rainstorm. Do you ask a series of questions? Do you criticize her for not wearing a raincoat? Do you say, "I'll let you in, but first you have to agree to certain terms"? No, you take her in and wrap her in a blanket.

True acceptance is like that. You open the door of your heart because the person is inherently worthy. No fine print. Come as you are. Green light all the way, not red, not yellow, not "proceed with caution." Full acceptance is the closest to the ideal of unconditional love that we are likely to find with another grown-up human being.

Does acceptance mean you consider the other person to be perfect? Of course not. It does not mean that their personality is without flaw or that everything they do is perfectly okay with you. It does not mean that you don't want them to be better. Human beings will always have qualities we don't like, characteristics we find annoying and behavior we wish they'd stop. Acceptance means that you recognize and acknowledge their essential worth and hold them to be deserving of your esteem and your love—despite their imperfections.

Needless to say, certain things are unacceptable. We all have our non-negotiable demands. Physical abuse should be one of them. Infidelity is usually a deal-breaker. Alcoholism or drug addiction may also be unacceptable. Accepting behavior that crosses the line you draw in the sand does not promote a healthy relationship, nor is it a mark of wisdom, tolerance or compassion. It is usually nothing more than an invitation to martyrdom. But, short of putting up with what is truly intolerable, the capacity for acceptance—hard as it sometimes is to achieve—is an essential ingredient of mature love.

The Quality of Constancy

We don't love qualities; we love a person; sometimes by reason of their defects as well as their qualities.
—JACQUES MARITAIN

In psychology, the term "object constancy" is used to describe a quality that is essential for acceptance: the ability to maintain a strong emotional connection to another person even when he or she disappoints you. It implies a certain kind of wisdom, one that recognizes that individual traits and actions are just isolated waves on a sea of innumerable traits and actions. Some of those waves may be displeasing, but the person with object constancy is able to keep the larger perspective in view. If they find the great majority of waves acceptable and desirable, their emotional bond with the other person remains intact. Those who lack object constancy can't maintain their connection when faced with inappropriate behavior or unappealing traits. Their disappointment is so great that they can't see the ocean for the waves: "To hell with it, I don't have to put up with that."

With mature love you understand that you can accept the essence of another person without approving all their individual traits. We don't find it difficult to achieve that attitude toward children. One of the staples of good parenting is saying to your kids, "I always love you, but I don't like it when you don't share with your sister," or, "I can understand why you're angry, but I don't like what you do when you're angry." It is vital to distinguish the person from the action because otherwise children take the slightest criticism as a rejection of them as a whole.

> **USABLE INSIGHT**
>
> *Young love is loving someone because of what they do right. Mature love is loving someone in spite of what they do wrong.*

It's not just with children that we find it easy to have object constancy. If you saw someone urinating against a building or shouting obscenities at passersby, you would be inclined to condemn the person—but not if you learned he was mentally impaired. The realization that he can't control his impulses dramatically alters your expectations. Now, instead of wanting to beat him up or scream at him, you want to take him to your heart and say, "It's not a good idea to do that sort of thing, it could get you into trouble." We grant the same tolerance of unacceptable behavior to the elderly, to victims of tragedy or oppression, to people from cultures unlike our own and others to whom we are willing to give the benefit of the doubt.

It is not as easy with lovers and spouses. Not only do we have more at stake when they display their flaws and foibles, we have higher expectations of them. Sometimes too high. Sociologist and historian Stephanie Coontz, the author of *The Way We Never Were* and *The Way We Really Are*, says that the postwar period from the late 1940s through the 1950s was an aberration in America. Those who grew up during that time of unprecedented prosperity and we-can-do-anything optimism were raised to have unrealistic expectations in everything from job security to romance. We expected marriage to bring us happiness beyond its capacity to deliver, and we did not learn to deal well with disappointment.

And so, for many of us, it is hard to fully comprehend that the people we love can drive us crazy and still deserve our unqualified acceptance. But without that foundation of deep acceptance, it's hard enough to be neighbors, let alone lovers.

You Accept Me, You Really Accept Me

It's an extra dividend when you like the girl
you're in love with.

—CLARK GABLE

Being accepted is liberating. You feel safe to be real, free to make mistakes, to be silly, to be quirky, to reveal your authentic individuality without running the risk of rejection. "I love my husband because he lets me be myself," is a remark I've heard countless times from thankful women. And I've heard from grateful men, "With her I can be exactly who I am." That is acceptance, and it is priceless.

With acceptance there is peace. Without it there is tension. If you want to see the look of acceptance, watch a husband and wife who have been together happily for many years. Look at the loving couples in a retirement home, for instance, or the old folks sitting on park benches. See what happens when they hold hands. See how they smile when their partners do or say something they've done or said a thousand times before. See how relaxed they are. That's the aura of acceptance.

The bonus is, once a baseline of absolute acceptance is established, the other person is more likely to change the traits you find difficult to tolerate. Knowing that they are fundamentally acceptable, they feel secure enough to listen to constructive criticism. They're more willing to make the effort to modify certain habits just because it would please you or make your life easier. They're also more likely to recognize that at least some of your feedback is designed to make them better people. Such generosity of spirit is not likely to blossom when someone is made to feel unacceptable to the core.

Whereas acceptance smooths and polishes a relationship and brings out the best in each party, its absence is abrasive. Over time, lack of acceptance brings out the worst in people. When you're with someone who doesn't fully accept who you are, you tend to walk on eggshells. Depending on the extent of their disapproval, you have to pick and choose what you say and restrain many of your natural impulses. To a certain extent, of course, thinking before you speak and minding your manners is just being considerate. But when you don't feel acceptable, you move through life in fear that if you say or do the wrong thing you'll get a double-barreled shot of contempt. It makes you act artificially, forcing you to play a role rather than be yourself.

The bigger the masquerade, the more you come to resent it. Then the retaliation and revenge begin. How can you restrain your criticism when you're being criticized? How can you tolerate someone who's intolerant of you? How can you accept someone who finds you unacceptable? Unless you're prepared to smother your authenticity and accept your partner's lack of acceptance, you can stand it just so long before your self-regard forces you to either leave or turn the tables.

"There aren't many places in life where I get to relax and just be who I am," an embittered spouse named Raymond told me. "I should at least be able to do it in my own home." He said he felt like he'd been under constant surveillance for years.

Raymond started reeling off everything about his wife that he found unacceptable. They were all things that he'd found easy to overlook or tolerate early on, before his wife's relentless criticism drove him to the breaking point. "I feel like she's locked the best part of me out of the house," he said. Then, pausing, he looked away, conjuring an image in his mind. He tried not to smile because he knew that what he was about to say had dreadful implications, but he couldn't help it. "There's this woman at the office," he said. "We've had lunch a few times. When she looks at me, it's like . . . I don't know what it is, but it makes me feel great. My wife hasn't looked at me that way in years."

What that look conveyed was admiration and acceptance. What he got from his wife was disapproval and derision.

An honorable man, Raymond was terrified by the feelings he had when he was with the woman at work. He was on the fast track to adultery and he was hoping I could help him get off before it was too late. We were able to avert the train wreck only because his wife was willing to come to counseling and address the fundamental issue of acceptance.

Keeping Score

Marriage must incessantly contend with a monster
that devours everything: familiarity.

—HONORÉ DE BALZAC

Almost from the start, without meaning to, both members of an intimate relationship start to accumulate a list of their partners' unacceptable traits. They're the adjectives that follow the "but," as in, "He's wonderful, but . . ." and "She's incredible, but . . ." At first, it's little things like the fact that he's a bit sloppy or unkempt, or that she tends to be late all the time. Then, as the partners relax and reveal more of their true nature, and the smoke of passion stops clouding their vision, more serious reservations start to register: "Sometimes he seems a little controlling," or, "She can be pretty demanding at times." After a while, you have to ask yourself, "Is that acceptable? Can I live with that? Will it change?"

Often, the very things that attracted you to the person in the first place become unacceptable later on. That's because our greatest strengths become our Achilles' heels when we take them a step too far. The man that seems controlling now was probably very appealing when you first saw his strong, decisive, take-charge personality in action. The woman who seems demanding now was probably admired for being honest and knowing what she wants. A man whose sensitivity and warmth was so comforting at first may later seem weak or wimpy. The vivacious woman who dazzled you with her perky charm may later seem loud and verbose.

> **USABLE INSIGHT**
>
> *Keeping score in the game of love is the surest way to lose in the end.*

This pattern is exacerbated when opposites attract. Hal, for example, was a screenwriter who tended to be flighty and unfocused. When he fell in love he thought it was a perfect match, for Emily, a financial planner, was practical and sensible and always down-to-earth. Two years later, when they came for counseling, Hal complained that Emily was cold and analytical, completely out of touch with her feelings. Emily's story was the flip side. She'd never met anyone as affectionate as Hal, and she was awestruck by his spontaneity. When I met them, she said that Hal was just an impulsive dreamer. Their sources of inspiration had become sources of irritation. They had to accept that they could not have their lover's endearing qualities without the dark side that was revealed when those same qualities were taken to an extreme.

The Mars-Venus Factor

Before marriage, a man declares that he would lay down his life to serve you; after marriage, he won't even lay down his newspaper to talk to you.

—HELEN ROWLAND

We all want to be appreciated for what we are and accepted for who we are. But men and women tend to differ on *how* they want to be appreciated. As mentioned earlier, most women want to be cherished and most men want to be admired.

When we cherish something, we consider it precious. We treat it with special tenderness and affection. When we admire something, we have a high opinion of it and treat it with a certain amount of honor. Where people are concerned, we tend to cherish those who have certain qualities of the soul, such as decency, goodness and kindness. We admire those whose actions or talents are exceptional.

As it happens, the qualities we *cherish* are the kind that little girls are typically praised for, and the qualities we *admire* are those we tend to single out in boys. Those distinctions may sound archaic, but they still hold true for a great many people. Girls are often adored by their fathers just for being good daughters; boys are showered with admiration by their mothers for every achievement. And since our relationship to the opposite sex is largely determined by how we're treated by the opposite-sex parent when we're young, it's no wonder that women need to be cherished by men and men need to be admired by women.

When we fall in love, we're usually cherished or admired as if we'd written the script ourselves. That's one of the reasons early love is so charming. We don't think, "Wow, she admires me just like my mother did," or, "No one's cherished me like this since my father," but we feel it deep down inside, where our positive early experiences cry out to be repeated. That's why it's so upsetting when you no longer feel quite so cherished or quite so admired—and so painful when the appreciation stops and acceptance is hanging on by a thread. "She used to look up to me," I've heard men moan, "but now she looks down on me." "I don't care if he treats me as a possession," women have cried, "I just want to be treated as a *prized* possession again."

You may be surprised to hear that lack of acceptance hits men harder than it does women. There are several reasons for this. One is that boys usually have to work hard to win the admiration of others. Whereas girls are more likely to gain approval for looking good and behaving nicely, boys are raised to link their self-esteem to outer achievement. They're constantly compared to other boys and encouraged to compete. What did you accomplish today? Did you win? Did you work hard? The evaluation is relentless. This makes for men who are highly vulnerable to signs that they don't measure up.

"If You Really Loved Me, You'd Change"

Look, I can't promise I'll change, but I can promise
I'll pretend to change.

—ROBERT MANKOFF

Another factor that contributes to sex differences in acceptance is this: Women tend to have greater expectations for men than men do for women. When a man gets married, his expectations usually center on certain "feminine" traits; he wants his wife to look good, be a good mother, behave with kindness and decency and treat him well. Sure, most modern men also admire accomplished women and take pride in their wives' achievements, but the standards they apply in those areas are not as high as women's standards for male achievement. Since women's survival, and that of their children, often depend on male proficiency, it is understandable that they would be threatened by signs of incompetence.

The expectations issue is compounded by the fact that girls are still raised to pin their hopes on finding Prince Charming. By the time they're old enough to date, their fantasy of Mr. Right is a guy who's sensitive, strong, a great provider, a perfect friend, a stud in bed, a terrific father and a hunk they're proud to be seen with. Boys have fantasies too, but they don't extend far beyond the pages of a supermodel calendar.

For all those reasons, the conventional wisdom is mostly true: women try to change their men, and men try to keep their women the same. Women are much more likely to enter marriage with a secret list of improvements they intend to bring about in their husbands, as if they had purchased a house that needs fixing up. You seldom see that attitude in men, except in Pygmalion-like cases, when a mature man marries a younger woman or a sophisticated man marries someone from a sheltered background. For the most part, if you ask a woman what she wants to change about her man, you might get a list. If you ask a man what he wants to change about his woman, the answer is likely to be, "I want her to stop trying to change me."

The problem is exacerbated because men are much more sensitive to criticism, even of the most constructive kind. Women don't like being criticized or disapproved of either, of course, and no one wants to be dominated or controlled. But men not only hate it, they strongly resist it. It makes them feel more unacceptable than their partners actually think they are.

When many men hear, "Can you wear another shirt?" or "Let me show you how to do that," they don't hear a reasonable suggestion, they hear, "You're doing it wrong." They feel scolded. They experience the remark as an attack on their competence. Men don't interpret being corrected and asked to do things a different way as welcome help. It doesn't make them feel protected or guided or taken care of. They take it as a threat to their control over their own lives. They feel watched over and intruded upon, as if their mothers were still telling them how to get ready for school. In a word, they feel like an infant—and that is a big blow to their self-esteem. After all, the day a boy graduates from that kind of close supervision by his mother is a big moment. It's a sign of maturity, of being a man instead of a boy, and no man wants to be made to feel like a child again.

Sometimes, a woman who insists on changing her man is being flat-out unreasonable; her fantasies have not been met and she's using criticism and harassment to try and turn him into the man of her dreams. The man is often caught by surprise, since he seemed to be accepted without reservation when they were dating. The comments of a beleaguered husband named Walter were typical: "She didn't complain before the wedding, but then she started showing her true colors—demanding, manipulative, picky picky picky. I feel that I can't do anything right in her eyes."

Ah, but that's just his side of the story. A woman may be perfectly justified in wanting to change her guy. He may have grown careless or lazy or crude or abusive since they fell in love, and the decline of acceptance is well deserved. "It's like he was on his best behavior at first, a real prince," said Walter's wife, who was so fed up she was contemplating divorce. "Then he started taking me for granted, and now he's on his *worst* behavior all the time. I can't just shut up about that."

In many cases, both scenarios can be operating at the same time in a continual feedback loop: her criticism gives him license to mistreat her, and his mistreatment provokes more criticism.

Mama's Boys and Daddy's Girls

But my heart belongs to Daddy.

—COLE PORTER

Sometimes, a man's need to be admired is so great that nothing short of worship can satisfy it. In a poignant example, a thirty-year-old research scientist named Stanley complained that Jill, his fiancé, no longer looked up to him. With tears in her eyes, Jill said, "I think what you really want is for me to adore you all the time. But I can't do that. I can't be that phony. It makes me very sad, because you are a wonderful man, and I admire you a great deal. But I can't keep you on a pedestal and bat my eyes all day and call you 'my hero.'"

The key to the survival of that relationship was for Jill to convince Stanley that she accepted him even though she didn't approve of everything about him or gush with admiration all the time—and for Stanley to accept that his need to be constantly venerated had to be ratcheted down to a level appropriate for an adult relationship between equals.

Stanley was a mama's boy. As a child, he received not only the unconditional acceptance and love that every youngster should have, but outright adulation. And it didn't change as he grew older. In the eyes of his mother he could do no wrong. She expected nothing of him and demanded nothing from him except to smile at her and be a good boy. Discipline and life lessons were left to his father.

For a mama's boy it is bliss to be bathed in the unwavering warmth of a mother's adoration—just as it is for a daddy's girl to be adored by a father. The problems come later in life, when they hook up with love partners and find that they are not adored to quite the same extent. Adults evaluate each other. They judge their partners by what they actually do and what they give. They expect more than a smile and a hug in return for their love. This can be a rude awakening for a mama's boy or a daddy's girl. Some never get used to the fact that their lovers will not and cannot give them the kind of unqualified approval they got from their mother or father.

Mama's boys and daddy's girls are spoiled—not necessarily in the material sense, but emotionally. They feel entitled to have what they want and need emotionally without necessarily having to earn it or give much of anything in return. It's simply what they were programmed to expect from the opposite sex. In most cases they also have a hard time admitting they're wrong. It's always the other person who's at fault and the other person who has to apologize. If they do say "I'm sorry," it's usually with reluctance and a tone of insincerity—something they say to end the unpleasantness, not something they deeply feel. They are simply not used to looking at themselves with a critical eye. They might be self-reflective in other settings—at work, for instance, or with their same-sex friends—but not in the context of a love relationship.

In addition to having inflated expectations for approval and acceptance, many mama's boys and daddy's girls bring another pattern to relationships: they apply impossible standards to their partners. Naturally, as children they saw the mother or father who adored them as perfect. Now their love partners are expected to measure up to that standard—something no mortal human should be asked to do. The problem is compounded if the idolized parent dies before the child can discover that Mom or Dad had clay feet; they get frozen in memory as perfect beings, idealized and beatified. Daddy was generous, protective and strong; he made the world safe, comfortable and fun. Mommy was unfailingly loving, kind and nurturing, never critical, always encouraging. With models like that, future love partners don't stand a chance. Without being conscious of it, daddy's girls and mama's boys try to mold their lovers into their image of the idealized parent, and they are invariably disappointed.

As a cute, playful little girl, Cynthia was doted on by her father. He was a hardworking stockbroker who had three sons before his only daughter was born, and he raised those boys with a firm hand. Because in his mind girls did not need strength and discipline to make their way in the world, he showered Cynthia with love and gave her whatever she wanted. When Daddy came home from work, his sons would snap to. Cynthia would run to his arms and make him smile.

When Cynthia was fifteen, her father died. She never got to see his weaknesses, and she never had a chance to rebel. By age twenty-four, she had discarded a long list of ardent lovers who seemed wonderful at first but ended up disappointing her. Then she met Luke, who was a kind, sensitive, romantic man. He could sense the pain of loss deep within Cynthia's heart and was moved to heal it and to create a happy-ever-after life with her. But his best intentions crashed into an immovable wall of expectation.

Luke could never love his wife enough. He could never be warm enough, tender enough, understanding enough. Nor could he be generous enough, ambitious enough, successful enough or strong enough. Cynthia felt perfectly justified in calling attention to the shortcomings she perceived. Luke was not permitted that luxury. He adored Cynthia and cut her more slack than other men had, but if he ever got annoyed or irritated or tried to point out ways that she could do better, he was attacked. After all, Daddy never talked to her that way.

In one counseling session, Cynthia tore into Luke for always forgetting things. The look on her face was of angry frustration. The look on Luke's face was of bewildered anguish. "Why are you so mad at me all the time?" he said. His pain did not register on his wife. "I'm not mad," replied Cynthia, "you're just always screwing up."

This brought Luke to the edge. He realized that he had never been totally acceptable to Cynthia and perhaps he never would be. Somehow this insight strengthened him. "I've done the best I could to love you well," he said. "Maybe there's someone out there who can do it better, but I'm tired of disappointing you." And he got up to leave.

Some daddy's girls would have said, "Fine, go, there are plenty of men out there," and there would be little hope for the marriage. Fortunately, Cynthia had greater awareness and depth of feeling than that. Taken aback by Luke's statement, she said, "Please don't leave, I didn't mean to hurt you."

It was a start. To take advantage of the moment, I asked Cynthia if she had ever known anyone who constantly made her feel unacceptable, as if she just didn't measure up no matter what she did. "I had a boss like that once," she said. I asked how it made her feel at the time. "I felt horrible," she recalled. "I was always frustrated, always on edge."

"I'll bet you felt infuriated sometimes, and defenseless and totally unappreciated." She said yes, she had felt those things. "Would you want to make anyone else feel that way?" I asked.

> **USABLE INSIGHT**
>
> *You can't compete with a mama's boy's mama or a daddy's girl's daddy.*

That's when she really got it. She looked at Luke with compassion for the first time. "Is that how you feel?" she asked. He nodded. Cynthia cried. Because she was finally willing to look at herself honestly and consider Luke's feelings, there was hope. What followed was their first truly honest conversation; it turned the tide of their marriage.

Cynthia and Luke were lucky enough to catch the pillar of acceptance before it toppled completely. Had their situation continued unchanged for much longer, it would have been irreversible. The reason Luke was able to stand up and walk toward the door was that he'd realized something vital. "I was so busy trying to not be unacceptable to my wife," he said, "that I was blind to what was really going on: *she* had become unacceptable to *me,* and I couldn't take it anymore." Unfortunately, that's what often happens to the partners of daddy's girls and mama's boys.

When You're Not Being Accepted

*Do you know what it means to come home at night
to a woman who'll give you a little love, a
little affection, a little tenderness? It means that
you're in the wrong house, that's what it means.*

—HENNY YOUNGMAN

There are two areas to work on to shore up a weakening pillar of acceptance: the things your partner finds unacceptable about you, and the things you find unacceptable about your partner. Let's begin with what to do—and not to do—when you're the one on the firing line.

The first thing to avoid is denial. You'll only make the problem worse by pretending it doesn't exist. Even if your partner is coy about making his or her disapproval known, your internal prompts will call your attention to it. You may choose to ignore those signals because they're hard to face. You might try to talk yourself out of it ("Oh, he's just touchy," "I'm being too sensitive"). You can suppress your hurt, but it will simmer inside you and eventually make you resentful.

Denial usually occurs when a partner's lack of acceptance is not openly expressed. When it roars forth in criticism or demands, the usual reaction is defensiveness. The cliché, "The best offense is a good defense" usually backfires when applied to relationships. Defensiveness is perceived as an attack. It invariably begets a counterattack, which begets further defensiveness, another attack and . . . well, if you want your relationship to be like a football game, by all means continue. If you have a more peaceful image in mind, though, defensiveness is a recipe for disaster.

If you're defensive, your partner will think you're saying, "I'm right and you're wrong." More than likely, what you really mean to convey is simply, "I'm not wrong," or, "I'm not unacceptable" or "I'm feeling under attack and I need to set the record straight." But by responding defensively or

> **USABLE INSIGHT**
>
> *When you're not being attacked, being on the defensive comes off as offensive.*

belligerently to signs of disapproval, the wrong impression is conveyed and the other person strikes a warlike posture.

Don't Be a Rebel Without a Pause

The rebel can never find peace.

—ALBERT CAMUS

Another thing to avoid is rebelling against legitimate requests. Some of the traits your partner has trouble accepting may be well worth your effort to change. They might even make you a better person. The problem is, you can feel so ticked off at having someone try to change you that you resist out of sheer spite. Then your partner is likely to find you *more* unacceptable because you're dismissing their concerns or making excuses for yourself.

"If you don't want to be treated like a child, don't act like one." That's what Sharon said to her husband, Fred, when he complained that she was nagging him. Fred had regressed after they got married, she claimed. "He walks around the house like a total slob, belching and farting whenever he feels like it, leaving a trail of junk food behind him and expecting me to clean it up. He's a big baby. You should see his study, it's somewhere between a playpen and a pigpen." In short, Fred was acting like a ten-year-old who needs his Mommy but doesn't want her to tell him what to do.

While Sharon had a lot to learn about the way she made her disapproval known, most of what she asked of Fred was not only reasonable but good for *him*. Over and above the childish behavior, he was slacking off at work. Fred snarled at her concerns and balked at her suggestions. It was that attitude that Sharon found most unacceptable. "I can put up with a lot of immature stuff," she said, "but I can't accept someone who's not interested in improving himself."

As I questioned Fred, it became clear that there was a lot more going on than simple rebelliousness. He was misbehaving to test his wife's limits. In his mind, it was easy to be accepted if you did everything just the way the other person wanted you to. But he wanted to be loved with no strings attached, something he never got as a child. Both his parents were demanding, verbally abusive taskmasters who made him earn every compliment and every sign of affection—which they gave away about as often as birthday presents.

I asked Sharon if she ever complimented her husband. "I used to do it a lot," she said, "but he never appreciated it. He'd get embarrassed and say things like, 'You're just saying that,' and, 'I know what you really think.'" Learning that Fred had trouble receiving compliments was the missing piece of the puzzle. "I think you're afraid of acceptance," I told him.

"What are you talking about?" he said. "Acceptance is what I *want!*"

I told him that one of the reasons we hunger for acceptance is that we want to be able to lower our guard. It can be awfully tiring to go through life protecting ourselves from disapproval and rejection. But for many people, like Fred, the prospect of dropping their guard is terrifying. They have no defense against the consequences of acceptance.

What consequences could there possibly be? Being accepted should make you feel safe and secure, not threatened. That's true, but for people who have never felt safe in their entire lives, it can be scary. "If you were ever to feel truly accepted," I told Fred, "it would be safe to feel all your feelings—including all the terrible emotions you swept under the rug because you didn't want to upset Mom or Dad, or because you didn't want your friends to think you were weak, or because you couldn't bear the pain. I think you're afraid that if you ever felt completely accepted by Sharon, the pain would overwhelm you."

Fred broke down and began to sob. He realized that he was fighting the very thing he craved, resisting every reasonable attempt by his wife to make him more acceptable. It was a crucial turning point in the couple's journey to lasting love.

Are you afraid to let your guard down? Are there other reasons you resist doing what it would take to earn the complete acceptance of your mate? When you catch yourself instinctively rebelling, stop. Pause for a moment and ask yourself if your resistance is purposeful or self-defeating. The following list will help you identify why you might be resisting.

- You think what's being asked of you is unfair and unreasonable.
- It's not unreasonable, but you don't like your partner's attitude or tone of voice.
- You think your partner's demands are petty—not worth the time or effort.
- You're afraid that if you give in, you'll end up being dominated or controlled.
- You don't feel you're strong enough to change, and if you try you'll only fail.
- You feel that you don't deserve complete acceptance.
- You don't accept yourself, so why should anyone accept you?

Becoming aware of why you're resisting change will help you work with your partner on mutual acceptance.

An Ounce of Prevention

Marriage is the alliance of two people, one of whom never
remembers birthdays and the other who never forgets.

—OGDEN NASH

Let's say you know that some of your traits drive your partner crazy. Let's say the changes he or she would like to see in you are fair and reasonable. Let's say you're willing to make the effort, but you know that old dogs don't learn new tricks easily. In the meantime, you'd like to avoid the hostile confrontations that arise when you don't get it right. The key is to anticipate the problem and defuse the tension in advance.

Three times a year, for two consecutive years, Gerald got it wrong. Birthday, anniversary, Christmas—on every occasion that called for a present, the one he got his wife ended up returned. It was a minor offense, to be sure, but to Carol it was symptomatic of a larger problem: she felt that Gerald didn't care enough to pay attention to her or try to understand her needs and wants. Through couples counseling, Gerald came to appreciate his wife's concerns. He was making progress toward becoming a better listener and a more attentive partner in general. Now Carol's birthday was coming up, and the gift decision was making him so nervous you'd think it was a matter of life and death.

He decided on a completely different course of action. Over a quiet dinner at Carol's favorite restaurant, he said, "I've been racking my brain for a birthday gift that would let you know how thankful I am for having you in my life. But my batting average has been pretty bad and I don't want to disappoint you again. I really want you to be happy on your birthday, not have to pretend that you like what I got you when you don't. So, what can I give you to make your birthday special? I know you'd rather be surprised, but until I get really confident in this department, I'd like your help."

This was not Carol's ideal scenario. But she was deeply moved by Gerald's willingness to share his struggle in such a vulnerable way, and she appreciated that he was making a sincere effort to make her happy. It turned out to be her best birthday since they met, and she knew the next one would be better.

Gerald's example helped Carol make some changes of her own. On previous occasions, when she had to accompany her husband to a social affair with his business colleagues, they had fought over her choice of clothing. A sculptor and art teacher, Carol was the jeans-and-sweat-shirt type. She bristled at the corporate dress code. Because her version of a compromise outfit was not quite formal enough for Gerald, getting dressed for these affairs was like negotiating a Mideast peace accord. Carol knew that it meant a lot to Gerald that she fit in, and she knew that her resistance made him feel that she didn't care about his career. But she hated him hovering over her and making suggestions as if he were dressing a Barbie doll. By the time they were ready to leave, the tension would be unbearable.

The next time the situation came up, Carol decided to be proactive. A week ahead of time, she sat Gerald down and said,

> **USABLE INSIGHT**
>
> *Think of what matters to them ahead of time and you'll matter to them all the time.*

"That company dinner is coming up soon. I know I tend to get resentful and uncooperative, and I've spoiled things for you in the past. I don't want that to happen again, so instead of waiting till the last minute and making ourselves crazy, why don't you tell me now what you'd like me to wear. I want to be a good sport, and if we work it out in advance, we might even be able to have some fun."

If you anticipate areas where your habits and personality traits are likely to meet with disapproval, take command of the situation and be proactive. An ounce of prevention will save a pound of wear and tear on the pillar of acceptance.

When You Can't Quite Accept Your Partner

What counts in making a happy marriage is not so much how compatible you are, but how you deal with incompatibility.

—DANIEL GOLEMAN

What can you do when you find yourself struggling to accept your partner? One thing you should *not* do is make your disapproval known through nagging, complaining, insulting or manipulating. When you do that, you're making demands in a way that does not exactly invite compliance. You may think you're merely trying to correct unacceptable behavior, but the target will take it personally. They'll hear it as an assault on their basic worth. They might hit back, or dig in their heels and keep right on doing what you don't want them to do just for spite.

The other extreme to avoid is suppressing your disapproval in hopes that your partner will see the light and change on his or her own. Sometimes we hesitate to make our feelings known because we don't want to cause a confrontation or hurt the person we love. So we hope they'll get the message through osmosis and change automatically. If you cling to that hope long enough, you might even start resenting them for not taking a hint.

Your partner may not know exactly what you're thinking and feeling, but sooner or later they will sense that something is wrong. Your tone of voice and body language will slowly but surely drive home the message, "You are not acceptable." Then, without quite knowing why, your partner will start pulling away from you. If it gets bad enough, he or she will eventually do what kids do when their playmates don't accept them: take their marbles and go play someplace else.

That is, if *you* haven't already left. One of the more heartbreaking experiences I encounter as a therapist is when someone whose spouse or lover has just dumped them cries, "Why didn't he tell me it was bothering him? I could have changed."

In sum, you have to let your concerns be known, but do it in a way that fosters change while treating your partner with dignity.

Changing Your Default Position

When we are no longer able to change a situation,
we are challenged to change ourselves.

—VICTOR FRANKL

In *Get Out of Your Own Way,* I wrote: "If you expect people to change, you can drive yourself crazy waiting for it to happen. If you try to *make* them change, you will drive *them* crazy. But if you accept them as they are and tell them that you *hope* they'll change, they just might do it." This is never more true than in a love relationship. If you're thinking that you can't accept your partner until he or she changes, see if you can reverse your default position: accept first and then see about encouraging change. (The exception is when abuse, infidelity, addiction or some other absolutely unacceptable behavior is involved.) If you can convert the *demand* for your partner to change to the *hope* that he or she will change, you can preserve the acceptance that keeps a relationship intact.

Claude was a highly successful engineer with a gifted intellect and a highly trained capacity for analysis. But his emotional IQ did not reach triple digits. He was kind and considerate by nature, but understanding human feelings was just not his forte. This drove his wife crazy. "I wish he was abusive," Kathleen told me. "I wish he was a slimeball. Then it would be much easier, because then I could leave him. But he's a fine person and a very responsible husband and father, and I know he loves me." It's just that when conflicts or disagreements arose, or problems came up involving their children or other family members, Claude could not relate on an emotional level. He tried to turn everything into a puzzle that could be solved with logic.

Kathleen was troubled for several reasons. An editor of novels, she knew that human life can't be reduced to equations. She also felt that Claude looked down on her for getting carried away by emotion. Mostly, she felt a great gap in her life; she wanted to be able to speak from the heart and know she was being understood.

Kathleen eventually found acceptance by learning not to take it personally when Claude failed to understand her way of relating to the world. She came to appreciate his struggle to make sense of things and how hard it was to bring the mysteries of the human heart into his comfort zone. She also realized that Claude was not going to change in that regard; his way of relating to the world was hardwired into his brain. As for the lack she felt, she learned that there were ways to make up for that. She started reaching out more to her female friends and took an office downtown instead of working at home so she could meet more people. Claude was a lot of things—a lot of very good things—and it was unreasonable to expect him to be all things. She could learn to live with what he couldn't give because what he did give was more than acceptable.

One thing that helped Kathleen come to that awareness was taking a good long look at her own shortcomings. In examining the ways that she might be disappointing to her husband, she had a revelation. "I'm far from perfect," she said, "and Claude doesn't seem to have a problem accepting me."

> **USABLE INSIGHT**
>
> *Just because you think you can't accept doesn't mean you can't.*

A funny thing can happen if you work at becoming more accepting. The person you have trouble accepting may become not only tolerable but worthy of admiration. As Henry Miller observed, "What seems nasty, painful, evil, can become a source of beauty, joy and strength, if faced with an open mind."

The Gift of Appreciation

The deepest principle in human nature is the craving to be appreciated.

—WILLIAM JAMES

Julia and Bob had been married for more than fifty years. Acerbic and eccentric, they seemed to be so much at odds with each other that everyone wondered how they managed to live under the same roof for so long. They reminded me of Jack Benny's line about his long marriage: "The word divorce never entered my mind," he said, then paused and added, "Murder, yes."

They came to see me because Julia was suffering from depression and refused to leave the house. When Bob described how sad it was to take his daily walk by himself for the first time, it was clear that underneath the couple's sniping and smart-aleck remarks lay a powerful love and an ironclad devotion.

"Bob," I said, "has Julia ever told you that you're the best man she's ever known and that she considers herself extremely lucky to be married to you?"

His jaw dropped. He was about to make a sarcastic comment, when he looked over at his wife and saw that her eyes had filled with tears. I had expressed what she felt, and it pained her to realize that what she thought was obvious all those years was news to Bob. "He's right," she told him. "Marrying you was the best decision I ever made."

Bob turned to me with a smirk. "I guess that's why she's been picking on me for fifty years. 'Don't do this, don't do that . . .'"

"I'm a picker," said Julia. "I pick on everyone. That has nothing to do with it. You're a wonderful man."

For the first time, Bob was at a loss for words. I stepped into the silence by asking Julia, "Has he ever told you that you're the greatest thing that ever happened to him? That without you, his life would be an empty shell?"

"Yeah, sure," said Julia.

"What are you so surprised about?" said Bob. "Before you, I never had a moment of joy or tenderness in my life. If it wasn't for you, I'd be cardboard. You made me a better man. Just because you're a pain in the neck doesn't mean I don't love you."

For half a century, neither one of them had ever openly expressed the deep, profound appreciation they felt for one another. As a result, they had spent those years feeling tolerated, not accepted.

The best and quickest antidote for lack of acceptance is a regular dose of appreciation. It's impossible to express appreciation for someone and at the same time communicate that he or she is not acceptable to you. And what goes around comes around: When your heart is uplifted by your partner's appreciation, your first instinct is to find a way to express appreciation in return.

Practicing the Three A's

Be quick to praise. People like to praise
those who praise them.

—BERNARD BARUCH

The kind of appreciation that will make your partner feel fully accepted is a three-step process:

STEP 1: AWARENESS. If you look for things that are unacceptable, you can always find them; if you look for things to feel thankful for, you can always find those too. It's a matter of choosing what you want to look for.

One reason we tend to find fault is that we're problem-solving creatures by nature; we have our eyes peeled for threats to our safety and security. Another is that it justifies our discontent. Depression, anger or frustration may have built up for reasons having little to do with your partner, but rather than delve into the real causes, you take the convenient way out and blame it on the handiest target.

But by far the most common reason we are blind to our partner's positive traits is that they're not as noticeable as the bad ones. Some we simply take for granted, like the furniture and artwork in our homes that we hardly notice until a visitor tells us how beautiful they are. Others are simply hard to spot. You notice when he doesn't clean up after himself, but not when he does. You notice when she's a back seat driver, but not when she sits calmly in the passenger seat the entire trip. You notice when he spends money on a gadget that he doesn't really need, but not what he *doesn't* buy because he bought you something instead. You notice that she's ten minutes late, but not when she gives up something in order to be on time. And so, one of the most frequent remarks I hear from exasperated spouses is, "No matter what I do it's always wrong."

People who take up bird-watching find that once they start training their eyes, they see more and more birds where before they saw only trees. Keep your eyes open for the not-so-obvious signs of decency, generosity and goodness, and you'll start finding lots of them.

STEP 2: ADMIRATION. Your partner may have worked hard to develop some of the traits you like. It may take a good deal of effort and commitment to live up to certain values or standards of behavior. It might require a good deal of compromise and sacrifice to make you happy or safeguard your family or preserve the dignity of your relationship. Those efforts are worthy of admiration.

Take your awareness of your partner's positive traits to the next level by walking a mile or two in his or her shoes. Chances are, you don't really understand the pressures they face or the demands on their time and energy. With that in mind, ask yourself:

- Does he/she make sacrifices to improve our life together?
- Does he/she refrain from saying or doing certain things to keep the peace in our relationship?
- Does he/she work hard to be a better person?
- What compromises does he/she make on behalf of our relationship?
- What does he/she have to put up with to be with me?

STEP 3: ACKNOWLEDGMENT. Don't keep your appreciation to yourself. Express it to your partner.

> **USABLE INSIGHT**
>
> *Appreciation that is left to the imagination is the same as no appreciation at all.*

Are you reluctant to acknowledge your partner's positive traits? Would you rather focus on what you find unacceptable? In my experience as a therapist, the most common reason for that is the fear of lowering our guard. We're afraid that if we let people off the hook we'll get disappointed or hurt again. We think the best way to protect ourselves is to keep our partners on edge, forcing them to toe the line by letting them know what they're doing wrong. With a boot-camp strategy like that, you're likely to end up like Julia and Bob, appreciating each other in secret for fifty years. That is if you're lucky enough to stay together that long. If the goal is to grow together in a loving atmosphere, positive reinforcement—acknowledging good behavior—is much more effective.

Changing What Can Be Changed

Love is what happens to men and women who
don't know each other.

—W. SOMERSET MAUGHAM

Let's face it, no matter how hard you work at being more accepting, some of each other's traits may still be hard to tolerate. Rather than let the damage pile up, it makes sense to encourage one another to change in those problem areas. Here is a series of steps that will increase your chances of success:

I. MAKE YOUR WISH LIST. Write down all the things about your partner that you have trouble accepting and wish that he or she would change. Don't censor yourself at this stage. Don't stop to ponder each item or analyze whether it's feasible. Just put down your wishes, and be as specific as possible.

When you've written everything down, sort the list into three categories (if they apply):

• Level 1. It would be nice if they changed, but if they stay the same, it won't alter your love or your basic acceptance.

- Level 2. You can live with them, but the pillar of acceptance will be seriously damaged if they don't change.
- Level 3. Absolute deal-breakers: if they don't change, you're out the door.

2. PUT YOURSELF IN YOUR PARTNER'S PLACE. Now, write down all the actions and attitudes that you think your partner finds unacceptable about you. Again, get everything down in detail, then rearrange the list into those same three categories.

Here are sample items from the lists made by a couple named Irene and Jack, who put themselves in each other's place. First, Irene:

What Jack finds unacceptable about me

- Level 1. I make too many social obligations.
- Level 2. I run up big credit card bills every month.
- Level 3. I drank again, even though I said I'd stop.

What Irene finds unacceptable about me

- Level 1. I dominate the conversation when we're with other people.
- Level 2. I don't spend enough time with the kids.
- Level 3. The time I slapped her.

The primary purpose of this step is to increase your empathy for your partner and to add perspective to your own demands. Many people find that they become more tolerant of their partners' faults as soon as they list their own. Once you've made this list, go back and re-examine the first one.

3. THINK IT THROUGH. Before beginning your conversation, ponder these questions:

- Why do I want so much for my partner to change?
- Is what I'm asking for good for him/her, or only for me?
- Am I being unforgiving?
- Are my expectations too high?
- Can the behavior or attitude actually be changed, or is it a permanent feature of his/her personality?
- Am I blaming my discontent on my partner?
- Am I fooling myself into thinking that if my partner changes all my troubles will be over?
- Am I willing to make an equal effort to change?

4. START THE DIALOGUE. Once both of you have completed steps one through three, set aside an uninterrupted hour or more to discuss the issues raised in this chapter. Needless to say, calling attention to the traits you're struggling to accept is delicate; make sure you stick to the principles of good communication on page 26 and the dialogue guidelines in other chapters. In addition, try not to sound as though you're complaining, criticizing or making demands. And try to avoid expressions such as, "You always . . ." or "You never . . ." General statements like those harden resistance and encourage retaliation.

5. MAKE A COMMITMENT TO ACTION. Even after a deep and meaningful dialogue, it would be unreasonable to expect each other to work on all the desired changes at once. One way to get the process off to a good start is to make an explicit agreement to focus on one thing apiece. Here are some examples of tradeoffs that my clients have made:

- He stops gambling; she cuts back on her spending.
- He tries to stop smoking; she tries to lose weight.
- He stands up for her when his family criticizes her; she tells her mother to stop coming over without calling first.
- He helps more around the house; she stops making fun of him in public.

After some reasonable progress has been made, begin to add other traits to your working agreement.

6. BE PATIENT.   As mentioned earlier, research shows that it takes thirty days for a change in behavior to become a habit, and six months to a year (if not longer) for a habit to become part of your personality and a way of doing things. That's why, in twelve-step programs, participants get a special acknowledgment when they've achieved thirty days of sobriety. It's also why counselors recommend avoiding intimate relationships for a year when you are battling an addiction. It simply takes that long for changes to be internalized and integrated into your personality. So bear in mind that change isn't easy and progress is not always smooth and linear. Be prepared for some backsliding.

7. REINFORCE THE DESIRED BEHAVIOR.   Instead of looking for signs that your partner is slacking off or regressing, try to catch each other getting it right and acknowledge the effort that went into it. My friend Heidi Wall, the president of the Flash Forward Institute, says there are three parts to an effective acknowledgment. The first is simply to acknowledge what the other person did: "Thank you for not criticizing me in front of those people," "Thank you for not betting on the Superbowl."

The second part is acknowledging the effort it took for the person to do it: "I know you were disappointed in how I handled the situation. It took real restraint not to say something right on the spot." "I know you were tempted to make a bet, especially with all your buddies goading you on. That took strength."

The third part is acknowledging what the person's action means to you personally: "It's good to know that I can make a mistake without being embarrassed in front of others. It makes me feel safe, so I can relax and enjoy myself," "It's a great relief to feel that I can plan our finances without worrying that you're going to lose money gambling. It means a lot to know that you're a man of your word."

By acknowledging your partner's effort on all three levels, you reinforce the positive behavior and give him or her added incentive to keep on trying to change.

You now have two areas to work on to increase the acceptance in your relationship. One is learning to be more accepting of your partner while offering patience, tolerance and encouragement as he or she works on the changes you wish to see. The other is changing what your partner finds hard to accept about you.

You both may be surprised to find that you are able to change in ways you did not think possible. You might also find that you *like* those changes; more often than not the things our partners find hard to accept in us are things we don't like about ourselves. In addition, you will probably find that it is much easier to accept one another than you thought it was before. What seems to be unacceptable becomes much more acceptable when you're working together to CREATE a love that lasts.

6

Trust

Believing and
Being Believed

The best proof of love is trust.
—DR. JOYCE BROTHERS

How much do the following statements apply to the way you think or feel about trust in your relationship?

	Hardly Ever 0	Sometimes 1	Almost Always 2
1. My partner and I can confide shameful thoughts to each other.	____	____	____
2. We will not use anything we've shared in confidence against one another.	____	____	____
3. I trust that my partner will not hurt me.	____	____	____
4. My partner trusts me not to hurt him/her.	____	____	____
5. I keep my promises to my partner.	____	____	____
6. My partner keeps his/her promises to me.	____	____	____
7. I trust my partner when we are away from each other.	____	____	____
8. My partner trusts me when we are away from each other.	____	____	____
9. I don't bad-mouth my partner behind his/her back.	____	____	____
10. My partner doesn't bad-mouth me behind my back.	____	____	____
TOTAL:	____	____	____

SCORING:
  0–6   In God you may trust, but not each other.
  7–13   Trust me, this is a satisfactory score.
  14–20 In trust you love. Congratulations on a solid foundation.

A skeptic is someone who is reluctant to trust. A cynic is someone who refuses to trust. Show me a skeptic and I'll show you someone who once trusted and was hurt. Show me a cynic and I'll show you someone who once trusted and was devastated. But deep inside all skeptics and the majority of cynics is a deep, abiding ache to trust once more, but safely, without the fear of being hurt or devastated again.

Trust speaks to the deepest and most primal of human needs: the need for safety. "At the bottom of the heart of every human being from earliest infancy until the tomb," wrote the French philosopher Simone Weil, "there is something that goes on indomitably expecting, in the teeth of all experience of crimes committed, suffered and witnessed, that good and not evil will be done to him. It is this above all that is sacred in every human being." That expectation takes shape in our capacity to trust, without which the dependency of childhood would be a ceaseless horror and adult life would be bleak and fearful.

Trust means different things to different people. Depending on our individual values and needs, each of us determines whom we can trust and what limits we should place on our trust. Generally speaking, trust implies faith and confidence. When you trust people you have confidence that you can rely on their integrity, ability or character. You have faith that they will uphold the standards and principles that matter to you. You believe that you can count on them, if not at all times then at least in specific circumstances.

In the context of a love relationship, trust has additional

connotations as well. At the very least, trusting our lovers or spouses means having faith that they will honor their sacred vows and keep their promises. We feel confident that we are safe and secure with them. We believe they will not hurt us. At its best, trust is liberating. It allows us to be ourselves, free to be open with our thoughts and feelings; free to bare our souls; free to reveal our hopes and fears, our doubts and dreams, knowing that we will not be judged or demeaned; free to be vulnerable without having our vulnerability used against us.

When trust is damaged, the cement that binds two people together is ruptured. And the space is quickly filled by fear: fear of being hurt—by infidelity, physical or emotional abuse, abandonment, humiliation and other sources of pain. We also may suffer fear of loss—the loss of love, home, family, money and other essentials that nurture and sustain us and make us feel safe in the world.

> ### USABLE INSIGHT
> *Without emotional trust, you cannot have emotional intimacy.*

Often, the fear is more subtle. You may trust your partner to be faithful, truthful and dependable in a crisis, but you may not trust them emotionally. That may translate to a fear of not being understood, or not being appreciated for who you are, or not being able to share your sorrows and secrets. It may involve a fear of being judged, rejected, ridiculed or betrayed when you are most vulnerable. Without emotional trust, you cannot have emotional intimacy. You might have sex, you might have children, you might have a sound and trustworthy economic partnership; you may respect, enjoy and accept one another; but if one or both of you is withholding trust on an emotional level, something precious will be absent and you will yearn for it, even if you can't quite identify what's missing.

The consequences of a lack of trust are felt not only by those who can't trust their partners but also by those who are not trusted. It hurts to know that you don't fully enjoy your partner's trust because of a perceived character flaw or something you've done in the past. It hurts in a different way when the lack of trust is unexpressed—when you sense it and feel it but don't know what you did to warrant it. And it hurts even more when you feel you don't deserve the mistrust.

Not being trusted leads to a number of possible reactions: you can become *determined* to prove that you are trustworthy; you can become *depressed* and lose your self-esteem; you can become *defiant,* making no effort to remedy the lack of trust and perhaps even making things worse; or you can become *devious* and start looking for someone else to give you the trust you feel you deserve.

The Varieties of Trust

It is an equal failing to trust everybody,
and to trust nobody.

—ENGLISH PROVERB

You can trust a person in some ways and not in others. You might, for example, trust someone to be honest and forthright, but not to pay their bills on time or remember where the car keys are. You might trust someone to be punctual, but not to come through in times of need. You might trust a lover's fidelity, but not his or her ability to keep a secret. You might trust a spouse to bring home the bacon and protect your children, but not with your deepest feelings.

To illustrate the subtleties of trust, consider Miranda and Patrick. Patrick was a former collegiate basketball star who was channeling his high-powered energy into a new fitness business. As a take-no-prisoners entrepreneur, he trusted no one. Self-sufficiency and personal strength were the qualities he valued above all others, in himself and anyone who entered his life. After a disastrous marriage to a dependent woman who had neither of those attributes, he was thrilled to meet Miranda. Not only did she share his zeal for physical fitness, but she was a go-getter who became a partner in her law firm before she turned thirty. What Patrick did not bargain for was that Miranda was as needy emotionally as she was self-sufficient financially.

Miranda was able to keep that aspect of her personality under wraps in the heady early days of their relationship. But once Patrick settled back into his usual workaholic mode, Miranda's insecurity and neediness emerged. As soon as Patrick's commitment to his business started putting some distance between them, Miranda felt abandoned. The more she asked of his time and attention the more Patrick backed away, and the more detached he seemed the more desperate and clingy Miranda became.

What does this familiar pattern have to do with trust? To begin with, Patrick's unbending philosophy of self-reliance was rooted in a basic sense of mistrust. It began in childhood when his mother died and his father left him and his sister on the doorstep of a child welfare agency. He spent his youth going from one foster home to another, learning along the way that he could count on no one. As an adult, he was charming and likeable, but he was so mistrustful that he kept friends and lovers at arm's length emotionally. It was safer that way.

Just as Patrick needed to mistrust because he was afraid to be abandoned, Miranda needed to trust because she had an insatiable need for affection and could hardly stand to be alone. She had grown up excessively close to her father, who showered her with attention as a child and was almost flirtatiously devoted to her when she entered adolescence. As Miranda developed into a sexy teenager, her father panicked. Terrified of the feelings she aroused in him, he tore himself away, becoming remote and seemingly indifferent overnight. Then he packed Miranda off to a boarding school for safekeeping. Ever since, she craved the attention and affection of men, entrusting them with her heart too quickly. At the first sign of their pulling away, her fear of being hurt again would kick in and her naïve trust turned to an almost paranoid *mis*trust.

As he got to know Miranda, Patrick was thrilled to learn that he could trust her in ways he could not trust his first wife— to hold her own financially, to show up on time, to encourage his ambition and not turn him away sexually. But after a while, Miranda's neediness made him feel invaded. "She's like a parasite," he said. "She's sucking the life out of me." He could not trust her to be part of his life without metastasizing like a tumor and taking over his freedom.

For her part, Miranda learned early on that she could trust Patrick to protect her and stand up for her—he'd nearly pulver-

> **USABLE INSIGHT**
>
> *Defenses that kept you safe in the past might make you sorry in the future.*
>
> —

ized an obnoxious drunk who came on to her in a bar. She could trust him to be honest, to treat her like an equal and to respect her commitment to her career. And she sensed that she could trust him to be a good father should the relationship ever come to that. But she was not sure she could trust him to be faithful, or to be there when she needed a good listener or a shoulder to cry on.

Had they met a few years earlier, Patrick and Miranda would have been doomed to a quick, tempestuous breakup. But they had been through enough to know that an attraction as strong as theirs deserved a fighting chance. To work things out, both of them had to demonstrate that they could be trusted in the ways that mattered to the other. Equally important, they had to show that they were capable of trusting.

Trusting Too Much or Too Little

You may be deceived if you trust too much, but you will live in torment if you do not trust enough.

—FRANK CRANE

Trust is usually not part of the package that brings two lovers together; we hold it in abeyance because it's risky to give it away too soon. Instead, we test, evaluate and shadowbox until we're sure the other person deserves it. The scrutiny is partially rational; we make inferences based on our observations of someone's behavior under different circumstances and, like scientists, we test our hypotheses. But it is also intuitive. We feel out whether we can trust them. Gut feelings and hunches whisper, "It's okay, you can trust this one," or, "Look out!" When we get a strong, persistent signal of mistrust, we are well advised to take it seriously, even in the absence of tangible evidence. Many a love boat has been wisely returned to shore on the feeling that, "He/she is terrific, but I'm not sure I can trust him/her."

The opposite feeling—"I think I can trust this person"—is like a strong gust of wind, propelling the love boat further into the deep waters of commitment. We can't fully commit to someone unless we have trust. When you sense a certain integrity, decency, honesty or kindness that signals trustworthiness, it's usually a significant turning point.

The sizing up process has key moments, such as the first time the person keeps or breaks an important promise and the first time he or she has to demonstrate courage. But the truly key moment comes when you let your guard down emotionally and reveal something unflattering about yourself, or share something embarrassing or painful—something that could be a turnoff or scare the person away.

Does he or she appear to be preoccupied? Indifferent? Annoyed? Judgmental? Halfway out the door? Such responses normally trigger the gut reaction, "This is not someone I can trust with my heart." But if he or she responds with interest, understanding and respect, you get on the phone to your best friend and say you think you've found a gem. Assuming the other pillars are strong, when that gut feeling, "I think I can trust this person," becomes the firm conviction, "I *know* I can trust this person," we drop our defenses, send the security guards home and turn off the alarm system.

As most of us remember, new lovers can be overly generous with their faith. In the flush of romance and passion, we're willing to trust because we *want* to trust. We want to believe that this is *it* and the feeling will last forever, and we can't believe such things unless we're prepared to believe that the beautiful person lying next to us in the morning is worthy of our trust. But it doesn't take more than one or two broken hearts for us to reset the gauge. By the time we're twenty-five or thirty, most of us have learned to run a long series of safety checks before we give our trust away.

We meet someone we're attracted to and the detective in our brain starts to run every observation of every nuance through our mental data bank: Is that response similar to that of someone I was able to trust or someone I couldn't trust? To a certain extent, vigilance is a mark of wisdom. Taken too far, it's a curse. It limits you to arm's-length relationships in which you're not alone but you're not completely, wholeheartedly with your lover either. You just can't let yourself trust enough to be vulnerable again.

> **USABLE INSIGHT**
>
> *Trust too much and you end up hurt. Trust too little and you end up alone.*

This is especially true if you've had the misfortune of giving away your trust to a user, a manipulator or an outright psychopath. The truly dangerous ones often pass the initial trust tests with flying colors, exhibiting care and concern and making you feel safe, accepted and even special. They're so charming and disarming you feel like you've won the love lottery. You open up completely, only to get crushed by betrayal and deceit. A few relationships with people like that and you end up with scar tissue over your heart, a barricade to future love. In some cases, the pain is so great we vow never to trust again.

Every day in my therapy practice I see wounded veterans of the love wars struggling with intense ambivalence. Whether married or single, they've become trust misers, aching for deeper intimacy but unable to open up completely because they're afraid of being hurt or disappointed again.

When Trust Is Betrayed

Trust everybody, but cut the cards.

—FINLEY PETER DUNNE

Someone once said that it takes seconds to lose trust and years to rebuild it. One careless deed, one selfish act, one failure to live up to a promise or expectation, and all the hard work of earning someone's trust can go down the drain. Whether or not it's irretrievably lost depends on several factors: the severity of the act and its importance to the other person; whether it's part of a pattern or an isolated incident; and the other person's willingness to forgive enough to trust again.

As a young film producer whose star was on the rise, Tom was tireless in his pursuit of new stories, hot talent and lucrative deals. "His cell phone is like an appendage," complained his wife, Janice. "He won't even turn it off when we make love." One Sunday morning that appendage changed the life of their family forever. Tom and Janice had just had brunch with an important agent and were strolling through Beverly Hills with their five-year-old son. At one point, Janice wanted to try on some clothing. She asked Tom to walk their child to a toy store up the street, where she would meet them later.

On the way, Tom's restless mind clicked into overdrive. He took out his cell phone and called his assistant. She told him that the star of one of his movies was in a snit about the director. Tom called the set. The conversation got heated. The loud barking of a dog made it hard to hear. Annoyed, he ducked into the entranceway of a store. Then he heard screams. He turned in the direction of the sound, just in time to see the dog's teeth tearing into the flesh of his son. The child, tired of waiting for Daddy, had strolled away to play with the dog. He nearly lost a finger and his face was badly scarred.

Janice's trust was shattered. She could barely conceal her contempt for her husband. To say that Tom was contrite is an understatement. Despondent and depressed, he couldn't stop saying "I'm sorry." He promised to turn over a new leaf. Janice didn't buy it. She would not let Tom be alone with their son, and she put their plans to have a second child on hold indefinitely. "How can I have another child with someone I can't trust to be a responsible father?" she said. Her attitude about children was understandable, even to Tom. What was harder for him to comprehend was how Janice could let one incident, horrible as it was, carry over to other aspects of their lives. A year later, she still did not trust Tom on any level. She did not trust him to drive safely, handle their money responsibly or even follow through on minor promises. With each passing day, the destruction of trust placed so much stress on the other five pillars that the entire marriage was seriously threatened.

When you look at a story like Janice and Tom's, where do you place the lion's share of responsibility for the long-term breakdown of trust? On Tom for behaving in such a way as to destroy his wife's faith in him? Or on Janice for generalizing from Tom's behavior in one tragic

> **USABLE INSIGHT**
>
> *Trust is in the eye of the beholder, and also in the behavior of the beheld.*

instance to all other aspects of their marriage and clinging to distrust for so long? In intimate relationships, the dance of the truster and the trusted is intricate indeed.

The Measure of Distrust

There can be no deep disappointment where there is not deep love.
—MARTIN LUTHER KING JR.

When you want something and you don't get it, you're *disappointed*. When you need something and you don't get it, you're *depressed*. And when you absolutely have to have something and you don't get it, you're *devastated*. That is the formula I give my clients to help them set realistic goals and avoid the devastation of unfulfilled desires. The same reasoning applies to trust. In an area where we would *like* to trust someone, getting let down is annoying but tolerable; the loss of trust is usually minimal and temporary. When you *need* to trust the person, the letdown is more damaging; the anger and disappointment linger, and the loss of trust may be extended to other areas of your relationship. When you *must* have trust because it is vital to your well-being, you will be devastated by a betrayal and your trust will be hard, if not impossible, to earn back.

Suppose you want your partner to pick you up at the train station because your car is being repaired. If he or she forgets, or shows up twenty minutes late, you'll be annoyed, but you'll get over it. If they do such things repeatedly you will stop trusting their punctuality. If you're reasonable, though, you'll learn to accommodate that weakness and you won't assume they're undependable in other areas. "I discovered a long time ago that I can't trust my wife to be on time for anything," said one client. "I've learned to adapt to it in various ways, like telling her we have to leave twenty minutes earlier than we really do." It was easy for him to live with this because he trusted his wife in other areas where it really mattered.

Now suppose you're about to attend a high school reunion and you're nervous about seeing your old classmates. You ask your partner to go with you. "I need you to keep me calm," you tell him, "and it would mean a lot to me if you could meet certain people." Then he backs out at the last minute. Unless there's a darn good reason why he let you down, your basic trust in him could suffer a blow. "Can I count on him to come through when I need him?" you may wonder. "Can I trust him to understand what's really important to me?" Still, you're not likely to withdraw your trust entirely or generalize your mistrust to other aspects of life unless it's part of a pattern of unreliability.

Then there are areas where you *absolutely* must trust your partner. Without trust in aspects of your relationship that touch on core values or on physical and emotional safety, life together would be painful, anxiety-filled and possibly untenable. Trusting your partner to be faithful is an obvious example. So is trusting him or her not to be violent. Another might be substance abuse. "I can't trust her to behave herself in public," said one client about his wife. "I lost a promotion because she got drunk at my boss's birthday party and created a scene." For his wife, the issue was money. "I can't trust him to spend within our means," she said, "or to not lose our savings on another high-risk investment."

Disappointments that fall in the middle of the continuum are the most confusing. The minor letdowns won't destroy your trust entirely, and the major ones leave little room for doubt. It's the in-between areas that create ambivalence and uncertainty. If I trust him, will I be setting myself up for another, bigger disaster? If I don't, will it destroy the relationship? If I can't trust her in that way, can I trust her at all? These are complex questions. The waters of trust can be difficult to navigate, and intelligent, reasonable people will arrive on different shores, just as the American public did during the Clinton sex scandal, to cite a famous example. Some felt that a man who cheats on his wife and lies about it can't be trusted to run the country; others felt perfectly comfortable with an adulterer setting national policy, as long as he stayed away from their daughters. It depended on how they viewed the man as a whole. For the most part, Americans trusted the president not to jeopardize their safety or security even if they couldn't trust him not to act foolishly.

In most love relationships it is not a single instance that destroys the bond of trust but an accumulation of experiences, and the severity of the damage depends on the partners' history.

In the end, it comes down to individual judgment. We can err by being too trusting or by being too stingy with our trust.

Going Beyond Belief

Trust, but verify.

—RONALD REAGAN

Deborah was a plain-looking, introverted computer consultant who, at age thirty-one, had not had a relationship in years. She worried that she might never find the love she craved. When she met Allen at a software conference it seemed like a wish come true. "It's the revenge of the nerds," she said. "We're perfect soul mates." For several months, her awakened passion was so consuming, and her dreams of everlasting love so blinding, that she exiled her sharp analytic skills to the basement of her mind. Sure, Allen didn't always follow through on his word, and sometimes he forgot things, but you have to cut geniuses some slack. After all, Einstein was absentminded too!

Time after time, as Allen broke one promise after another, Deborah ignored the feeling that he couldn't be trusted. But Allen was not an absentminded genius, he was a narcissist. He made promises to win favor or to get something he wanted, and he had no intention of following through if it was inconvenient to do so.

It was not just her desperate need for love that made Deborah keep on trusting a man who was unworthy of her faith. It was also that the promises Allen failed to keep were relatively insignificant—cancelled trips, broken dates, last-minute changes of plans and the like. But as the relationship progressed, so did the offenses. And so did the inconsistencies in his alibis. Despite catching Allen in lies, Deborah kept on trusting. If she couldn't trust this man, she thought, she might as well join a convent.

As the little heartbreaks mounted and her doubts fought their way to the forefront of her mind, her friends urged her to see a therapist. That's when I met her. In our first session, her description of Allen matched that of either a compulsive or pathological liar who did not care about the effect of his actions on other people. When I told her this, Deborah was indignant. "I believe in him," she declared. "I know I can trust him when it matters most."

Deborah cancelled our next appointment. Clearly, she was afraid to confront the truth. But the truth confronted her a few weeks later. Bedridden with a nasty stomach flu, she assumed Allen would do the things that loved ones do: drive her to the doctor, pick up some food, keep her company, etc. Instead, he treated her illness as an inconvenience. When he didn't even call for two days, Deborah was forced to ponder whether she had been wrong about him all along. Still, she gave him the benefit of the doubt. Then, when she recovered, the other shoe fell. Hard.

She wept uncontrollably when she told me what happened. Allen stopped calling and did not respond to her messages. When she tracked him down, she discovered that he had moved back home—with his wife. The wife had kicked him out just before he met Deborah, after discovering he was having an affair. Allen had told Deborah he'd never been married.

Deborah was an example of someone whose need for love was so great as to make her gullible. She had to learn to trust enough to let love in without opening the door to scoundrels.

Refusing to Take the Leap of Faith

What loneliness is more lonely than distrust?

—GEORGE ELIOT

Terri was the antithesis of Deborah. At forty, she had been single for nine years, ever since the breakup of her second marriage. Beautiful and sophisticated, she did not have to do much to attract the attention of men, and as a Hollywood publicist she was constantly meeting new ones. For years she was satisfied with casual relationships. She said they fulfilled her needs for sex and companionship without complicating her life. Then the ticktock of her biological clock shifted her priorities. She wanted a permanent mate with whom to build a family. But, she said, every likely prospect fell short of her standards. "Isn't there anyone out there I can trust?" she asked. "Every promising guy ends up letting me down."

Few of those potential mates did anything outrageous to betray her faith. They never had the chance. A few minor disappointments would quickly cascade into blanket mistrust. As I listened to her tale of woe, I realized that the problem was not that the pool of available men was filled with slime, nor that Terri made bad choices. The problem was Terri herself.

She was one of the people I referred to earlier who bear the scars of heartbreak and carry the cynical attitude that lovers can't be trusted into each new relationship. Mistrust was a survival mechanism. But, by creating an emotional wall between her and the men she dated, it became a self-fulfilling prophecy. Her wariness made her seem demanding and manipulative. Sensing that *she* could not be completely trusted, men were not willing to give to her what they otherwise might have given. For Terri, that was only another reason not to trust them.

Terri was also a victim of her own perfectionism. This had its advantages in the business world, where she'd earned a reputation for flawless work, but in her personal life it was a drawback. She expected perfection from everyone. For her lovers, that meant being practically psychic—anticipating her every need. Needless to say, this was a recipe for frustration. Terri marked each disappointment in the "Can't Trust" column. Subconsciously, her reasoning was: "If he really cared about me, he would take the trouble to know me, and he would not do things that upset me. Therefore, he must not care. So how can I trust him with my hopes and dreams?"

Terri had to look long and hard at her inflated expectations and self-defeating mistrust. She also had to come to terms with the old hurts that had created such a deep sense of fear in her. Her new relationships were dying for the sins of the old ones.

Terri was the equivalent of someone who burns her hand on a hot stove and now only eats takeout. Her fear of getting burned again was keeping her from getting the nourishment she needed. Instead of "Don't trust men," the better lesson would have been to learn how to tell who could be trusted and who could not. She didn't have to drop her guard completely. She had to learn to lower it enough to see other people clearly.

> **USABLE INSIGHT**
>
> *After you've been hurt, the wrong lesson is "Don't trust again." The right lesson is, "Trust wisely."*

Sometimes trust is not deserved and we are wise to withhold it. Sometimes we mistrust for the wrong reasons and end up tossing out a diamond thinking it's glass. Knowing the difference takes maturity, self-awareness and the right mix of cold reason and intuition.

Restoring Trust

*Trust men, and they will be true to you; treat them
greatly, and they will show themselves great.*

—RALPH WALDO EMERSON

If the trust between you and your partner has been damaged, or if it has never fully ripened, your job as a couple is to look at both sides of the issue: the person who is not trusted and the person who is not able to trust. Chances are, each of you falls into both categories.

If you are not trusted, you must:

- acknowledge that your partner may have reason not to trust you in certain ways
- look honestly at what you've done—or continue to do—to damage that trust
- be willing to do what's fair and reasonable to earn your partner's trust

If you don't trust your partner, your task is to:

- make clear the reasons for your lack of trust
- state what you need in order to trust again

- be open to the possibility of forgiveness and the restoration of trust

- be willing to examine your own capacity to trust

Taking Inventory

As we've seen, people can be more trustworthy in some areas of life than others. The beginning of wisdom in this area is to determine exactly what you can trust your partner for and what you can't—and vice versa. Let's begin by taking inventory.

On a piece of paper or your computer screen, create three columns. The left-hand column is called Trust Inventory. Head the middle one What I Can Trust My Partner To Do, and the one on the right What I Can't Trust My Partner To Do. Now divide the page into sections by listing the following categories down the left column:

- Understanding
- Finances
- Taking responsibility
- Communication
- Honesty
- Forgiveness and tolerance
- Practical matters

For each category, list what you can trust and what you can't trust about your partner. Here are some examples from my clients' Trust Inventories:

Trust Inventory	Why I Can Trust My Partner	Why I Can't Trust My Partner
Understanding	• Shows compassion when I'm upset • Listens patiently without trying to fix everything • Knows when I need to be comforted	• Gets impatient when I need to be heard • Can't relate to strong emotions • Doesn't take my worries seriously
Finances	• Doesn't spend foolishly • Invests intelligently without taking unnecessary risks • Is generous within sensible limits	• Acts penny-wise and pound-foolish • Can't keep track of where the money goes • Takes too many risks
Taking responsibility	• Apologizes for mistakes • Shows remorse when he hurts me • Willing to work on her weaknesses and shortcomings	• Blames others when things go wrong • Can't say "I'm sorry" • Makes excuses
Communication	• Lets me know what she wants and needs • Expresses feelings honestly • Tells me when he's upset without getting nasty	• Interrupts all the time • Hides his feelings • Has temper tantrums when she's upset
Honesty	• Admits when he's wrong • Tells it just like it is • Won't even cheat on his taxes	• Would rather lie than admit she's wrong • Often evasive • Beats around the bush when he's embarrassed about something
Forgiveness and tolerance	• Once something is resolved, she's over it for good • Puts up with all my flaws • Never brings up the past	• Drags out old issues whenever she's upset • Holds grudges forever • Relentlessly critical
Practical matters	• Gets things done promptly • Knows what has to be done without being told • Sees what's wrong and calmly finds a solution	• Procrastinates • Says he'll do it and doesn't follow through • Panics when things go wrong

When you've completed the inventory of your partner's traits, take a break and start thinking about yourself. When you're ready to be perfectly honest, create a new chart listing what *you* can be trusted for and what you can't. Think of it this way: As your partner's friend, what would you want him or her to know about you in the area of trust? The headings would now be Why I Can Be Trusted and Why I Can't Be Trusted.

Talk About Trust

After you and your partner each fill out your inventories, set aside a block of time to share your thoughts and observations. Bearing in mind the principles of good communication, discuss your feelings about the issue of trust. These are some of the areas you might want to explore:

- Do your assessments of what you can trust and what you can't trust match the other person's self-assessments? If there are discrepancies, discuss the reasons for them.
- Of all the ways in which one of you can't be completely trusted, which can the other one live with and which would be impossible to live with?
- Which untrustworthy qualities can be changed and which are permanent parts of your personalities?
- What would it take to earn each other's trust?
- What is each of you willing to do to earn the other's trust?
- Where you are *not* willing to make the effort, is it because you don't think you can change, or because you don't think you should *have* to change?

- In which areas should the person who does not trust learn to be more trusting?

If you approach your heart-to-heart talk with love and kindness, you will find that the trust between you has already been magically strengthened. You have learned that it is safe to entrust each other with intimate feelings and candid thoughts.

Once you reach an understanding about the work that each of you needs to do, it is extremely important to follow through. You'll each be keeping an eye peeled to see if your partner is being diligent or whether they're slacking off—in short, whether they can be trusted. Make sure the effort is not one-sided. Trust builds on trust, and it can grow rapidly. But distrust builds on distrust as well, and the decline can be precipitous. The place to be vigilant is in monitoring your *own* behavior, not your partner's.

> **USABLE INSIGHT**
>
> *Being trustworthy is not about having the right thoughts and doing the right things. It's about having the* wrong *thoughts and doing the right things.*

The Four H's and the Four R's

The stupid neither forgive nor forget; the naïve forgive and forget; the wise forgive but do not forget.

—THOMAS SZASZ

If there has been a serious breach of faith, do not expect immediate forgiveness and restoration of trust. After a big hurt there is usually a big chill. It takes time for the pain to sink in and for the violation to be seen in the clear light of day. Only then can the healing begin.

The first step in the recovery of trust is for both parties to understand that the injured one will probably go through four emotional stages. I call them the four H's: hurt, hate, hesitation and holding on:

1. HURT. It is deeply painful to have your trust betrayed by a loved one. The wound can be deep and the emotional bleeding can be hard to stop. Compounding the pain is the terrifying realization that you *can* be that badly hurt. The bubble of safety that you thought the relationship provided has burst. The damage may prove to be fixable, but at the time of the hurt you feel as shattered as Humpty Dumpty.

2. HATE. As many sharp observers of human nature have noted, love contains the seeds of hate. We place our deepest needs and most sacred values in the hands of those we love. If they betray our trust, the hatred we feel is as strong as the love had been. You may be mad as hell when someone you don't care about harms you in some way. But when your spouse or lover betrays your trust, there is an extra measure of revulsion and loathing because they stole your sense of safety: *How could you do this to me!* The hatred can be confusing to both partners because it does not necessarily obliterate the love. Affection and animosity can coexist, creating tremendous ambivalence in the hurt person and making the offender feel uncertain, awkward and even paranoid.

3. HESITATION. When you fall off a bicycle, you hesitate before you get back on. When you dive into shallow water and bang your head, you test the depth very carefully before diving again. And when you've been betrayed or severely disappointed, it's only natural to withdraw your trust and lock it away until you feel safe enough to bring it out again.

4. HOLDING ON. If the hurt is really bad and the hatred is strong, you may be unable to let go of your grudge. There is a certain comfort in staying mad; it gives victims a sense of power over the victimizers. It's a form of revenge, a way of punishing those who hurt you. It is also a form of self-defense: *As long as I hold this angry posture, I can't be hurt again.* It is an illusory defense, however, and if it goes on for too long it can add fuel to a crisis that's already aflame. Nevertheless, by making a vulnerable person feel safer, it can be a necessary phase in healing.

If your trust in your partner has been shattered, expect that you will experience all four H's in one form or another. If you're the one who broke the trust, understand that your partner is going through these stages. Don't expect him or her to get over it quickly. "I'm sorry" will not be enough. You can get away with a simple apology for minor offenses, but not the big trust-busting hurts. For those, you have to *show* you're sorry.

> **USABLE INSIGHT**
>
> *Being in love means always having to show you're sorry.*

If you've damaged your partner's trust and want to earn it back, you have work to do. To counter the four H's, you need to perform the four R's: remorse, restitution, rehabilitation and requesting forgiveness.

1. REMORSE. You have to let your partner know that you understand the pain you've caused and that it gives *you* pain to have made it happen. This is not the time for explanations, and certainly not excuses. It's a time to acknowledge that you were wrong and that the damage you inflicted matters to you. Remember Tom, the workaholic father whose negligence caused his son to be mauled by a dog? His remorse was obvious. Anyone who knew him could tell he was in agony over what had happened. He would break down and cry at the sight of his son's wounds and repeat over and over again, "What kind of a father can't protect his child from danger?" It's not always that obvious, though. You may have to go out of your way to show your partner that you feel genuine remorse. And you may have to do so not once, not twice, but many times because he or she may not believe you. This can be exasperating, but if you lose patience—*How many times do I have to say "I'm sorry" for God's sake?*—you will only reinforce their suspicion that you don't understand and you don't really care.

2. RESTITUTION. The dictionary defines restitution as "the act of making good or compensating for loss, damage or injury." It implies something tangible. Restitution can take many forms depending on the nature of the injury and the extent of the damage. If you cause a business associate to lose money, a check for the appropriate amount will do nicely. Where lovers and spouses are concerned, the formula is seldom that neat. For minor injuries, a token gift or a bouquet of flowers might suffice. For bigger hurts, something more is required. Don't just think diamond necklaces or the new camera he covets. Expensive presents might work in some instances, but they can also backfire by being seen as a crude attempt to buy back trust. More imaginative gestures may be needed, and those can cost as much in emotion as a diamond does in dollars.

For example, Megan, who got drunk and embarrassed her husband by having a temper tantrum in public, wrote a note of apology to everyone who witnessed the spectacle. Scott, who forgot to show up at the restaurant for dinner with his fiancé's visiting relatives, made up for it by flying to their hometown just to meet them. As for Tom, finding a satisfactory way to make restitution for his son's permanent injuries was not easy. He made several heartfelt gestures, which helped, but the form of restitution that worked best is one I've recommended in many cases of serious betrayals, especially infidelity. He agreed to let Janice vent her anger at him without answering back or defending himself—not just once, but whenever she needed to let loose. It was not easy for a proud guy like Tom to listen to the same venomous comments over and over again, but he bowed his head and endured the barrage until Janice had spent her rage. Sometimes, the only satisfactory restitution is to let the victim hurt you back by expelling all the feelings that your action gave rise to.

3. **REHABILITATION.** Just as "I'm sorry" is not enough, neither is "I'll never do it again." In order to trust you, your partner has to know that you'll walk the walk, not just talk the talk. You need to demonstrate that you've learned your lesson and are capable of behaving differently should the same situation arise. Not just until the storm blows over, but forever. Moreover, your partner needs to see that you actually prefer the new way of behaving and are not just doing it to appease or to feel less guilty. Otherwise he or she will not feel safe enough to let you back in. This can take time.

Megan had to show that she could attend social events without becoming an obnoxious drunk. Only then did her husband feel safe to be with her where liquor was present. Scott had to find ways to show that he cared about his girlfriend's family and could be counted on to honor his commitments. In both cases, the hurtful behavior had been part of a pattern, not a one-time occurrence; rehabilitation was necessary to show that the pattern had truly changed.

Tom's rehab had several components. He agreed to Janice's demand that he have private psychotherapy in addition to couples counseling. He had to leave his cell phone home whenever he was with her or their child. And he had to demonstrate that he was not totally work-obsessed. To free up time to spend with his family, he took on a young, aggressive partner to take over some of the 24-7 aspects of his business. It was a long time before Janice allowed Tom to be alone with their son outside their home. On the first occasion, she was a nervous wreck until she saw them drive safely into the garage. Once the ice had been broken and Tom had passed the test, the time was right for step four.

4. REQUESTING FORGIVENESS. Tom had frequently hinted that he wanted to be forgiven. But he could never bring himself to ask for it directly, and Janice never offered it. In fact, she thought she might never be able to. But the healing power of time coupled with Tom's track record with the first three R's had brought her to the brink of forgiveness. The evening after his first outing with his son, Tom said to Janice, "I know I can never make up for what I did. I know how much pain I've caused you and the damage I've done to our son. I'll live with regret for the rest of my life. But it's been over a year now, and

I think I've shown that I can be trusted. Janice, I need you to forgive me."

Janice could not do it, not yet. Fortunately, Tom had discussed that possibility with me in advance. He kept his cool and said, "I was hoping that wouldn't be your reaction, but it doesn't change what I said. I'm sorry, and I always will be, and someday I hope to have your forgiveness." Two days later, Janice came to him and said, "I forgive you." She needed it to come from her side, without feeling pressured.

If Tom had never asked, he might have waited forever for Janice to offer forgiveness. Once he did ask, and she refused, if he had lost patience and said something like, "You're just not capable of forgiveness," or, "What do I have to do, beg? Forget it!" it would have been another setback for their already shaky marriage. He had to first demonstrate that he was worthy of being forgiven, then make the request graciously and wait for Janice to be ready. From her side, Janice had to feel absolutely certain that it was safe to give up her grudge.

The final step for her was to make her feelings crystal clear. "I can forgive you now," she told Tom, "but you have to understand that if you ever cause harm to our child again, I won't be able to forgive. This is not an ultimatum. I'm simply telling you that it's hard to trust you now, and the next time it will be impossible. Do you understand?" When Tom said that he not only understood but would feel the same way if he were in her position, she was finally able to trust him.

When Enough Is Not Enough

It is impossible to go through life without trust: that
is to be imprisoned in the worst cell of all, oneself.

—GRAHAM GREENE

In most cases, if you have a good track record with the first three
R's—remorse, restitution and rehabilitation—you will have earned
the right to request forgiveness and trust. That does not mean you
will get it. The willingness to trust again depends upon a mysterious combination of upbringing, experience, values and personality traits that vary from one individual to the next.

Felicia was shopping for a wedding dress when she found out
that her fiancé had slept with his ex-girlfriend the previous weekend. Devastated, she called off the wedding and told Charles she
never wanted to see him again. He called her repeatedly to apologize and beg for her forgiveness, but she would not take his calls.
He had bouquets of flowers delivered in waves. He sent long let-
ters that gushed with adoration for Felicia and disgust with himself. He swore that except for that one moment of weakness he
had been faithful for the three years they were together. He got
cold feet, he said, and succumbed to a foolish urge to assert his
independence. In message after message, he declared his love and
vowed he would never hurt her again.

Felicia stuck to her guns. But she missed him. She wanted to
believe him and take him back, but she was scared.

Finally, Charles convinced her to see him. She had never seen
this thick-skinned real estate broker cry before. His remorse was
clearly sincere. They started dating again, with Felicia keeping a

close check on her heart and a watchful eye on Charles. With an instinctive understanding of the need for restitution, Charles showered her with gifts and took her out on the kind of dates she liked instead of imposing his taste on her, as he had in the past. When Felicia asked him to go to couples counseling, he swallowed his pride and tagged along. This alone scored him restitution points. Then, at my urging, he held his tongue and let Felicia uncork all the malice she felt toward him for what he'd done.

Charles's rehabilitation proceeded at a fast pace. Felicia used to tolerate his occasional displays of macho, chalking it up to his working-class background. Now she saw that behavior as symptomatic of an attitude that sanctioned disrespect for women. Charles gave it up. He cut out the bar hopping with his old buddies, canceled his subscription to *Penthouse,* tried to open up emotionally in therapy and generally treated Felicia with a newfound sensitivity. Clearly, a corner had been turned.

Soon, Charles proposed again. Felicia said no.

He begged for her forgiveness. She wouldn't grant it.

Felicia simply could not bring herself to trust him. She tried. She struggled mightily to overcome her resistance. A religious woman, she prayed for the strength to be merciful and forgiving. Desperate, she asked me to teach her how to trust. I was obliged to tell her that there was no magic formula. We worked at it, but succeeded only in gaining clarity on the bitter truth: She just could not trust Charles, and there was nothing more he could do to prove himself worthy.

If you have fulfilled the four R's with sincerity and consistency for at least six months, the burden should shift to the other person. If he or she still can't forgive or trust, it is not because you are unforgivable and untrustworthy. You've done as much as you can; it is up to them to let go of their resentment and take the leap of faith. If they can't, it is not that they're bad, defective, pitiless or hard-hearted. That's what Felicia had to understand about herself—and you do too, if you're having trouble finding it in your heart to trust again after being wounded.

You have a right to keep your guard up if that's what you need to feel safe. You also have a right to stand by your moral principles. Just be aware that playing defense all the time can prevent you from scoring goals, and holding rigidly to one principle can mean violating another. In Felicia's case, Charles's infidelity was so offensive to her values that she could not get over it. Couple that with a childhood in which she saw her mother suffer with a philandering husband, and trusting Charles again was a lost cause.

For his part, Charles came to see that he faced an uphill battle he might never win. Satisfied that he had done everything he could to earn Felicia's trust, he had at least won back his self-respect. He realized that he had done a bad thing, but he was not a bad person. Just as Felicia had the right to protect herself by withholding her trust, he had the right to be with someone who trusted him. The breakup was sad, but inevitable. I'm confident that they had done all they could to save what could not be saved.

> **USABLE INSIGHT**
>
> *When you've earned forgiveness and your partner still won't forgive you, you're not unforgivable, they're unforgiving.*

They emerged from their efforts better equipped to create the kind of love they wanted in the future.

Resisting Resistance

The only way to make a man trustworthy
is to trust him.

—HENRY LEWIS STIMSON

It is very easy to find reasons not to trust someone who's hurt you. The urge to cling to hatred like a life raft is a mighty temptation. That's why it's crucial to examine your resistance to forgiving. Holding a grudge gives you the alert feeling of vigilance, as if you have sentries on duty at all times watching out for another attack. It's also a terrific form of revenge. We punish those who hurt us by refusing to forgive and letting them know we don't trust them.

It is important to remember that forgiveness does more for the forgiver than the forgiven. Holding in all that anger will eat you up alive; it can turn into physical illness and almost surely lead to emotional stagnation and depression. As Archbishop Desmond Tutu said when he and Nelson Mandela established South Africa's Truth and Reconciliation Commission, "Without forgiveness, resentment builds in us, a resentment which turns into hostility and anger. Hatred eats away at our well-being."

Remember Janice, the mother of the boy who was disfigured by a dog? A turning point in her willingness to forgive her husband came when she realized that if she continued to hold her grudge, it would destroy her and her family, not just Tom.

Forgiveness does not mean that you exonerate the guilty person or absolve him of responsibility for what occurred. As in a court of law, you can hold the perpetrator accountable and still show mercy in your sentencing. You can opt for rehabilitation instead of life in prison.

It's vital to understand that you can forgive and still feel safe—as long as you take effective steps to guard against a repeat of the incident that destroyed your trust in the first place. Nor do you have to forget what happened or pretend that it never did. "Forgive and forget" is a nice saying, but it's not very practical. If we had to forget in order to forgive, we would all be slaves to our anger. You can clasp the memory of your pain to your bosom like a sacred amulet

> **USABLE INSIGHT**
>
> *It is better to have trusted and been hurt than never to have trusted at all.*

and cling to it until you no longer need to remember—and still you can forgive.

If you find yourself unable to trust again, examine the reasons for your resistance:

- Are you holding your forgiveness as a bargaining chip to get something you want?
- Are you using anger as a weapon to gain revenge on the person who hurt you?
- Are you afraid that if you get hurt again the pain would be so overwhelming it might destroy you?
- Do you fear that forgiveness would let the other person off the hook and embolden him or her to hurt you again?
- Do you think that trusting would brand you a wimp, a fool or a pathetic doormat?

- Does withholding your trust give you a sense of power or control over the other person?
- Do you enjoy feeling like a victim?
- Does holding a grudge shield you from having to see weaknesses and flaws in yourself that you can't forgive?
- Would you rather be right than happy?

Your motives for clinging to mistrust may not be worth the price of encasing your heart in armor. If you want a love that will stand the test of time, you need a strong pillar of trust. You owe it to yourself to give it your best shot.

Build Trust by Entrusting

The highest compact we can make with our fellow is,
"Let there be truth between us two forevermore."
—RALPH WALDO EMERSON

Trust is the single most important sign that a derailed relationship is back on track. But it is important not to rest on your laurels and settle for bringing the trust level back to where it was before. Instead, try to deepen it by building on the goodwill you have just created. If you succeed, you will find that your trust will be strong enough to withstand just about any crisis that comes along.

The best way to deepen your trust is to share the unsharable. Talk to each other about things that frighten you, things you're ashamed of, things that cause you pain, things that could be used against you by someone who can't be trusted. Frequently, what interferes with the full blossoming of trust is when one or both partners wants to reveal something and is afraid to open up. The truth that can't be spoken sits between them like a Cyclone fence, allowing them to see and touch one another but not completely embrace.

Getting difficult truths out into the light of day is not necessarily easy. There is always the possibility that the other person will be frightened, or disgusted, or clueless, or uncaring. The risk is well worth taking. In my experience, once a basic level of trust has been established, couples invariably find that opening up further brings them closer than they ever dreamed possible.

Donna and Ben had been married for just over a year when they went to a party at the home of one of Ben's old college buddies. Not normally drug users, they felt a bit adventurous that evening, so when marijuana was passed around they took a few puffs. They learned too late that it was laced with angel dust. Meanwhile, in the throes of an unfamiliar high, Donna's tongue loosened up. When Ben's old pals started teasing him, she joined right in. Ben did not find her jibes amusing. Seething, he whispered, "Would you stop please." She kept on blabbing. He squeezed her arm to get her attention. "I said, shut up," he hissed.

"Screw you, I'm only kidding," said Donna. She tried to yank her arm free. Ben squeezed so tight she could feel the pressure on her bone. "I told you to shut the hell up." Writhing in pain, Donna cursed at him. He shoved her so hard that she crashed into an end table, knocking beer bottles to the floor and bruising her face.

Ben had crossed a line he never thought he'd even get near. To him, the drugs were no excuse. He hated himself for hurting his wife. But what he damaged more than her arm was her trust. As a social worker, Donna had seen the ravages of domestic violence all too often. She had wondered at times if Ben were capable of lashing out. He was high strung, after all, and sometimes needed to burn off the stress of his sales job by whacking a racquetball or pounding a punching bag. Now she was so wary that their home became as tense as a demilitarized zone.

Ben worked his way through the stages of remorse, restitution and rehabilitation. It was only when Donna had pushed his buttons on a number of occasions and seen that he could control his anger that she opened up to trusting him again. In counseling one day, he asked for her forgiveness. "I know there is no way I can convince you with words that what happened will never happen again," he said. "But I love you way too much to ever hurt you. Will you forgive me?"

She did. Now their trust was restored to its pre-fight status. What followed was one of the most remarkable instances of taking it to another level that I've ever seen. In the atmosphere of safety that had been established, Donna revealed for the first time why the incident had been so traumatic. When she was fourteen, her older brother got hooked on methamphetamine and tried to rape her. Her parents, fooled by their son's affable nature, told her she was imagining things. As for the bruises, they said she should stop making her brother mad. Then he *did* rape her. Donna was too ashamed to report it. Her brother was soon arrested on drug charges and Donna was safe from further assaults. She vowed that no man would ever mistreat her. But ever since, she felt like damaged goods.

As Donna wept in her husband's arms, it was clear to me that she had done more than explain why it had been so hard to trust Ben. By making herself vulnerable, she was testing him further. Could he be trusted to hear her truth and not judge her or reject her? He came through with flying colors.

When they arrived for their next session, I could see that something was on Ben's mind. I encouraged him to speak up. He said that Donna's revelation about her past had started him thinking about his own childhood. His father's idea of discipline was to smack him around, he told us, and his idea of making a man of his son was to provoke him into fights. His dad would antagonize him with demeaning insults, and when Ben got mad he'd say, "Come on, be a man, hit me." If Ben hesitated, his father would call him chickenshit and sissy. When Ben finally lashed out, his father would cuff him around and knock him to the ground. When Ben gave up, he'd call him a quitter. If he cried, he'd sneer contemptuously and say, "Go play with the other girls."

As he told this heartbreaking story, Ben lay down on his side with his head in Donna's lap. At one point, he closed his eyes and curled into a fetal position. When he finished speaking, he started flinching and wincing. Stunned, Donna looked at me as if to say, "What's going on? What should I do?" I motioned to her to hold him. She held him and stroked his head reassuringly. Gradually, his twitching ceased and he started to weep, moaning softly as he clung to his wife.

When the time was right, I asked Ben what had happened. "I don't know," he said, "I just wanted to curl up like a baby." I asked him why he'd been flinching and wincing. "When my father hurt me," he recalled, "I'd run to my mother and cry on her lap. One day my father saw me and put a stop to it. The next time I tried to do it, my mother smacked me and shoved me aside and said, 'Act like a man.' That's why I was flinching. I expected Donna to hit me or push me away.

"I live with this all the time," he continued. "I have to fight this voice inside my head that says a man's not supposed to show weakness. That's why I lost it that time, when Donna was putting me down. The voice said, 'Act like a man.' Only afterward I hated myself. I felt like my father."

He looked at Donna, expecting her to be ashamed of him. Instead, she said she loved him for having the guts to reveal such a painful truth. "I'll tell you something else," said Ben. "I've always had a fantasy about how I want to die. I see myself at the moment of my death, with my head in my wife's lap, and I'm just crying and crying, and I cry myself to sleep and never wake up." By then, Donna and I were crying too. "I have so much pain inside of me," said Ben, "and I've never been able to tell anyone because men don't do that. I thought if the last thing I did on earth was cry in my wife's arms, I would die in peace because I wouldn't have to worry that she'd walk out on me."

> **USABLE INSIGHT**
>
> *Baring your neck is the quickest way to tell if you can trust someone with your heart.*

Ben and Donna had entrusted one another to look into their

shadows, and the quality of love that burst through the darkness was majestic. I told them I would miss seeing them, but there was no need to continue in therapy.

You build trust by entrusting. When you learn that you can bare your necks to each other without getting your heads chopped off, you will feel truly free to love, maybe for the first time.

7

Empathy

Walking a Mile in Your Partner's Shoes

> *Love is what is left over in a relationship after all the selfishness is taken out.*
>
> —NICK RICHARDSON

How many of the following statements apply to how you think or feel about empathy in your relationship?

	Hardly Ever 0	Sometimes 1	Almost Always 2
1. I feel my partner understands me.	____	____	____
2. My partner feels understood by me.	____	____	____
3. I try to think of what's important to my partner.	____	____	____
4. My partner tries to think of what's important to me.	____	____	____
5. When we're in conflict, I consider my partner's point of view as much as or more than my own.	____	____	____
6. When we're in conflict, my partner considers my point of view as much as or more than his/her own.	____	____	____
7. I know how I frustrate, frighten, disappoint and anger my partner.	____	____	____
8. My partner knows how he/she frustrates, frightens, disappoints and angers me.	____	____	____
9. I know my partner's sensitivities and take them into account during confrontations.	____	____	____
10. My partner knows my sensitivities and takes them into account during confrontations.	____	____	____
TOTAL:	____	____	____

SCORING:

0–6   You presume to know each other much better than you actually do.

7–13   With some effort, you have the skill, if not the desire, to understand each other.

14–20   You've walked miles in your partner's shoes.

If any of the six elements of CREATE can be called the most important, it is empathy. Empathy is not just an essential ingredient for a healthy and enduring relationship, it is a practical tool for achieving it. If I had to name one single practice that can be used to solve any relationship problem, the answer would be to ask yourself, "What is it like for my partner right now?" "It" equals the problem as viewed or felt by them. "Right now" signals you to pause and stop digging in your heels.

Empathy involves temporarily relinquishing your own point of view to tune in to someone else's. It means identifying with their situation, feelings, and motives to gain a level of insightful awareness greater than ordinary understanding. It is one thing, for instance, to understand that you can be difficult to your partner. Being empathic would be feeling *how* your partner experiences you as difficult.

Empathy is not an attitude, it is a way of perceiving. Experiencing something the way someone else experiences it is a tuning-in process, not an analytic process. It is an attempt to answer the question "What is it like for them?" *not* "Why are they like this?" or "What makes them do that?" Unlike compassion, sympathy or pity, empathy is essentially a neutral act. It is value free and judgment free. While it is most often motivated by love, the act of empathy itself is as dispassionate as looking through a pair of binoculars. However, the *result* is seldom neutral. Empathy enhances emotional involvement, creating in most cases not only understanding but deeper love and greater compassion.

Like running or singing, empathy is an ability all human

beings have, although it comes more easily to some than to others. But anyone with motivation can develop the skill and improve their ability to apply it.

Empathy Counters Antipathy

If you do not understand a man you cannot crush him. And if you do understand him, very probably you will not.

—G. K. CHESTERTON

Early in my career it became evident to me that many couples who come for counseling bring with them a truckload of animosity. Each partner is geared up to blame and criticize the other, and to defend him- or herself against the other's blame and criticism. If I allowed each of them to vent their hostility, it would take a long time, perhaps several sessions, before they could relate to one another in a constructive way. That realization led me to develop what I call Empathogenic Therapy. I had clients do what you've been doing in previous chapters: answer questions from the point of view of the other person. Instantly, the sessions were transformed from debate to dialogue, from competition and antagonism to cooperation and goodwill.

When Miriam and Ralph entered my office, for example, it was clear within seconds that coming to see me was her idea and he had been dragged along reluctantly. She marched in with a purposeful air, shook my hand firmly and grabbed the best seat in the room. She was ready to get down to business. Ralph hung back with a cautious, wary demeanor. As he tentatively grasped my hand, he looked me over carefully, then glanced around like a soldier scoping out potential danger.

I asked some preliminary questions to break the ice and see how the couple interacted. Ralph answered curtly, revealing as little as possible. Miriam couldn't wait to tell me what she thought was wrong with their relationship—mainly Ralph. Instead of letting her unload indefinitely, I asked, "What would Ralph say if I were to ask him why he thinks that being here is a waste of time?" Taken aback, she asked me what I meant by the question. I rephrased it: "If I were to ask Ralph why he is skeptical that coming here will do any good, what would he say?"

"Well," said Miriam after contemplating a moment, "he'd probably say that the last time we did this he felt like the therapist and I were ganging up on him. He'd say we were trying to turn him into something he's not." This was enough to get Ralph to perk up; suddenly, his expression shifted from guarded to intrigued.

"Anything else?" I asked Miriam.

She shuffled nervously. "Well, maybe he'd say that I wanted him to come here so I can dump on him and accuse him of stuff where he can't . . . well, yell at me and walk away, like he does at home."

Now Ralph was more than intrigued. The fact that his wife actually knew how he felt softened him. I could tell he was thinking, "Maybe this isn't a waste of time after all." Miriam had softened too. Having been forced to put herself in her husband's shoes, she loosened her grip on her hostility.

Rather than break the momentum to see what Ralph had to say about Miriam's comments, I used the empathogenic process on him. I had noticed that when Miriam mentioned Ralph's tendency to scream at her she chose her words very carefully, as if afraid to say the wrong thing. I said to Ralph, "If I were to ask Miriam what frightens her the most about you, what would she say?"

Clearly, being empathic did not come easily to him, but he could not very well refuse to give it a shot once Miriam had done it. "Well, you know, I have kind of a short fuse," he said. "When I get mad, I kind of go over the top and I shout a lot. I guess that can be pretty scary."

"Is that all?" I asked. "Would she say anything else scares her?"

He gave it serious thought. "Well, maybe she'd say it scares her when I break my promises, like saying I'm going to do something and not doing it. She probably thinks it's scary to rely on someone you can't always count on."

Now the power of empathy had worked its magic. Not only had it exposed meaningful issues that might have taken several sessions to turn up, but Ralph's defensiveness and Miriam's animosity had all but disappeared. Miriam was deeply moved to find that Ralph understood something she thought he could never grasp—and that he cared enough to pay attention to her feelings.

Ralph tried to hide it, but he was clearly embarrassed about revealing a personal weakness. Miriam looked as though she wanted to comfort him, whereas a few minutes earlier she seemed ready to smack him. She even defended him. "Sure he makes me crazy when he breaks a promise," she said, "but when the chips are down, he'll be there for me."

Such is the peacemaking power of empathy. It almost always makes the recipient want to return the favor.

Empathy Heals Deep Wounds

*The capacity to give one's attention to a sufferer is a
very rare and difficult thing; it is almost a miracle;
it is a miracle.*

—SIMONE WEIL

I have used Empathogenic Therapy hundreds of times, and it
rarely fails to bring two antagonists closer together. It works just
as well with long-held anger over major betrayals as it does with
accumulated resentment over minor disappointments, as with
Miriam and Ralph. Take Stuart and Sally, a husband and wife in
their mid-fifties who ran a popular night spot in Los Angeles.
Working long hard hours together while raising a pair of kids
had not been a problem for the first thirteen years of their marriage, but the last three had been such a nightmare they were
thinking of either selling the business or getting a divorce.

It was obvious that something had happened three years earlier to drastically alter the landscape of their marriage. Rather
than ask outright, I chose to introduce the element of empathy.
Turning to Stuart, I said, "If I were to ask Sally to name the most
upsetting thing you've ever done—something that if you ever
did again, it would all be over—what would she say?"

This was not easy for him. He cleared his throat, thought for
a moment, then cleared his throat again. "The *most* upsetting
thing?" he asked. I nodded. In fits and starts, he proceeded to
confess something he'd never told a soul except Sally. Three years
ago, when Sally was fighting breast cancer, he'd had an affair. It
was agony for him to tell me this, but there was no other possi-

ble answer to my question and he knew that Sally would not respect him if he dodged it in the context of counseling. So he stammered out the truth. Then came something so moving I get chills whenever I think of it. "What would Sally say about it?" I asked him.

"She'd say it was the most horrible thing anyone had ever done to her," said Stuart. "She'd say the person who was supposed to be by her side in sickness and in health betrayed her." He started crying. "She'd say I turned my back on her when she needed me the most." Now he was sobbing so hard he could barely make himself heard, but he had to continue. Speaking directly to his wife, he said, "I'm sorry, I'm so so sorry. I know how devastating it was for you. It must have been more painful than the cancer and the chemo. You probably wanted to kill me. You probably thought of taking the kids and never seeing me again. I wouldn't have blamed you. I don't know where you found the strength to even look me in the eye again. I'm just grateful that you didn't leave me." The sobs were now too overwhelming for him to speak. Like most men, Stuart wanted to be a hero to the woman he loved. When, instead, he acted like a scoundrel, he felt contemptible.

> **USABLE INSIGHT**
>
> *When what your partner hears shows that you care, it reduces their fear that you don't.*

Sally was quietly weeping, her face a mixed portrait of relief and astonishment. Stuart had said he was sorry before, but always in a tone that implied, "Can't we just move on?" Sally was never sure that he understood just how much pain his betrayal had inflicted. Now she saw what she needed to see.

Just as resentment triggers resentment, understanding triggers understanding and empathy triggers empathy. For the first time, Sally could feel the torturous guilt and the ceaseless pain that Stuart had felt ever since his brief affair. She had never seen him cry before. In the flow of tenderness that followed, the couple was able to begin the work of repairing the other five pillars, each of which had been shattered by Stuart's betrayal. It took some time, but without that empathic breakthrough they might never have been able to trust, respect, accept or enjoy each other, or fully embrace as lovers ever again.

The Roots of Empathy

Shallow understanding from people of good will is
more frustrating than absolute misunderstanding
from people of ill will.

—MARTIN LUTHER KING JR.

It is rare for people to spontaneously ask about someone, "What is it like to be her right now? What is he feeling? What thoughts are going through her mind?" It is not a natural way of thinking, with one beautiful exception: parents instinctively make the effort to know what their children feel and think. If we could do it that naturally with friends, lovers and colleagues, the world would be a better place.

For most human beings most of the time, empathy goes

against our animal instincts, which drive us to seek pleasure and avoid pain. We are basically self-centered creatures. When we feel hurt, confused or upset by others, rather than try to understand what it's like to be them, we focus on our own feelings and our personal needs. When we're engulfed by anger, pain and other difficult emotions, we turn our energy toward self-protection (however we define it at the time). But there is another aspect to human existence: the urge to rise above our physical and emotional reflexes and give expression to our higher nature.

One way we do that is by cultivating the capacity for empathy. We can train ourselves to transport our awareness into the mind and heart of another human being. Ironically, developing that seemingly selfless skill might be the best thing you'll ever do for *yourself*. The rewards are greater than you can imagine, especially in an intimate relationship. Offsetting the natural tendency to self-centeredness, empathy gives rise to generosity, consideration, compassion and tenderness—and inspires the other person to give back all of the above.

Those for whom empathy comes easily usually learned the skill from childhood role models. To see how that might happen, imagine you're six years old. At school one day you wet your pants. The humiliation is so overwhelming you run to the bathroom and cry your eyes out. After school, the other children make fun of you, taunting you so mercilessly you run away, thinking you never want to go back to school again. Finally, you make it to the shelter of your home and tell your parents what happened. Now, imagine these possible reactions:

1. "I told you to go to the bathroom before you leave for school. Go to your room and change your clothes, now!"
2. "For God's sake, I just did a wash, now I have to do another one. Just go change and get ready for dinner."
3. "Don't you worry, honey, I'm going to call your teacher. We'll make sure those awful kids don't make fun of you again."

In the first scenario, you are blamed. In the second, you are made to feel like a burden. In the third, you are taken off the hook and others are blamed. None of those reactions addresses the awful shame and pain you feel inside. If any of those styles were the norm in your household, you probably internalized that form of behavior. You may blame your love partners when things go wrong, or make them feel like a burden, or bail them out by making excuses for them and shifting the blame to outsiders. You probably did not learn to empathize.

Now consider this scenario:

Your parent immediately sees that something is wrong, drops everything and looks you in the eye: "What happened, honey?" You're too embarrassed to talk about it, but your parent holds you and whispers reassuringly, "It's okay, you can tell me." You feel their firm resolve to get to the bottom of what happened and know what you are feeling. "Tell me more . . . Then what happened? . . . Oh, it must have felt terrible . . . How awful was it?"

You can see how parents like that would not only make you feel safe and taken care of, but would instill in you the habit of trying to know what someone else is going through.

Having empathic role models is the best training ground for

empathy. That is one of the main reasons why psychotherapists in training are urged to have therapists themselves, and why the best coaches and mentors in all fields of life are those who were well coached themselves. If your parents did not model empathy, you may have been fortunate enough to learn the skill later in life, from another relative perhaps, or a teacher, a neighbor, a pastor or the parent of a friend—someone who was empathic toward you and made a difference in your life. In my case, it was a mentor in medical school.

He was the dean of students, William McNary, a man of rare character and integrity. I was having a difficult time of it. Depressed, confused and unsure if I had what it took to be a doctor, I was on the verge of either dropping out or being kicked out. Dr. McNary asked to see me. I expected him to express disappointment, perhaps even reprimand me. What I got instead was compassion, acceptance and empathy. "Mark, you're messed up right now," he said, "but I think you can get un-messed up, and if you do, you would make a fine doctor, one this school would be proud to have trained."

That vote of confidence alone would have been precious, but it would not have been enough. "And even if you *don't* get your act together," added Dr. McNary, "you are the kind of person I would be proud to know, because you are kind."

He was so empathic that he knew exactly what I felt at that moment: worthless. And he knew what I needed: to have someone of his stature tell me that I did, in fact, have value. It changed my life. Because of Dr. McNary I stayed in medical school, switching my specialty to psychiatry and becoming a psychotherapist. Now, when I work with couples or individuals, his memory motivates me to do for them what he did for me: put myself in their shoes to see what they're feeling and what they need, and most of all to never give up on them.

You can do the same. Think of the people in your past to whom you are grateful—those who made a difference in your life. Ask yourself, "What is it about them that I'm most grateful for?" You will probably realize that they cared enough to look at life through your eyes. Perhaps they acted unselfishly to help you in a time of need, or believed in you when you didn't believe in yourself. Remembering those people does three things: First, it can soften your heart when you might otherwise feel bitter or spiteful. Second, it can motivate you to be generous with your own empathy, knowing that they would be disappointed if you were to be petty or vengeful instead. Third, you can emulate their behavior.

What exactly did those people do to put themselves in your skin? How did they discern what was upsetting you? Chances are, one thing they did was to drop whatever they were doing and focus on you. That's usually the first step in being empathic: being willing to give your attention completely to the other person. Another quality they probably had was curiosity, asking questions to find out what made you tick. They also made you feel safe to speak your truth. And they probably took themselves out of the equation; they didn't ask what was in it for them, and they didn't manipulate you in a direction that would serve their interests. They may even have been willing to sacrifice something to help you do what was best for you.

Let those role models inspire you to cultivate and practice the skill of empathy. Why not honor their memory by being as empathic toward your mate as they were toward you?

Practice Makes Perfect

Practice and thought might gradually
forge many an art.

—VIRGIL

Empathy is not typically present at the very beginning of a relationship. It may appear to be, because you finish each other's sentences and anticipate some of each other's needs, but that powerful sense of commonality and connectedness is not the same as empathy. The ability to empathize naturally grows the more you're exposed to a person. It comes from observing how they respond to different situations—what they say, what they do and what emotions they express. But only if you're motivated will your understanding rise to the level of empathy. You have to care enough to observe the person carefully and consistently.

You also have to be unselfish enough to truly see through their eyes and not what you *want* to see or what will work to your advantage. There is a big difference between empathy and projection. Projection is knowing what *you* would feel if you were in someone else's place. When you project, the other person does not necessarily feel understood or cared for; they might, in fact, feel patronized, manipulated or judged instead.

A good way to develop the skill of empathizing with your partner is to prac-

> **USABLE INSIGHT**
>
> *Your partner won't care how much you know until he knows how much you care.*

tice in situations where you're not involved and where you have nothing at stake. If, for instance, your partner is having difficulty with a parent, observe them during a phone call with that person. Try to imagine what they're going through, what they're thinking and feeling, and what they really want to say: "I'll bet that no matter what she says, her mother will make her feel that she's wrong," "He must feel totally drained by his father's complaints." Be as specific as possible, and as soon as it's appropriate, test out your hypotheses on your partner—not by making it seem like some kind of game, but rather as part of a conversation in which you are trying to gain a deeper understanding.

Finding the Right Words

Even if you're skilled at using empathy, it can be hard to get a solid grasp on what your partner is experiencing at any given moment. The following sentence fragments may help you penetrate the mystery. Complete the ones that apply to the present situation, *as if you were your partner.*

I have trouble forgiving because _____.

I feel hurt when _____.

What disappoints me most is _____.

What frightens me most is _____.

What really makes me mad is _____.

What I feel underneath my anger is _____.

What it makes me want to do is _____.

I'm having trouble deciding _____.

What confuses me is _____.

At times, you may have a sense of what your partner is feeling but not be able to find the right words. Consulting this list of negative moods and emotions will help:

abandoned	afraid	alone
ambivalent	angry	annoyed
anxious	betrayed	bitter
bored	burdened	cheated
combative	confused	defeated
diminished	disappointed	distraught
disturbed	empty	envious
exposed	exasperated	flustered
foolish	forgotten	frantic
frustrated	furious	grief
guilt	hateful	helpless
horrified	ignored	impatient
inadequate	insignificant	intimidated
isolated	jealous	lonely
mistreated	neglected	nervous
oppressed	outraged	panicked
persecuted	petrified	pressured
quarrelsome	rage	rejected
resentful	restless	sadness
self-hatred	shocked	sorrow
spiteful	stressed	tense
threatened	unappreciated	unloved
used	vengeful	worried

Use Analogies

*The end of understanding is not to prove and find
reasons, but to know and believe.*

—THOMAS CARLYLE

Contrary to popular opinion, men and women are actually from
the same planet. Both sexes share the same fundamental needs—
to be loved, cared for and understood; to gain material comfort
and spiritual sustenance. We also share the same set of emotions:
men and women alike get sad, angry, hurt, disappointed, scared
and embarrassed; we all feel guilt, shame, joy, enthusiasm and the
rest of the spectrum of feelings. We may seek to satisfy our needs
in different ways, and some needs may be more important to
women and others to men. The emotions of each sex may be
triggered by different kinds of experiences and get expressed in
different ways. But the fundamental things apply to all humans.
Drawing on this common ground can help you and your partner
find empathy for one another.

One excellent method is to use analogies to translate one
person's feelings into the emotional language of the other. When
you're struggling to understand what your partner is going
through, try to think of an analogous situation in your life and
recall how you felt under those circumstances. If no analogous
experience occurred in your past, think of a hypothetical situation and imagine how you *would* feel. Here's how it worked with
two clients of mine, Elaine and Sid, who came to see me shortly
after their first wedding anniversary.

A freelance graphic designer who worked at home most of the time, Elaine complained that she felt unimportant to Sid. "We used to do things together," she said. "Now I never see him. He spends all his free time messing around with his motorcycles or watching ball games with his friends." She said she felt like a mere appendage to her husband's life, whereas before they were married she felt like the centerpiece.

Sid objected to his wife's use of "never." "We still spend time together," he argued. "Why does she object to my hobbies and my friends? I work hard all day. I need to unwind." Soon, some of his deeper feelings came out: "She's getting to be a real pain. 'Where'd you go? Who were you with?' If she'd been this nosy and possessive before we were married, I never would have gone through with it."

It was a classic conflict. Inside both men and women live two conflicting needs: for intimacy and for independence. In general, though, intimacy tends to mean more to women and independence means more to men. Women react more strongly when they're ignored by their mates; men react more strongly when their mates threaten their autonomy. Elaine and Sid could not understand each other on this issue; they needed empathy to bridge the gap.

My first step was to get Sid to recall a situation in which he was ignored and made to feel unimportant. Like most men, he immediately thought of work. In one of his early jobs, he was the youngest staff member and his colleagues paid no attention to what he said at meetings. How did it make you feel? I asked. "Totally useless and unimportant," he replied.

Armed with that memory, it was not much of a leap for Sid to imagine how Elaine felt when he ignored her.

Now it was Elaine's turn to empathize. I asked her to remember a time when she felt that her sense of independence was threatened. What came to mind was her mother, an overbearing woman who made Elaine account for every minute of her time and told her exactly what to wear every day. How did that make her feel? "Invaded," she said. "Like I wasn't allowed to have a mind of my own." She looked at Sid. "Is that how I make you feel?"

"Not quite," he said, "but it's getting there."

Their smiles contained the seed of hope. The analogies enabled them to empathize enough to stop feeling like victims. Sid promised to spend more time with Elaine and include her more in his life; Elaine vowed to be less meddlesome and to respect Sid's need for some autonomy.

Analogies are powerful tools for achieving empathy because they help you penetrate to the commonality of human feeling. This lowers the voltage in volatile situations because you can't hate or resent someone while you are trying to understand what he or she is feeling.

When they came to see me, the needle on Nancy and Chris's voltage meter was crossing into the red zone. Nancy was furious because Chris had promised to be friendlier at social gatherings, but at a recent party he had reverted to his old behavior—aloof and uncommunicative. Chris was livid too. He resented that Nancy expected him to be Mr. Congeniality, and he hated the way she hovered over him at social events, like a classroom monitor on the lookout for bad behavior. "I'm a chemist," he said.

"I'm comfortable in lab clothes, dealing with test tubes and computer printouts. I'm not good at socializing, and she makes it worse by keeping me under constant surveillance."

Nancy was quick to say that she understood Chris's discomfort. But she did not see anything wrong with expecting her husband to be gracious about attending events that meant a lot to her. He could at least try, instead of acting as though he were above it all and would rather be someplace else.

I asked Chris if he and the other scientists in his department ever had to make presentations to colleagues or funding sources. Many times, he said. I asked how he would feel if someone on his team dressed sloppily and made inappropriate remarks at such an event. "Embarrassed," he said. "Maybe even betrayed." And if it happened repeatedly, reflecting badly on your reputation? He got the point: His sullen behavior was as much a threat to Elaine's friendships as an antisocial colleague would be to his professional relationships.

Now it was important for Elaine to feel what Chris felt, namely that he was being subjected to intense evaluation in an area he wasn't particularly good at. Did she ever feel that way? At tax time, she said. Every year, Chris and their accountant would scrutinize Elaine's figures and invariably find discrepancies. "I'm not that good with numbers," she said. "I'm an English teacher. I deal in words. But my schedule is more flexible than Chris's so I do the tax stuff." How does it feel when they sit down with the accountant? "I hate it," she said. "I get so nervous I can't remember where I filed things."

"That's how I feel when I go to a party and you watch over me like I'm about to humiliate you any second," Chris explained. Her scrutiny, he said, makes him more nervous than he would otherwise be, so he clams up.

Thanks to the use of analogies, the animosity they came in with had dissipated. Now Chris and Elaine were able to calmly discuss how to handle future social events.

Which analogies are most effective depends on the personalities and life experiences of the people involved. Generally speaking, you can't go wrong using relationship analogies for women and career analogies for men. Of course men care about relationships and women care about their careers, but there are still differences in the relative weight they give to those areas of life. Women tend to evaluate themselves according to how well they relate to others, while male self-esteem tends to revolve around work and money.

Analogies can be used in both directions. Just follow these steps.

If you feel you are not being understood:

1. Identify what you're feeling.
2. Think of a situation in your partner's life in which he or she might feel the same emotions.
3. Ask your partner to remember what it was like or to imagine what it would be like.

If you need to empathize with your partner:

1. Look at what's going on in his or her life.
2. Try to identify what your partner is feeling (ask directly if appropriate).
3. Remember or imagine a situation in your life that would evoke the same feelings.

USABLE INSIGHT

*Men and women
are not from
different planets.
They're both
from Earth.*

The following Gender Equivalency Guide will help you construct analogies for most situations in your life as a couple. Bear in mind that these are generalizations, not absolutes; in specific instances, they might not fit and might even be reversed. However, while they don't apply 100% in every case, they can still be useful vehicles for improving empathy.

Women	Men
Fear abandonment	Fear humiliation
See-hear-feel-know-do	See-hear-think-know-do
Rules obstruct relating to others	Rules promote relating to others
Ashamed of being emotional but lacking warmth	Ashamed of being angry but lacking courage
Sexual shyness	Emotional shyness
Threatened by male sneakiness	Threatened by female intrusiveness
Control is about safety	Control is about power
Generalize about things, detailed about people	Generalize about people, detailed about things
Play house	Play war
Guard the hearth	Guard the perimeter
Lifestyle section	Sports section
Communicate to connect and increase intimacy	Communicate to compete and establish pecking order

Know Your Partner

If we could read the secret history of our enemies, we should find in each man's life sorrow and suffering enough to disarm all hostility.

—HENRY WADSWORTH LONGFELLOW

Becky said she was thinking of leaving her husband. She was afraid of his explosive temper. Rod had never hit her, but his behavior was getting scarier and scarier. Several times in recent weeks he had lost his temper. With the veins on his face bulging, he would shake his fists violently in the air and scream so loud it awakened their kids. Becky was afraid he would lose it one day. "I'd die before I'd harm her," Rod insisted. "I just blow off steam sometimes because I can't stand her picking on me." He said he felt oppressed and harassed by Becky's constant criticism.

Neither one could comprehend why the other couldn't just stop doing what they did. It was only when we explored their family backgrounds that the roots of their behavior became clear. One of Becky's earliest memories was waking up one night hearing screams. She ran to her parents' bedroom and saw her father in a drunken rage, screaming at the top of his lungs and beating her mother with his fists. That trauma was repeated on a regular basis. Her mother, terrified that her husband would walk out and leave her destitute, cowered in his presence and meekly obeyed his commands. But sometimes she couldn't take it and her contempt would leak out in the form of demeaning remarks.

From those role models, Becky learned that men are dangerous and a woman's only defense is verbal warfare. Vowing not to repeat her mother's mistakes, she never put up with abuse or domination. But she imitated the wisecracks and relentless fault-finding, and when Rod lost his temper, visions of her mother getting battered rushed to her mind and she was terrified.

As for Rod, his mother was a caustic alcoholic and his father a hardworking factory hand whose way of coping with his wife's erratic and spiteful behavior was to withdraw into a shell. Once in a while, though, when the rage inside reached the breaking point, he would start screaming and punching the air with his fists. Rod managed to escape many of his father's tendencies, but not the fist-shaking explosions.

The revelations about their childhood experiences laid the groundwork for empathy. The couple's habitual patterns did not disappear overnight, of course, but their newly heightened awareness enabled them to be less reactive when emotions ran high. They were able to stop their conditioned responses before they got out of hand and sense what it was like to be the other person at that moment.

What was life like for your partner growing up? Were his or her parents kind? Loving? Generous? Domineering? Abusive? Neglectful? Was he or she spoiled? Ignored? Criticized? Did siblings make him or her feel safe and wanted? Or were they resentful and cruel? Was there alcoholism, drug abuse or violence in the family? Was there a divorce or early death? In your partner's adolescence, did he or she suffer humiliation or ostracism at the hands of peers? In early adulthood, did he or she endure failure? Heartbreak? Loss?

By asking such questions, and perhaps doing some research to fill the gaps in your knowledge, you can gain a deeper understanding of the forces that shaped the person you live with. This database can help you identify the roots of behavior patterns that might otherwise perplex you and drive you crazy. It will be enormously useful when it comes time to feel what your partner is feeling and think what he or she is thinking.

> **USABLE INSIGHT**
>
> *It takes minutes to love the way someone makes you feel, but years to feel the way they love.*

Put Yourself in Your Partner's Place—Literally

Not even one's own pain weighs so heavy as the pain one feels with someone, for someone, a pain intensified by the imagination and prolonged by a hundred echoes.

—MILAN KUNDERA

It is not always possible to get a true taste of another person's life, but if it can be arranged there is no quicker route to empathy. To illustrate the point, meet a couple who were given that opportunity by fate.

After the birth of their third child, Faith and Leland agreed that it would be okay for Faith to quit her job as a sales representative to be a full-time mom. Two years later, they were at each other's throats. Leland complained that Faith never had dinner ready when he got home from work, that she left errands undone and, worst of all, had become short-tempered and irritable. "Cut me some slack, I'm under a lot of stress," Faith would say. Leland's response was, "What do you know about stress? My company is downsizing, the Internet is cutting into our sales . . . I wish the only pressure on me was showing up on time for the car pool."

He got his wish the hard way. He got laid off. Faith was lucky enough to get her old job back, and Leland became a househusband while figuring out what to do next. Within three weeks, he was reeling. A stiff-upper-lip Englishman, he had always taken pride in being calm and collected. Now he was petulant and grumpy. Always well organized, he now had loose ends everywhere. Always loose under pressure, he was now as tight as a drum for fear of making a mistake that could harm one of his children. One day, he got distracted by one child and another slipped and fell in the bathtub. Just a lump on the head, but enough to make Leland's worst nightmare a bit more real.

"This job is more overwhelming than anything I've ever done," he confessed to Faith. "I'm sorry I gave you so much grief. I had no idea what your life was like."

That wasn't the only difference. While Leland played the role of stay-at-home dad, Faith was playing breadwinner mom. She saw what it was like to bear the pressure of supporting a family by herself. Since her income was based on commissions, she found herself working extra hours, bearing down more heavily on her clients and sometimes being tempted to compromise her ethics. When she came home after a hard day and the house was a mess and the kids were unruly and there was nothing warm to eat, she did not like it one bit. One night, downing a martini after an exhausting day, she had an empathic epiphany. "Were you ever terrified that you wouldn't be able to pull it off and the kids would go hungry?" she asked Leland.

"Yes," he said, "all the time."

"Did you feel trapped?"

"Like I was sentenced to twenty years of hard labor."

"Did you resent me for putting you in that position?"

"Yes," Leland confessed.

"Now I know how you felt," said Faith.

Six months later, their lives reverted to the original plan; Leland found a new job and Faith quit hers once again. But their life together was vastly different this time around. Now they could empathize. They had taken a trek in one another's shoes.

It's not always possible, of course, but if you and your partner can arrange to spend a day, a week or even longer experiencing the parts of one another's lives that affect your moods the most, you will find yourselves enriched with natural empathy.

Ask the Right Questions

Knowledge is of two kinds. We know a subject
ourselves, or we know where we can find
information upon it.

—SAMUEL JOHNSON

When it comes to human beings, the best place to "find information upon it" is usually the horse's mouth: How did you feel when I said that? What were you thinking when that happened? What does it feel like now? The right questions can open the door to your partner's mind and heart.

In building empathy, there are basically three areas to cover: thoughts, feelings and actions. Getting your partner to talk about those three aspects of a particular issue or event will help you fill in the blanks of your empathy. Try to ask questions that get at all three: What else do you feel when I do that? What goes through your mind when I say those things? What does it make you want to do to me? If you make a sincere effort to inquire, your partner will feel known. More important, he or she will feel that you *want* to know—and that, as we saw earlier, matters more than *what* you know.

How much you learn depends not only on the actual questions you ask but also the manner of asking. Coming on strong, like an interrogator or a prosecutor, won't get you very far. The key is to make it safe for your partner to be honest. Your body language and tone of voice should communicate that you're not out to gain an edge, or to dominate or control, but rather to find out the truth because you truly care about the person.

Suppose your partner comes home from work and barks at you over something trivial. You could become defensive and snap back at him, but before long you'll be fighting. Instead, you could put yourself in his shoes. What's going on with him right now? Why is he in that mood? You might not know the answer, but you can hypothesize. For instance, you might ask, "Did something go wrong at the office?"

"My boss can be a real jerk sometimes," replies your partner.

Now, you could say, "I'm sure it will work out. What should we do about dinner?" Or, worse, "That's too bad, but don't take it out on me."

But you could also say, "I'm sorry to hear that. Tell me what happened." That invitation to elaborate immediately conveys that you care. Then, suppose your partner responds, "It's no big deal.

Let's eat out." You could take him at his word and drop your inquiry. Or, you could ask yourself, "What's it *really* like for him right now?" You might discern that he still feels bothered. If you then said, "Really, I want to know. Tell me what happened," you would be conveying not only that you care but that you understand that he's upset and you're willing to take the time to listen. He may still choose not to say more, but he will have felt your empathy, and that alone will make a difference in your relationship. And if he *does* need to get something off his chest or solicit your advice, you will have given him permission to do so.

Suppose he then tells you what happened. "During the presentation, when we were projecting the charts, someone pointed out a typo. My boss turned to me and said, 'I told you spelling counts.' He said it with a smile, like he was joking, but everyone in the room knew he was pissed."

"That must have felt awful," you say. That alone would be empathic. But you could take it to a higher level by asking, "How bad did it feel?" A question like that shows that you're interested in the depth of his feelings and are prepared to hear the entire story.

You can encourage him to go deeper by asking questions such as, "Did you feel belittled?" "It was humiliating, wasn't it?" "What else did you feel?" "Were you scared?" Gently and patiently, try to get your partner to dig as deep as possible: "What was scary about it?" "What was the most frustrating part?" "How did it make you feel physically?" The more penetrating the questions, the more you will learn and the more your partner will feel valued.

Right about now one point needs to be emphasized. *Being empathic does not mean letting people get away with bad behavior. The* husband in this example was rude when he came home from work. He should not be given a free pass no matter how com-passionate your empathy makes you feel. After you've defused the situation and made him feel understood, look him in the eye and say, "You know, when bad things happen at work, I'd really appre-ciate it if you don't take it out on me. I'm on your side."

Don't you think he'll be less likely to unload on you in the future than if you'd skipped the empathy part and let him have it on the spot? And don't you think he'll be more inclined to cut you some slack the next time *you* vent some anger or frus-tration?

Using Empathy When You Need It Most

If one does not understand a person,
one tends to regard him as a fool.

—CARL JUNG

The most important time to use empathy is also the hardest time to use it: when you or your partner feel hostile toward one another. As the adrenaline pours into your system, urging you to raise your voice in anger, empathy may seem like the property of saints, not ordinary mortals like you. And, when you're being accused of causing your partner pain, it's hard to empathize because you don't want to admit to yourself that you can be hurtful to someone you love. In either case, if you can find the presence of mind to pause and reflect for just a moment, you can inject some powerful medicine into your relationship. During that pause, ask yourself this simple question: If I do or say what I'm about to do or say, what effect will it have on my partner?

The answer is probably not, "He'll hear what I'm saying and agree with me and everything will be fine." More likely it will be, "He'll get defensive and start hollering back," or "She'll get scared and walk away, and she won't speak to me for days," or "He'll be very hurt, and he'll start pouting and this conflict will just drag on," or "She'll start crying and I'll feel like a jerk, and I'll apologize, but nothing will be resolved." Is that the result you want?

Then ask yourself, What is more important, venting my anger or creating peace? Would I rather be right at all costs or genuinely resolve the conflict?

It may seem impossible to stop in the heat of an argument and ponder those questions. But you'd be surprised how quickly you can do it once you develop the habit. In fact, the simple mantra, "What effect will it have on my partner?" can have a powerful impact even if you don't run through the rest of the sequence. It triggers the feeling tone of empathy, and that alone can transform a battlefield into a healing zone.

The reason empathy is so powerful is that it is totally opposite to the destructive attitudes and actions that drive people apart. It is psychologically impossible to be empathic and at the same time attack the other person. You can't embrace someone's point of view and simultaneously push them away. You can't reject them while you're feeling what they feel. When you are

being empathic you're not competing, you're not being adver-
sarial, you're not judging. On an emotional level, it is as though
you have sat down beside the person and put your arm around
their shoulders. The immediate effect on the recipient is to call a
cease-fire and drop their defenses.

> **USABLE INSIGHT**
>
> *You can't put your-
> self in someone's
> shoes and step on
> their toes at the
> same time.*

Empathy softens the self-centered
"What's in it for me?" attitude that poi-
sons relationships. For that moment, at
least, instead of seeing your partner as a
perpetrator who caused you pain, you see
him or her as a fellow sufferer. Instead of
"He's to blame" or "It's all her fault," it's,
"Look what we've done to each other."
The simple act of seeing through the eyes
of another takes you right to the heart of the Golden Rule.

8

How to Stay in Love

Keeping the 6 Secrets

> *Love does not consist in gazing at each other, but in looking outward together in the same direction.*
>
> —ANTOINE DE SAINT-EXUPÉRY

Congratulate yourselves for having made it to this point.

You have tried diligently to talk *with* instead of at or over each other. You have had dialogues and discussions, not debates and diatribes. You have discovered how, in the past, the six pillars of love were damaged, and you've worked hard to make the needed repairs. You've corrected misunderstandings, shared deep feelings and peered deeper into each other's hurts, hopes and fears than you ever did before. You have resolved old conflicts and agreed to put the past behind you rather than continue to resent one another and squander your future. You have learned to ask, "What is it like for my partner right now?" Your conscientious efforts on behalf of your relationship have been noticed, appreciated and willingly reciprocated by one another.

Quite possibly, you have fallen in love again. At the very least, you have created a solid foundation on which your love can grow—and on which you can take a well-earned rest from the struggle and strife that had marked your relationship in the past. Enjoy what you have and take pride in what you've accomplished. But don't rest on your laurels. The challenge now is to build on that foundation—to not only guard against messing up what is beautiful and precious, but to stay in love and grow in love. Unlike pillars of stone, the pillars of love do not have to deteriorate over time. If you protect them, refurbish them and reinforce them on a regular basis, they can keep on getting stronger.

Building an Eagle's Nest

Avoid the reeking herd,
Shun the polluted flock,
Live like that stoic bird,
The eagle of the rock.

—ELINOR HOYT WYLIE

One of the most inspiring people I know is Dave Hibbard, the founder of Profit Techniques, a consulting and training firm in Irvine, California. In helping companies become the best that they can be, Dave stresses the importance of building an eagle's nest rather than a crow's nest.

Everything about an eagle's nest communicates that this is a class act. Integrity, quality and positivity are present in every corner and corridor. People want to get into eagles' nests; that's why GE, IBM and other outstanding companies with good reputations never lack for high-level job applicants. Think of the businesses in your area that everyone respects, whether repair shops, supermarkets or multinational corporations. They reflect positively on everyone associated with them. Their employees are proud to tell people where they work. Many consider it an honor to be there.

With crows' nests, it's an embarrassment to be there. These are the unethical, dishonest companies with a reputation for poor quality and low integrity. Filled with blamers, victims and negative thinkers, crow's nests suck the life out of everyone in them. Employees hope that no one asks where they work because they're ashamed to be there. They can't wait to get out, but they worry that their reputations will be so marred by the association that no one will want them. People in eagles' nests take care not to do shabby, sleazy, shoddy things that would dishonor their organization. In crow's nests you find selfish, careless, sneaky, unethical, sloppy behavior. Inspired by this concept, I've tried to make my psychotherapy practice an eagle's nest. That does not mean that my office is as neat as a pin. It means that I honor my clients' trust, give them the full measure of my ability and always try to live up to the highest standards of my profession.

Why am I using business analogies in a book about love?

Well, if you and your partner have done the work in this book so far, your relationship is now an eagle's nest, or well on the way to becoming one. Don't do anything to dishonor it. Take pride in it. Respect the effort that has gone into your nest, and take care not to sully or shame it. The eagle is admired for its beauty, power and grace. It is inspiring in its majestic, soaring strength. None of which stopped it from becoming endangered. Protect your love with skill and steadfast effort.

> **USABLE INSIGHT**
>
> *Honor is a much better motivator than guilt.*

Those in eagles' nests feel like they are part of an elite division, as opposed to the ragtag mob in a crow's nest, they hold themselves to the highest standards and keep working to make it the best of all possible nests. If the six pillars of your love are sturdy and secure, you're in an elite group. You are now the couple that others envy and aspire to be like. Why not commit yourselves to the highest standards?

Take the High Road

*Be free, all worthy spirits, and stretch yourselves, for
greatness and for height.*

—GEORGE CHAPMAN

There will be upsets along the way. When
they crop up, you have a choice. You can
take the high road, or you can take the
low road. On the high road you acknowledge the upset, join with your partner to
deal with it, let go and move on. On the
low road you dwell on negativity, seek
victory or revenge over your partner and
remain stuck in the past. One way leads to
satisfaction and contentment in an eagle's
nest, the other to bitterness and depres-
sion in a crow's nest. That's your choice every time. Which will
you take?

> **USABLE INSIGHT**
>
> *The good news is
> that your relation-
> ship problems are
> not your fault. The
> better news is that
> they're not your
> partner's fault
> either.*

To help you make that choice, here is a list of contrasting
behaviors that characterize the low road and the high road.

Low Road	High Road
petty	gracious
controlling	trusting
abrasive	tender
scornful	compassionate
insensitive	sensitive
grudge-holding	forgiving

unappreciative	grateful
arrogant	confident
rejecting	accepting
roots against	roots for
blames others	accepts responsibility
dishonors	honors
makes excuses	accountable
defensive	remorseful
passive	takes initiative
manipulative	aboveboard
ego driven	principled
selfish	generous
prideful	humble
gives up	perseveres

In any given instance, you can always move from one column to the other. Try to move in the right direction.

The Three Good P's and the Three Bad P's

*Patience and tenacity of purpose are worth more
than twice their weight of cleverness.*

—THOMAS HENRY HUXLEY

To secure your eagle's nest on the rock of six strong pillars, you have to be *proactive, patient* and *persistent*—the three good P's.

BE PROACTIVE. Creating a love that soars takes strong intention, powerful will and determined follow-through. Don't just wait for problems to arise. Don't just do damage control. Don't fool yourself into thinking that the growth of love will take care of itself. It's not like a tree that takes root in the wild, it's more like a garden that has to be tended. Take charge. Initiate action.

BE PATIENT. "No thing great is created suddenly," said the Greek philosopher Epictetus, "any more than a bunch of grapes or a fig . . . Let it first blossom, then bear fruit, then ripen." Don't kid yourself. You will backslide. You will slip. You will momentarily forget what you learned. You will fall into the old patterns that caused so many problems in the past. You will have conflicts, arguments and maybe even fights. This is to be expected. Patience is an absolute necessity—but an alert, active patience, not a passive patience. As Thomas Edison said, "Everything comes to him who hustles while he waits."

BE PERSISTENT. The task ahead takes the kind of gritty, determined perseverance that all great achievements demand. Don't get discouraged when you run into snags. Dust yourself off and get back to work. "Fall seven times, stand up eight," says a Japanese proverb.

In practicing the three good P's, beware of the three bad P's: *perfectionism, procrastination* and *paralysis*.

"The essence of being human is that one does not seek perfection," wrote George Orwell. Take care not to seek it in yourself or your partner. It's terrific to have high standards, but not so high as to be unreachable. It's also good to have principles and policies, but not so rigid as to be inflexible and unbending. If you expect perfection, you're setting yourself up for a life of discontent.

Perfectionism can lead directly to the next bad P, procrastination. Perfectionists often hesitate on any action that is not likely to produce a perfect result. Rather than settle for less-than, they wait, hoping that a better alternative will turn up. The hesitation quickly becomes all-out procrastination. You'll know you're procrastinating if you find yourself thinking, "I'm upset and I really ought to talk to my partner about it," and you keep putting it off. Or, you rationalize, "Oh, he/she won't listen anyway." Initiate the action now. At the very least, commit to it, even if you can't actually do it immediately.

As mentioned earlier, if you avoid something long enough, it can turn into a phobia—a persistent, irrational fear. That's how procrastination can lead to the third bad P, paralysis. Put off working on your relationship issues long enough and eventually you won't just be stalling, you'll be stuck. When you're paralyzed, you can't take action even if you try.

You have acquired a wealth of new knowledge and an arsenal of new tools. Use them to practice the good P's and avoid the bad P's. As problems arise, go back to the appropriate chapters and make use of the insights and exercises. But don't stop there. Use the material even when things are going well—to learn more and grow more together. Many of the tools in the book can be used repeatedly, with new benefits to be gained each time.

Keeping Current

A successful marriage is an edifice that must be
rebuilt every day.

—ANDRÉ MAUROIS

Doctors run tests to look for warning signs and stop the disease process early. Gardeners check for weeds and pluck them out.

Eagles have to carry debris from their nests. And lovers have to monitor their relationships and eliminate emotional toxins when they arise.

The VD that destroys long-term monogamous relationships is not venereal disease but Vent/Dump disease. Venting is relieving yourself of tension, anger and other volatile emotions. Dumping is what happens when relieving yourself crosses over into abuse of the other person. If you don't find a way to deal with negative feelings or express them when they first arise, emotional pressure builds up inside you. When you finally can't contain it anymore, it erupts. And sometimes, it's such a relief to unburden yourself that you can't stop. You say things you later regret and wish you could take back.

Crossing the line from healthy venting to harmful dumping is like having a painful abscess that grows and grows until it has to be lanced. Once you stick a scalpel into an abscess and it starts to drain, there is no way to close it. You can't stitch it up, and sealing it with a bandage does no good. You have to insert an instrument in the opening so that all the pus drains out. The difference is, draining an abscess is necessary to heal the body. Dumping only makes an infected relationship worse.

The only way to prevent VD is to stay current in communicating your hurts to your partner. Unless you deal quickly and effectively with disappointments, upsets, frustrations and resentments, the pressure will build. Eventually,

> **USABLE INSIGHT**
>
> *The second most painful truth is that everything you say and do counts. The most painful truth is that everything you have already said and done has counted.*

you will have to vent, and if you can't keep the venting under control it will escalate into dumping. One way to maintain control is the technique we've used throughout the book: as soon as you feel that you might go too far, stop and ask yourself, "What is it like for my partner right now?" You simply cannot be receptive to what the other person is feeling and at the same time dump on them.

Even better is to prevent the toxicity from building to that point in the first place. Every time you justify something that upsets you, or rationalize it away with, "It will pass," or "It's not a big deal, it's just his way," or, "She's just had a hard day, I'll get over it," you add to the internal pressure that is building toward an explosion. Trying to avoid confrontation only delays the confrontation. And with each delay, you make it more likely that a manageable conflict will turn into an all-out melee.

That is why the curtain falls on many marriages in what seems to be an abrupt, dramatic fashion. What happens is this: You internalize upsets instead of dealing with them when they arise. Sooner or later, your partner realizes that something is wrong. On a conscious level, they see that you look less animated, less cheerful, less enthusiastic; perhaps you're brooding, or making negative comments, or not enjoying the things you used to enjoy. Unconsciously, they know even more. They know that every time they yelled at you or criticized you or let you down and you did not react, the emotions you were feeling had to go someplace.

"What's wrong," they ask. "Is something bothering you?" "No, no, I'm fine, just a little tired." Then some straw breaks the camel's back, and you start to vent. The relief of getting things off your chest acts like a drug, loosening all your inhibitions, and the dumping begins. And when you're seeing red, you can't see clearly. Next thing you know, you've gone from "I'm fine" to "I'm outta here!" Or, you're acting out in some other way—having an affair, or bad-mouthing your partner to other people or taking on some form of behavior that does more harm to the relationship than anything you might have said when you first got upset.

The key to avoiding a buildup of emotional toxins is to stay current with your upsets. Make a mutual commitment to:

> **USABLE INSIGHT**
>
> *Marriages don't end when two people stop loving each other but when they can't stop hating each other.*

1. express the things that hurt or disappoint you as soon as possible
2. listen patiently and carefully to the person who is upset
3. deal with the upset in a constructive manner, observing the principles of good dialogue
4. treat each other with love and respect throughout

If you observe those four rules when one of you says, "I'd like to tell you something I'm upset about," you'll avoid the Vent/Dump reflex that batters the pillars of love like a wrecking ball. Even if it causes a temporary upheaval, it won't be as inflammatory as what can happen if you let things build up on the erroneous belief that it will go away by itself.

When Help Is Needed

I believe that most couples who use this book wisely and diligently will be able to handle most relationship problems that arise. But there are limits to what a book can do. Under certain circumstances, the help of a qualified counselor or therapist may be necessary. Please understand that there is no shame in seeking help. It does not imply failure. You turn to plumbers, mechanics and electricians when you can't fix things on your own. You go to doctors when you're not feeling well. There is no reason not to seek expert help when your relationship is under the weather and you can't fix it on your own.

Generally speaking, you and your partner should consider seeing a couples therapist when:

- disagreements and conflicts deteriorate into battles that can't be resolved
- your ability to communicate is so poor that even a difference of opinion about a neutral subject becomes a hostile argument
- the information in this book makes sense and feels right, but you can't put what you've learned into action
- destructive patterns persist despite your efforts
- your core problems seem unfixable
- one or both of you has lost the motivation to keep on trying
- one or both of you resists working on an issue because you're afraid

If some deep-seated emotional block is preventing you from making progress on your own, a good therapist can serve as a catalyst, helping you to overcome your resistance. A couples therapist is part referee, part facilitator and part translator. That last function is frequently the most important one. Often, what we say is not what we mean. For example, when one person, out of self-protection, acts defensively, it can seem like an attack to his or her partner. A therapist's translation can ensure that both parties understand exactly what was meant and what the underlying feelings were.

When a therapist is working with an individual client, that person is the entire focus of concern. When a therapist sees a couple, the patient is the relationship itself. The therapist does not take sides; his or her job is to stand up for the relationship and protect it from abuse and neglect.

When Individual Therapy Is Needed

If one partner's behavior is disproportionately harming the relationship, it might be appropriate for that person to see an individual therapist. This can be done either instead of couples counseling or in addition to it. It would be a misuse of couples therapy, for instance, to expect it to resolve the painful tangle of emotions in someone who suffered significant abuse or neglect as a child. Similarly, if one partner has a deep-rooted fear of intimacy due to a past trauma—rape, or incest or violence at the hands of a previous spouse—couples work alone would be insufficient. In each of those examples, an unnecessary burden would be placed on both the therapist and the other partner.

In addition, certain destructive behaviors that cause havoc in a relationship should be dealt with individually. A pattern of uncontrollable violence, obsessive infidelity, alcoholism and drug addiction are examples of dysfunctions that are best treated in the context of individual therapy. In many cases, support groups can serve as a powerful adjunct to therapy for the person with the problem—and sometimes for the other partner as well. Many couples attend separate twelve-step meetings, with one partner going to, say, Alcoholics Anonymous and the other to Al-Anon.

Another situation that calls for individual therapy is the presence of an emotional condition with a biological basis. Depression, bipolar disorder (manic-depression), chronic anxiety and obsessive-compulsive disorder are among the common conditions that can destroy relationships if left untreated. The specialist best qualified to diagnose and treat such problems is the psychiatrist. Psychiatrists are trained in both psychotherapy and the neurochemistry of mental and emotional illness. Also, because they are medical doctors, they are the only mental health professionals who are permitted by law to prescribe medication.

Choosing a Therapist

There are several ways to get recommendations for a therapist. One is to ask trusted friends who have had good experiences in therapy. Another is your family doctor. A third is a local mental health clinic. One of my favorite methods is to contact the nearest medical school that has a department of psychiatry. Ask to speak to the chief psychiatric resident. He or she is at the highest level of training and is in a position to know the most respected mental health professionals in the community. Those experts tend to be affiliated with medical schools. Make sure the professional you select has all the appropriate credentials and is duly licensed by the state.

Your initial consultation should be viewed as an opportunity to get to know each other. Feel free to ask questions about the therapist's philosophy and approach to therapy. If you're looking for a couples therapist, you might also want to ask whether he or she is married and has children. That may not matter to you, and it is certainly not a prerequisite, but many clients feel more comfortable knowing that the therapist has been there and done that. I was able to help a great many couples with parenting issues early in my career, but I do a far better job of it now that I've had three children of my own.

You should also ask couples therapists about their philosophy of marriage and how they view their role in working with a couple. In my experience, the best therapists are neutral on the question of saving the marriage. Their job is to help you and your partner make your best possible effort.

Get a feeling for what it would be like to work with the therapist. Are you made to feel comfortable and at ease? Does he or she appear to have empathy and compassion? Do you feel safe to discuss your innermost thoughts and feelings? Your therapist should inspire trust. Even after your first session, you should have a reasonable amount of confidence that he or she understands where you're coming from and is capable of helping you go from where you are to where you want to be.

The therapist's statements should be understandable and his or her suggestions should seem doable. You may not be able to tell after just one session, but soon enough you will know if you can comfortably follow through on his or her recommendations. The guidance should make sense and feel right, inspiring confidence that it will lead to the desired outcome. The purpose of therapy is not simply to gain insight and understanding, it's to turn insight and understanding into practical steps to change your life.

It is perfectly appropriate to have initial consultations with two or three therapists to determine which, if any, is most suitable. If you meet several and have no confidence in any of them, it's time to ask yourself if you could trust *anyone*. If the therapists you've seen have good reputations in the community and were recommended by reliable sources, something within you may be keeping help and hope from getting close. That could be the first thing to discuss with a therapist, for that very pattern might be negatively affecting your relationship.

Hope is the feeling you have that the feeling you
have isn't permanent.

—JEAN KERR

Once you've made your decision, you and your partner should make a firm commitment to give it your best shot. You may feel hopeless. You may fear that therapy will prove to be a waste of money. A part of you may be convinced that the relationship has run its course and it's time to cut your losses and start a new life. Your therapist will help you sort through the turmoil of ambivalence, where hope and pessimism battle it out. If worse comes to worst and you decide that your relationship has no future, a good therapist will help you make the break cleanly, so you'll have as few regrets as possible. And if there is indeed hope for a fresh new start, the work you do in therapy can be indispensable in helping you forge ahead with greater purpose, greater awareness and greater commitment.

And in the End . . .

Success in marriage does not come merely through finding the right mate, but through becoming the right mate.

—BARNETT BRICKNESS

The Beatles had it right; the love we take *is* equal to the love we make. Remember the elderly couple we met in chapter 5? The ones who had been together for decades without knowing how much they were loved? Like someone who discovers too late that he has a bank account that's been gathering interest for years, you could wake up one day and realize how much love you could have enjoyed if only you'd appreciated what you had and taken proper care of it. It's very easy to fool yourself into thinking you have less than you do. You are now in a great position to avoid that fate.

Gardeners don't just pull weeds and destroy pests that threaten their plants. They prune, they spray, they plant fresh seeds, they fertilize the soil. Creating a love that lasts requires not just resolving conflicts as they arise, not just getting the help you need, not just monitoring the relationship for signs of damage. It also requires cultivation. In this regard, the spirit of John F. Kennedy's famous statement at his inauguration is the best formula for success: Ask not what your partner can give to you, ask what you can give to your partner.

You can give without loving, but you cannot love without giving.

—AMY CARMICHAEL

One of the unfortunate habits that couples fall into is communicating only the negative. We feel free to express critical thoughts toward one another, operating on the assumption that we don't have to mention our positive feelings because the other person surely knows about those. We probably do this because, when things are going smoothly and everything feels right, we take it for granted. It's the way things are supposed to be—just as feeling healthy is the way it's supposed to be. We seldom think, "I'm grateful that I'm feeling okay today," we just go about our business. Until we get sick. That, we notice. Illness is a blip on our radar screen. Similarly, when there's a blip on our emotional radar, we home in on it as if an enemy had invaded the continent of our contentment. It's a self-protective instinct that causes us to notice threats to our safety.

It takes some effort to look for the positive, but we need to give it equal time, or else, as Joni Mitchell warned us, we won't know what we've got till it's gone. You find what you look for. If you look for what your partner does right, you'll find it. If you look for reasons to respect, enjoy, accept and trust your partner, you'll find them. If you look for things that turn you on instead of what turns you off, you'll find them. If you look for opportunities to be empathic instead of self-centered, you'll find them as well. And once you find these things, let your partner know. Express your appreciation.

When you find yourself in a grateful mood, don't stop at feeling it and being glad that you're feeling it. Turn your gratitude into some kind of action. Actively do things for your partner without being asked. Be generous when you're not obliged to be. Nothing makes a person feel more special or more important than when someone goes out of their way to do something they don't have to do, simply as a gesture of appreciation. Write a note. Send an E-mail. Buy flowers. Suggest that you do something romantic together. At the very least, say it. Say that you're grateful to be graced by your partner's presence. Say it again and again. It will pay off, believe me. Nothing inspires loving behavior like knowing that you're loved.

> **USABLE INSIGHT**
>
> *Look for the negative and you'll find resentment; look for the positive and you'll find gratitude.*

Great athletes always say that the best strategy for success is not to think about what the opposition is doing, nor to worry about your teammates, but to focus on being the best that you can be. Everything else follows from that. Be the best lover, husband or wife that you can be, and as sure as night follows day, you'll inspire your partner to do the same. Someone has to go first. Why not you?

Index

About the Authors

MARK GOULSTON, M.D., is a board-certified psychiatrist and an assistant clinical professor at the UCLA Neuropsychiatric Institute. Dr. Goulston appears frequently on local and national television including *Today*, *Oprah*, *CBS News* and *ABC News*, and on CNN and MSNBC. He is interviewed on radio several times per week including *CBS Newsradio*, Westwood One, Infinity Broadcasting and *Talk America*. He has been quoted, been written about or written for magazines and newspapers including the *New York Times*, *Washington Post*, *Los Angeles Times*, *Biography*, *Wall Street Journal*, *Fortune*, *Newsweek*, *Time*, *Ladies' Home Journal*, *Cosmopolitan* and *Maxim*. He writes the Knight Ridder-Tribune syndicated college newspaper column "Relationships 101," and the *Emmy* magazine column "Question Mark." He is co-founder of www.couplescompany.com and has contributed on line to iVillage, Yahoo, Thirdage, Time Inc. and drkoop.com. He lives in Los Angeles with his wife and three children.

PHILIP GOLDBERG is the author or coauthor of many books including *Get Out of Your Own Way*, (with Mark Goulston), *Passion Play* (with Felice Dunas), *Pain Remedies* (with the Editors of *Prevention* magazine), *The Intuitive Edge* and *Making Peace with Your Past* (with Harold Bloomfield).